TWELVE
NEW TESTAMENT
STUDIES

STUDIES IN BIBLICAL THEOLOGY

TWELVE
NEW TESTAMENT
STUDIES

JOHN A. T. ROBINSON

WIPF & STOCK · Eugene, Oregon

Wipf and Stock Publishers
199 W 8th Ave, Suite 3
Eugene, OR 97401

Twelve New Testament Studies
By Robinson, John A.T.
Copyright©1962 SCM Press
ISBN 13: 978-1-60899-033-7
Publication date 8/17/2009
Previously published by SCM Press, 1962

CONTENTS

Preface   7

Abbreviations   9

   I The Baptism of John and the Qumran Community   11

  II Elijah, John and Jesus   28

 III The Temptations   53

 IV The 'Others' of John 4.38   61

  V The Parable of the Shepherd (John 10.1–5)   67

 VI The 'Parable' of the Sheep and the Goats   76

 VII The New Look on the Fourth Gospel   94

VIII The Destination and Purpose of St John's Gospel   107

 IX The Destination and Purpose of the Johannine
Epistles   126

  X The Most Primitive Christology of All?   139

 XI The Earliest Christian Liturgical Sequence?   154

 XII The One Baptism   158

Index   177

PREFACE

The twelve New Testament studies here collected are reprinted by kind permission of the editors of the journals in which they first appeared and to which reference is made at the beginning of each article. With occasional bibliographical additions I have left them substantially as they were written at their various dates of composition.

What unity they have is provided by an unsatisfied curiosity to push behind commonly accepted positions of New Testament study, and to explore and test alternative hypotheses.

I am deeply grateful to Miss Jean Cunningham of the SCM Press for her care in preparing the manuscript and making the index and to Professor C. F. D. Moule for sparing of his precious professorial time to correct the proofs.

JOHN WOOLWICH

ABBREVIATIONS

BA: *Biblical Archaeologist*
BASOR: *Bulletin of the American Schools of Oriental Research*
BJRL: *Bulletin of the John Rylands Library*
BZNW: Beiheft to *ZNW*
CDC: The Damascus Document or Zadokite Fragment
CSCO: Corpus Scriptorum Christianorum Orientalium
ET: English translation
EVV: English versions
ExpT: *Expository Times*
ICC: International Critical Commentary
JBL: *Journal of Biblical Literature*
JTS: *Journal of Theological Studies*
NEB: New English Bible
NS: New series
NTS: *New Testament Studies*
pars: parallels
1QH: The Qumran Psalms of Thanksgiving
1QM: The War between the Children of Darkness and the Children of Light
1QS: The Manual of Discipline
1QSa: The additional two columns associated with the Manual
RevB: *Revue Biblique*
RSV: Revised Standard Version of the Bible
RV: Revised Version of the Bible
SBT: Studies in Biblical Theology
SJT: *Scottish Journal of Theology*
Strack-Billerbeck: H. L. Strack and P. Billerbeck, *Kommentar zum NT aus Talmud und Midrasch* I–IV, 1922–8
TLZ: *Theologische Literaturzeitung*
TU: Texte und Untersuchungen zur Geschichte der altchristlichen Literatur
TWNT: *Theologisches Wörterbuch zum NT*, ed. G. Kittel, 1933 ff.
ZNW: *Zeitschrift für die neutestamentliche Wissenschaft*

I

THE BAPTISM OF JOHN AND THE QUMRAN COMMUNITY[1]

TESTING A HYPOTHESIS

THAT there was, as has been suggested,[2] an actual historical connexion between John the Baptist and the Qumran Community disclosed to us in the Dead Sea Scrolls is, and must at present remain, a hypothesis. The similarities to be found between them do not in any case depend upon this link being established. But I believe it to be one of those hypotheses which, once made, lead to further connexions and open up new and significant possibilities. It is therefore important to test it. And where direct historical confirmation fails, the only way to test a hypothesis is to push it to its limits and see how much of the evidence it can in fact explain. And to push it beyond its limits is not necessarily a fault: on the contrary, it is likely to be the best way of discovering where those limits lie.

According to the Lucan account, which there is no *a priori* reason for dismissing, John was born of ageing parents into a priestly family in the hill-country of Judaea and received his upbringing in the wilderness (Luke 1.5–80).[3] We next find him not,

[1]Reprinted from *The Harvard Theological Review* L (1957), 175–91.

[2]E.g. by W. H. Brownlee, 'John the Baptist in the New Light of Ancient Scrolls', *Interpretation* IX (1955), 71–90 (reprinted in *The Scrolls and the New Testament,* ed. K. Stendahl (1958), pp. 33–53); cf. his earlier article, 'A Comparison of the Covenanters of the Dead Sea Scrolls with Pre-Christian Jewish Sects', *BA* XIII (1950), 70–72; by B. Reicke, 'Nytt ljus över Johannes döparens förkunnelse', *Religion och Bibel* XI (1952), 5–18; by A. S. Geyser, 'The Youth of John the Baptist. A deduction from the break in the parallel account of the Lucan infancy story', *Novum Testamentum* I (1956), 70–75; by E. Stauffer, 'Probleme der Priestertradition', *TLZ* LXXXI (1956), cols. 143 f.; and, tentatively, by J. M. Allegro, *The Dead Sea Scrolls* (1956), pp. 163–5.

[3]This is not to deny that the Lucan birth narratives may be heavily overlaid with legendary and apologetic material. But they bear all the marks of a primitive Palestinian milieu, reflecting faithfully the unsophisticated piety of the circles in which they took shape. As both M. Goguel (*Au seuil de l'évangile: Jean-Baptiste,* 1928, p. 70) and C. Kraeling (*John the Baptist,* 1951, p. 23) admit, it is difficult to see what motive these circles should have had in making John the son of an obscure country priest if he was not. Cf. Stauffer, *op. cit.,* col. 143.

as we should expect, exercising his priestly office, like his father before him, in the Temple, but living as an ascetic prophet, preaching and administering a baptism of repentance in the Jordan valley. What has happened to produce this strange effect?

The hypothesis, which at any rate does violence to none of the facts, is that John was sent (on the death, perhaps, of his parents?) to be reared in the desert discipline of the Qumran Community. This Community had, as we know, considerable following among priestly families (which provided at least one for every ten or more of its members; 1QS vi.3; 1QSa ii.22; CDC xv.5),[4] and it appears more likely to have drawn this, not from the Sadducean priesthood it anathematized, but from those rural circles whose ideals of piety, as represented in the Lucan birth-narratives, are the closest approximation to those of Qumran to be found in the New Testament. It would, moreover, explain why he should come to have severed his connexion with the Temple cult and found himself fiercely opposed both to and by the Jerusalem priesthood (Matt. 3.7 = Luke 3.7; Mark 11.27–33 and pars; Matt. 21.32; cf. John 1.19).

This Community was situated at no great distance from John's home, and nearer still to his point of re-emergence in the wilderness of Judaea (Matt. 3.1). Provision is made in the additional columns to its Manual of Discipline,[5] for the training of those who come for instruction as children and for their assimilation by stages as adult members (1QSa i.4–18). And if, as I believe to be overwhelmingly probable, this Community was Essene in character, then we have the testimony of Josephus (*Bell. Jud.* II, § 120) that the practice of adoption was a customary one: 'They adopt other men's children, while yet pliable and docile, and regard them as their kin and mould them in accordance with their own principles.'[6]

Now it is equally clear that when John re-emerges into history he is *not* a member of the Qumran or any other community. In

[4]See Abbreviations for nomenclature, which is that set out by R. de Vaux, *RevB* LX (1953), 87 f.

[5]1QSa, published in *Discoveries in the Judaean Desert* (ed. D. Barthélemy, O. P., and J. T. Milik) I, pp. 108–18.

[6]This is said specifically of the non-marrying Essenes but, though it was obviously more necessary for them, there are no grounds for denying the practice to those who allowed marriage.

some way or other he has by then broken any connexion he may have had with them. He is an individual prophet, who, though he gathered disciples and gave them a discipline of prayer (Luke 11.1; 5.33) and fasting (Mark 2.18 and pars),[7] appears to have made no attempt to initiate them into any kind of order. In all that follows it must never be forgotten that John is a highly individual figure, whom neither Josephus nor anyone in the Gospels ever associates with any other group. Whatever he may have received from his association, if there was one, with Qumran, he remoulded into something quite distinctive and independent.

But when this has been said, there are many points in his teaching and ministry which are illuminated by the supposition of some such connexion.

However much he may have broken with the Community, he did not break with the desert and with the stress on asceticism, purification and separation from the evils of civilization which marked its discipline. Indeed, the great difference between John and Jesus lay in the fact that John remained in the desert and that men must come out to him: he refused to go to them, to eat and drink with the rest, or to mix with publicans and sinners. And his location in the desert was no accident. In fact, the very *raison d'être* of John's mission appears to have been grounded in the words of Isa. 40.3: 'A voice cries: "In the wilderness prepare the way of the Lord, make straight in the desert a highway for our God." ' This text is associated with him in all our Gospels (Mark 1.3; Matt. 3.3; Luke 3.4; John 1.23), and the most natural explanation of the connexion would seem to be, as the fourth Evangelist says, that it was used by the Baptist himself.[8]

Now in the use of this text we have our first direct, rather than purely circumstantial, evidence of a parallel between the Baptist and the covenanters of Qumran. For according to the Manual of Discipline they also used it to describe and justify what they aimed to do: 'Now when these things come to pass in Israel to the Community, according to these rules, they will separate

---

[7]There is nothing actually to suggest that John's disciples had any different regimen of fasting from other Jews. But it is at least conceivable that among the fruits John deemed worthy of repentance should have been counted an asceticism comparable with that for which he himself was known (Matt. 11.18 = Luke 7.33).

[8]So also Reicke, *op. cit.*, p. 14.

themselves from the midst of the session (or habitation) of per-
verse men to go to the wilderness to clear there the way of (the
Lord), as it is written:

> In the wilderness clear the way of (the Lord);
> Level in the desert a highway for our God.

That (means) studying the Torah (which) he commanded through
Moses, so as to do according to all that was revealed time after
time and according to that which the prophets revealed through
his holy Spirit.'[9]

Now, at first sight, it looks as if this is a description of the
present life of the Community. For they are out in the desert,
they are separate, and they are engaged in studying the Law (cf.
1QS v.1 f.). Certainly there is no doubt that it represents an ideal
which they are already seeking to practise and by constant
purification aiming to perfect. But it must not be overlooked
that the passage opens with the words, 'Now when these things
come to pass in Israel', a formula used twice again in neighbour-
ing passages (viii.4 and ix.3), and in the other two instances
evidently indicating a future and eschatological stage which has
not yet been reached. The conception in these three passages
appears to be that by its present life and discipline, and by means
of an inner group dedicated to perfection, a time will come when
the Community as a whole will stand forth, stripped and purified
of every contamination, to be the chosen instrument of Jahweh's
atoning work and judgment. *Then*, it seems, this wholly purified
remnant will complete its separation from the world and every
contact with evil (cf. ix.6) by marching out into the desert, ready
for anything Jahweh may require of it (presumably, to judge
from the War Scroll, for the final conflict with the sons of darkness),[10] and prepared for the coming of the Prophet and the
Messiahs of Aaron and Israel (1QS ix.11).

This interpretation, though it cannot be regarded as more than
probable, is, I believe, supported by the only other reference to
this moment of clearing a way in the desert—an exceedingly
obscure allusion in 1QS ix.20. In the context (ix.12–24) it is made

[9]1QS viii. 12–16. Tr. W. H. Brownlee, *BASOR*, Supplementary Studies
10–12 (1951).
[10]Cf. 1QM vii.5: 'They shall all be volunteers for war, blameless in spirit
and flesh, and ready for the day of vengeance.'

clear that in this present time the life of purification and perfection has still to be lived to a great extent 'in the midst of men of perversity'. But the ultimate purpose of all the teaching, instruction and discipline of the sect is to perfect a group which 'may walk perfectly each with his fellow in all that was revealed for them'. And *'that is the time* of clearing the way of the wilderness', i.e., when the perfect community is prepared and they are ready finally to go out from the world all together ('to separate from everyone') to meet the messianic age—a conception which may be reflected and rejected in the Gospels: 'If they say to you, "Lo, he is in the wilderness", do not go out' (Matt. 24.26).

Now, if we are right in stressing the eschatological context of this final withdrawal to the wilderness, then we *may* have the clue to why John went out from the Community. On this showing, he leaves the relative civilization and *corpus permixtum* even of Qumran because he becomes convinced, under the constraint of the word of God (Luke 3.2), that this eschatological moment is in fact nearer even than they believed: the axe is even now poised at the root of the trees (Matt. 3.10 = Luke 3.9). And so he deliberately goes out into the wilderness to prepare the way of Jahweh in the desert, to announce the imminent coming of the Prophet, and to gather the faithful of Israel for a final dedication to their God.

This he does by summoning the people to a baptism of repentance. So characteristic is this rite that it becomes inseparable from his very name. For Josephus (*Ant.* XVIII, 116), as for the Synoptists, he is John 'the Baptist' (Matt. 3.1, etc.) or 'the Baptizer' (Mark 6.14, etc.). The mere fact that it thus marked him out from others suggests that it was the most distinctive feature of his ministry. But even the most original and creative contributions do not drop from the blue, and the very success of his mission, attested again both by Josephus and the Gospels, bespeaks an environment where such a rite was immediately understood and accepted.

The evidence amassed by J. Thomas in his book, *Le mouvement Baptiste en Palestine et Syrie*,[11] makes it clear that at the turn of the era such an environment did exist. Baptism was very much 'in the air'—alike in the sects and in the great Church, where in

[11]Gembloux, 1935.

the course of the first century AD it came to assume a natural place in initiation both in Judaism and in Christianity. And yet, for all this, no really satisfactory explanation of John's activity has hitherto been found.

Attempts to derive it from proselyte baptism[12] or from the regular ablutions of Jewish worship[13] do not appear to allow sufficiently for the distinction between ritual impurity and sin. There is no evidence in orthodox Judaism that lustration, whether in proselyte baptism or elsewhere, was regarded as having power to deal with the latter, which was the function of sacrifice. One of the conclusions that emerges from Thomas' study is the tendency in the baptist sects to regard ablutions as taking the place or possessing the spiritual efficacy of sacrifice. Only when this assumption is made (as it appears to have been made at Qumran, but was certainly not in proselyte baptism), can one begin to account for the idea of baptism for the remission of sins.

The hypothesis that John was adapting to his own distinctive mission conceptions and practices which he had learnt at Qumran does, I believe, go further than any other to explain his peculiar activity in the Jordan valley.

But first, it is important once more to emphasize the distinctive character of John's action. As their buildings and their documents testify, the covenanters of Qumran centred their entire life in rites of moral purification. Nevertheless, we look in vain in their writings for the equivalent of a single baptism of repentance for the remission of sins. Corresponding, no doubt, to the different eschatological situation in which he saw himself standing, John

[12]There is a growing tendency among recent writers (cf. Kraeling, *op. cit.*, p. 204 n. 14) to reject proselyte baptism as a source for *John's* baptism, whatever may have been its influence upon later Christian practice. It is in any case extremely doubtful whether it can be established as existing at that date. Thomas concludes a very careful examination of the evidence with the words, 'The baptism of proselytes is attested at the end of the first century AD. It is possible that one could admit its existence from the beginning of the century. But there is little probability that it was universally accepted so soon and above all that it constituted a practice clearly distinct from ordinary baths of purification' (*op. cit.*, pp. 365 f.). Cf., most recently, T. M. Taylor, 'The Beginnings of Jewish Proselyte Baptism', *NTS* II (1956), 193–8, who reaches a similiar conclusion.

[13]N. A. Dahl, 'The Origin of Baptism', in *Interpretationes ad Vetus Testamentum pertinentes Sigmundo Mowinckel septuagenario missae. Norsk theologisk tidsskrift* LVI, 1–2 (1955).

was calling the people to something for which Qumran offered no parallel. His summons was not to a community life marked henceforth by constant rites of cleansing, but to a final purification of the nation against the imminent coming of the mighty one. There is a difference here that must not be obscured and which resulted in John's giving to the rite of baptism an isolation and a prominence which made him unique.

But, having said this, we must be careful not to exaggerate the difference from one of degree to one of kind. To those brought up in the Christian tradition there is indeed a decisive distinction between the single, once and for all, act of baptism and constantly repeated rites of ablution. And it is easy to read back the whole of this difference into the baptism of John.

But the Christian distinction rests upon two factors which have no relevance to John's baptism. The *theological* emphasis upon the unrepeatability of baptism, so important in the Christian tradition, derives, as the Epistle to the Hebrews makes clear (6.4–6), from the uniqueness of the Christ-event into which Christian baptism incorporates. But prior to the idea of a once and for all revelation, there is no evidence that any stress was laid on the unrepeatability of baptism, and there is in fact nothing actually to say that John's baptism was of this exclusive nature.

The other factor that in Christianity has isolated baptism as a unique event is its abandonment of the regular lustrations of Judaism, along with its food-laws and sacrifices. This repudiation goes back to Jesus' revolutionary disavowal of external washings as possessing any religious efficacy (Mark 7.1–15; Matt. 15. 1–11), and it is something that Mark, in one of his rare editorial comments, evidently regards as a distinctive characteristic of Christianity in contrast with the constant βαπτισμοί of 'all the Jews' (7.3 f.). Here, as in the closely connected matter of fasting (Mark 2.18), the disciples of John were without doubt at one with the Pharisees. According, at any rate, to the fourth Gospel, they were sufficiently involved in rites of purification to enter into controversy about them (John 3.25). And there is, in fact, every presumption that John's baptism did not stand alone, but was combined with other ablutions at least as frequent as those of the Pharisees. Certainly, in the closest parallel in all the baptist movement to the activity of John, the preaching by Elkasai in

AD 100 of a sovereign baptism for the remission of sins,[14] the rite itself (which was sufficiently decisive to be described, for Christians, as 'a second baptism') was supplemented by innumerable other baths of cleansing and healing.[15]

In admitting, therefore, a real difference of emphasis, it is important not to magnify it to a point of principle. For no such principle existed. Βάπτισμα and βαπτισμοί flowed into each other as naturally as the ever-running streams that supplied their constant source. None of the baptist sects appears to have had an initiatory rite which was never repeated again. Any decisiveness attaching to the first immersion lay rather in the repudiation it represented of the past than in the fact that it could not be renewed in the future. But *in this sense* the Community of Qumran does appear to have seen baptism as representing a decisive break for the individual, such as John could well have adapted as the basis of his call to repentance. For in 1QS v. 8 and 13 to 'enter the covenant' (or the Community) and to 'enter into water' should probably be read as parallel expressions (cf. iii.4–12). The solemn moment when a man was 'brought into the covenant, to turn from the truth and to turn away from all perversity' (vi.14 f.) was also that of his first entry into the water. And it would indeed be very strange if, with all their stress on water for purification, the covenanters had not used it to mark the initial break with the corrupt world.

If, therefore, John did modify the practice of Qumran, it was to give new emphasis to one element in it rather than to introduce any radical change. Indeed, the very fact that he was not gathering a community, but sending men back, as Israelites purified for coming judgment, to their ordinary occupations, must in itself have concentrated all the stress upon the single decisive immersion.

But the really interesting connexions are to be found not so much in the actual rite itself as in the meaning attaching to it. It is here that the parallels with the Qumran Community begin to be significant. Like John's, their washing was performed with strong insistence on the need for prior repentance (1QS v.13 f.;

[14]His language as preserved by Hippolytus (*Refut.* IX, 13.4) is strikingly similar: βαπτίσματι λαμβάνειν ἄφεσιν ἁμαρτιῶν.
[15]Cf. Thomas, *op. cit.*, pp. 140–9.

cf. i.24 f.):[16] there was no escaping the wrath to come by mere external ablution (iii.3–12). Again, unlike proselyte baptism, it was administered to those who were already Jews—to mark them out as belonging to the true and purified Israel. For them, as for John (Matt. 3.9; Luke 3.8), the true people of God was not to be built simply on the basis of racial inheritance. That this was the motive in John's preaching and baptism—to create a pure and penitent nucleus in Israel[17]—seems more likely than the explanation to which a parallel with proselyte baptism would force us, namely, that John was implying that all Jews were before God in the position of Gentiles.

These parallels are further confirmed by the baptism which both John and the Qumran covenanters envisaged as still to come, and of which there is no suggestion in the rite of proselyte baptism, *or in any other of the baptist sects.* For John, his baptism with water is but a preliminary purification, cleansing and marking out the true children of God for the day of that future, eschatological baptism to be administered by the one coming after him. When he, the mightier one, comes, he will baptize—with what? According to Mark (1.8), John (1.33) and Acts (1.5; 11.16) with 'holy Spirit'; according to Matthew (3.11) and Luke (3.16), with 'holy Spirit and fire'. Many critics have been reluctant to believe that John spoke of holy Spirit, and have seen in it a reading back of Christian theology. But now from Qumran we have clear evidence that the covenanters too regarded the dispensation of water, and with it all the present rules and discipline under which the Community lived, as being merely provisional till the coming of the messianic age (1QS ix.10 f.; CDC xv.4), when it would be superseded by a new dispensation of holy Spirit. 'And then [namely, at 'the season of visitation', when 'the truth of the world will appear for ever'] God will purge by his truth all the deeds of man, refining for himself some of mankind in order to abolish

[16]Cf. the insistence laid upon this by Josephus in his account of the Baptist (*Ant.* XVIII, 117). As has often been noticed, his description of John's baptism as being 'for the purification of the body when the soul had previously been cleansed by righteous conduct' is in striking accord with 1QS iii.8 f.
[17]Do the words ἀληθῶς 'Ισραηλείτης, ἐν ᾧ δόλος οὐκ ἐστιν (John 1.47) perhaps reflect the Baptist's ideal taken over by Jesus? Cf. the covenanters' aim of being a house of community 'for the Israelites who walk in perfection' in contrast with 'the men of deceit' (1QS ix.6 and 9).

every evil spirit from the midst of his flesh, and to cleanse him
through a holy Spirit from all wicked practices, sprinkling upon
him a Spirit of truth as purifying water' (1QS iv.20 f.).

Here are the characteristic themes of the Baptist's preaching—
refining, cleansing, water and holy Spirit—all set in the context
of the fire of judgment (iv.13),[18] the abolition of evil (iv.19 f.),
and 'the making of the new' (iv.25).[19] Here, I believe, is a much
more exact parallel for the Baptist's activity than anything we
have had before—even when full allowance is made for the
differences and for the highly striking and individual character
of John.

Moreover, and at this point I deliberately enter the field of
speculation, *if* John did see his mission in the same sort of categories as those of Qumran, then we may have a better idea of why
Jesus identified himself with it and, to the embarrassment of the
Church, himself underwent the baptism of John. Why should
Jesus, who later was to contrast himself so strongly with John,
have felt drawn thus to throw in his lot with the Baptist and his
movement?

From a remark recorded by Matthew (21.32) (and confirmed in
substance independently by Luke 7.29 f.; cf. 3.12), Jesus evidently
saw the mission of John as a path marked out for Israel by God:
'John came to you in the way of righteousness and you did not
believe him, but the tax-collectors and the harlots believed him;
and even when you saw it you did not afterwards repent and
believe him.' It is possible, incidentally, that in this expression
'the way of righteousness' we may have something more technical
than has hitherto been suspected. Just as both the covenanters
(1QS ix.18) and the Christians (Acts 9.2) knew themselves as
'the way', and dwelt strongly on the two ways (1QS iii.13—
iv.26; *Didache* 1–6; Matt. 7.13 f.), so 'the way of righteousness'
may well have been the popular name for John's movement.
According to the Manual of Discipline, the function of the Spirit

[18]Cf. the vivid description of the final judgment of the world by fire in
1QH iii.29–36.

[19]This is probably a reference to Isa. 43.19 (cf. the echo of v.10 of this
same chapter in viii.6), where it is significant that the 'new thing' that God
promises is precisely that he 'will make a way in the wilderness and rivers in
the desert'. This may be additional evidence that the time of the way in the
wilderness is 'the period of the decree', i.e., the End.

of truth in a man is to 'make straight before him all the ways of true righteousness, and to make his heart tremble with the judgments of God' (iv.2)—as good a summary of John's message as one could wish.

But, to return, something more seems to be required to explain Jesus' submission to John's baptism of repentance than that he evidently believed it to be 'from heaven' and not merely 'from men' (Mark 11.30 f.). It has indeed been customary to see in this act Jesus' first recognition of his redemptive mission and in this step of identification his willingness from then on to be 'numbered among the transgressors'. The difficulty is that there is nothing in the New Testament accounts to suggest that the Baptist's movement was in any way a redemptive group with which a man might identify himself from this kind of motive—in order, that is, to share in making atonement for the sin of Israel. But if there is behind John's mission the sort of thinking represented at Qumran, this missing link is supplied. For this Community saw its function precisely in these terms: 'to lay a foundation of truth for Israel . . ., to atone for all those who dedicate themselves for holiness in Aaron and for a house of truth in Israel' (1QS v.5 f.), 'to atone for the earth (or, the land) and to render to the wicked their desert' (viii.6 f.; cf. 1QSa i.3), 'to make atonement for the guilt of transgression and sinful infidelity' (1QS ix.4). If this was the kind of outlook in which John was nurtured and in some way also the *raison d'être* of his own movement—repentance, that is, not merely to escape the coming judgment, but to create a pure and purifying remnant—then we may have the clue to why Jesus felt compelled to associate himself with it.

It may also explain two other things. The first is the way in which later Jesus was to speak of his 'baptism' of suffering: 'I have a baptism to be baptized with; and how I am constricted until it is accomplished!' (Luke 12.50), and, 'Are you able to drink the cup that I drink, or to be baptized with the baptism that I am baptized with?' (Mark 10.38)—a passage that leads directly into the classic description of his death in terms of the suffering Servant: 'For the Son of man came not to be served but to serve, and to give his life as a ransom for many' (Mark 10.45). Why did Jesus thus think of his redemptive suffering in terms of his baptism? Presumably because he had already come to see his baptism in terms of redemptive suffering. What was to be 'accomplished' on Golgotha could only be understood as the full flowering of what was begun in Jordan. But that being baptized by John carried any such implications—that it involved in any sense setting one's foot on the path of redemptive suffering—of this there is no hint in the Gospels. But again the Dead Sea Scrolls may provide the missing link. For, according to the Manual of Discipline, the function of the inner group of twelve laymen and three priests, who were to embody the ultimate ideal of the whole Community, was 'to maintain faithfulness in the land . . . with a broken spirit, and to expiate iniquity through practising justice and through the anguish of the refining furnace' (viii.3 f.).

Secondly, new light may be shed on the connexion between Jesus' baptism by John and his subsequent baptism with the Spirit. This latter is accompanied by the declaration: 'Thou art my Son, the beloved, with thee I am well pleased.' It is generally recognized that behind these words stand those of Isa. 42.1: 'Behold my servant, whom I uphold, my chosen in whom my soul delights; I have put my spirit upon him, he will bring forth justice to the nations.'[20] But what is the link between Jesus' baptism with water and his anointing with the Spirit as the παῖς θεοῦ? The Gospels are content merely to stress the immediacy of the connexion (Mark 1.10). Part of the reason has already been suggested, namely, that the water baptism itself meant setting one's foot on the path of the Servant. But what is the relation between this baptism and that unique event which followed for Jesus but for none of the others who shared John's baptism?

Again the whole outlook of the Qumran sect is instructive. As we saw, they expected their present rites of purification to give place to a 'baptism' with holy Spirit that God himself would administer. All their activity was but preliminary to the time when the messianic age would dawn (1QS ix.10 f.; 1QSa ii.11; CDC ix.10 and 29; xv.4; xviii.8). And to hasten that day there was to be within the Community as a whole a dedicated nucleus, who in special degree were to embody to perfection the purifying discipline of the order. And then, 'when these things come to pass

[20] Cf. particularly O. Cullmann, *Baptism in the New Testament* (ET, SBT 1, 1950), pp. 16–22; J. Jeremias, *The Servant of God* (ET, SBT 20, 1957), pp. 81 f.

in Israel [i.e., when such purification and dedication is fully perfected], the Council of the Community [viz., the whole body] will have been established in truth:

> As an eternal planting, a holy house of Israel,
> A most holy institution of Aaron,
> True witnesses with regard to religion
> And the chosen of divine acceptance to atone for the earth
> (1QS viii.4–6).[21]

In other words, the final object of all the sect's discipline, repentance and purification is that the Community itself may become the embodiment of the Servant ideal, the Elect of God for his atoning work (cf. Isa. 43.10; 53.12). And in Jesus this ideal is *already declared* by the divine voice to have found its fulfilment: here and now, in this man, is God's purified instrument 'to serve the purpose of grace to make atonment for the earth' (viii. 9½) and to establish the new and eternal covenant (viii.10a). Baptized by John, and without further need to be made perfect, Jesus is designated what the covenanters, and (shall we say?) John too, envisaged as the agent by whom the messianic period would be ushered in.

But there is, perhaps, yet more exciting to come. For it may be that the sect actually expected that this Servant ideal would be embodied in the Community as a whole only through an *individual*, whom God must first purify and anoint with the Spirit, to be the means of communicating his knowledge of God to the rest. All here turns on a crux of translation and exegesis. But, whether it will prove itself or not, one cannot ignore the highly suggestive interpretation which Professor Brownlee has since placed[22] upon a passage quoted earlier. For if he is right, the sect had an expectation of an eschatological figure delineated in terms of the suffering Servant:

> And at that time God will purify by his truth all the deeds of *a man*; and he will refine him more than the sons of men, in order to consume every evil spirit from the midst of his flesh, to cleanse him through the holy Spirit from all wicked practices; and he will sprinkle upon him the

[21]Translation as revised by W. H. Brownlee, *BASOR* 135 (Oct. 1954), 34.
[22]*BASOR* 135 (Oct. 1954), 33–8. Reicke (*op. cit.*, p. 14) and J.-P. Audet ('Affinités littéraires et doctrinales du Manuel de Discipline', *RevB* LX (1953), 74) come independently to a similar interpretation.

Spirit of truth as purifying water so as to cleanse him from all untrue abominations and from being contaminated with the Spirit of impurity, so that he may give the upright insight into the knowledge of the Most High and into the wisdom of the sons of heaven,[23] in order to make wise the perfect of way. For God has chosen them to be an eternal covenant; and all the glory of Adam will be theirs; and there will be no more perversity, all works of fraud having been put to shame (1QS iv.20–3).

If this is the true sense of the passage, it gives a perfect connexion between the baptism of Jesus and his anointing with the Spirit as the Servant of the Lord for his consummating work of revelation and redemption. Moreover, it opens up the possibility that John himself, as the fourth Gospel asserts, should have been looking by revelation for precisely such a figure: 'He who sent me to baptize with water said to me, "He on whom you see the Spirit descend and remain, this is he who baptizes with holy Spirit." And I have seen and have borne witness that this is the Son of God'[24] (John 1.33 f.). The Scrolls, to be sure, have so far provided no exact parallel for the idea that it is *through* the 'coming one' that God would baptize his people with holy Spirit.[25] But given the fact that this was John's message—and such is the unanimous testimony of the Evangelists—we may now be able to see why he should have expected to recognize this figure in one who was *himself* to be baptized with the Spirit before he could communicate its gifts of wisdom and knowledge to others.

The purpose of John's baptism, we may say, was precisely to force the eschatological issue. The identity of the coming one indeed remained hidden from him as from the rest (John 1.26, 31, 33). What distinguished John was his certainty that this figure

[23]Cf. Test. Levi xviii.6–8: 'The heavens shall be opened . . . and the glory of the Most High shall be uttered over him, and the spirit of understanding and sanctification shall rest upon him (in the water). For he shall give the majesty of the Lord to his sons in truth for evermore.' (R. H. Charles' translation.)

[24]Originally again the παῖς θεοῦ as in the declaration 'Thou art my Son'? Cf. the v. l., ὁ ἐκλεκτός τοῦ θεοῦ, which Jeremias argues to be the true reading (*op. cit.*, p. 61), and Luke 9.35.

[25]The nearest apparent parallel is in CDC ii.10: 'And through his Messiah he shall make them know his holy Spirit.' (R. H. Charles' translation.) But this certainly refers, like the rest of the passage, to the *past* history of Israel. Millar Burrows, *The Dead Sea Scrolls* (1956), p. 350 (though not on p. 264), translates: 'And he caused them to know by his anointed his holy Spirit'; and C. Rabin, *The Zadokite Documents* (1954), p. 8, renders: 'By the hand of his anointed ones' (i.e., the prophets); cf. CDC viii.2; 1QS i.3; and Ps. 105.15.

now stood waiting only to be revealed (John 1.26). And so he emerges, at the prompting of God (John 1.33), to set the last things in motion by his baptism of water. For that was the necessary preliminary and pointer to that other 'baptism' by the Spirit, which was to consecrate the coming one for his mission (John 1.31), the ultimate divine mission of taking away the sin of the world (John 1.29),[26] and of pouring out upon men the holy Spirit of God (John 1.33).

Such is the reconstruction of the fourth Evangelist. Few modern commentators have been prepared to consider it seriously as history. But the new material must at least raise the question whether it does not in fact make surprising sense as an interpretation of John's work.[27]

It has indeed been widely, and increasingly, recognized that the early chapters of John embody a tradition remarkably well informed on southern Palestine prior to the fall of Jerusalem, and provide location and details of the Baptist's activity for whose inclusion there would appear to be no conceivable theological interest. But with this, paradoxically, has gone an estimate of the Evangelist's portrait of John as a picture drawn almost wholly from theological motives of a polemical nature and

[26]The title 'the Lamb of God' remains as mysterious as ever. But both C. H. Dodd (*The Interpretation of the Fourth Gospel* (1953), p. 238) and C. K. Barrett ('The Lamb of God,' *NTS* 1 (1955), 213) agree that it could plausibly have been used by the Baptist himself, standing in the apocalyptic tradition represented in Enoch and Revelation. The other echoes of the Servant language, if established, would reopen the question whether the phrase should not be traced to the Ebed Jahweh tradition of Isa. 53.7 and 12, and, for the first time, could associate the Baptist himself with this interpretation. In any case, the idea of a divine agent (whether corporate or individual) who would take away the sin of the earth (or the land) must not now be judged at all inconceivable on the lips of John. But, whatever the precise background, it is the abolition, as much as the redemption, of sin which is in mind. Though the Qumran group thought of themselves as making atonement for the faithful, they had no doubt that the only hope for there being 'no more wrong-doing' lay in the utter condemnation of wickedness (1QS iv.23; viii.9½). The prospects for the godless in eternal fire, both in their thinking (1QS ii.8, 15) and in John's (Matt. 3.10, 12 = Luke 3.9, 17), reveal a conception of the purging of sin which owes quite as much to Malachi (3.2 f.; 4.1) as to Second Isaiah.

[27]Thomas, *op. cit.*, pp. 86 f., cites John 1.31 and 33 as summing up very accurately the distinctive feature of John's mission, namely, that he alone within the Baptist movement (prior to the evidence of Qumran) justified his activity by reference to a coming messianic baptism.

possessed consequently of very little historical value. This assessment has been considerably influenced by the enormous gulf that appeared to exist between the eschatological prophet of the desert and that philosophical milieu of Hellenistic Judaism within which the fourth Evangelist was supposed to be writing: the religious outlook of the one could scarcely be reflected very accurately in the theological purpose of the other.

But the discovery of the Scrolls has not only made us review the historical accuracy of the account of the Baptist furnished by the fourth Gospel; it has revealed that *in theology* the language and outlook of Qumran have striking affinities not merely with those of the Baptist but even more with those of the Evangelist.[28] Perhaps the two were not so far apart, nor so unsympathetic, after all. Indeed, there is much to be said for the old view that the tradition at any rate behind the opening chapters of the Gospel derives from a follower of Jesus who had actually been a disciple of John (cf. John 1.35). And that that tradition should be marked both by the historical traits and by the theological character which it has is best explained if we can posit an earlier association between John and Qumran. For this Community is the common factor, and indeed the only common factor, between the stark prophet of the Judaean desert and those quasi-Gnostic forms of thought which hitherto had seemed so un-Palestinian

[28]Cf. K. G. Kuhn, 'Die in Palästina gefundenen hebräischen Texte und das Neue Testament', *Zeitschrift für Theologie und Kirche* XLVII (1950), 209 f.; W. Groussow, 'The Dead Sea Scrolls and the New Testament', *Studia Catholica* XXVI (1951), 295–9; B. Reicke, *op. cit.*, *Religion och Bibel* XI (1952), 15 f.; Lucetta Mowry, 'The Dead Sea Scrolls and the Background to the Gospel of John', *BA* XVII (1954), 78–97; F. M. Braun, O.P., 'L'arrière-fond judaïque du quatrième évangile et la Communauté de l'Alliance', *RevB* LXII (1955), 5–44; W. H. Brownlee, *op. cit.*, *Interpretation* IX (1955), 84–9; R. E. Brown, S.S., 'The Qumran Scrolls and the Johannine Gospel and Epistles', *Catholic Biblical Quarterly* XVII (1955), 403–19, 559–74 = *The Scrolls and the NT*, pp. 183–207; O. Cullmann, 'The Significance of the Qumran Texts for Research into the Beginnings of Christianity', *JBL* LXXIV (1955), 213–26 = *The Scrolls and the NT*, pp. 18–32; E. Stauffer, *op. cit.*, *TLZ* LXXXI (1956), cols. 136–49; G. Molin, *Die Söhne des Lichts* (Vienna, 1954); R. Gyllenberg, 'Die Anfänge der johanneischen Tradition', in *Neutestamentliche Studien für Rudolf Bultmann*, ed. W. Eltester (BZNW 21, 1954), pp. 144–7; M. Burrows, *op. cit.*, pp. 338–40; W. F. Albright, 'Recent Discoveries in Palestine and the Gospel of St John', in *The Background of the New Testament and its Eschatology*, ed. W. D. Davies and D. Daube (1956), pp. 163–71; J. Steinmann, *Saint Jean-Baptiste* (1956), pp. 58 ff.; E. Stauffer, *Jerusalem und Rom* (1957), pp. 88–93.

and so late. If Qumran does provide the unsuspected link, then it should no longer surprise us to find a document which appears to reveal an intimate and an accurate familiarity with both.

That there was such an association between the Baptist and Qumran still remains a hypothesis. But the function of a hypothesis, scientifically, is to enable us to correlate the data we possess and to perceive new connexions. It must be tested by its historical plausibility and its ability to provide this correlation. This study has attempted no more than to suggest some of the considerations relevant to this test.[29]

[29] H. H. Rowley in his article 'The Baptism of John and the Qumran Sect', *New Testament Essays*, ed. A. J. B. Higgins (1959), pp. 218–29, has subsequently mounted a scathing attack on any easy identification of John's baptism with the practice at Qumran. But my article had evidently not come to his notice, and I am not convinced that its thesis, particularly in relation to the theological connexions between the two movements, has been demolished.

II

ELIJAH, JOHN AND JESUS[1]

AN ESSAY IN DETECTION

I HAVE called this an essay in detection. That means it is a tale of some mystery and still more imagination. It must be left to the reader to decide whether it should properly be classed as detective fiction.

Let me start from what may not irreverently be called one of the most carefully laid clues in the Gospel story. Jesus has just seen off the emissaries of John the Baptist, who have been trying to probe the secret of his person; and, turning to the crowd, he says: 'Well, and what do you make of *him*? Why did you go out to him? To see a prophet? Yes, I tell you, and more than a prophet. This is the one of whom it is written, "Behold, I send my messenger before thy face, who shall prepare thy way before thee." Truly, I tell you, among those born of women there has risen no one greater than John the Baptist. . . . And if you are prepared to accept it, he is Elijah who is to come. He who has the ears to hear, let him hear' (Matt. 11.7–15). It is safe to say that the clue was lost as completely upon those who heard it as it is upon us who read it. It was lost upon the audience at the time, because it was so improbable as to be the sort of clue one can happily leave around without fear of anyone picking it up. It is lost upon us, because we are so familiar with the end of the story that we do not recognize it as a clue at all.

If the Gospel narrative can be read, as in a real sense Mark evidently intended it to be read, as a mystery story, with its centre in the messianic secret, then a subordinate and closely connected theme is the secret of this man John. Just who was *he*, and what is his relation to the main plot? Of course, for Mark's readers, as for us, it is an open secret: Jesus is the Christ, and John is his forerunner, the promised Elijah. That is how the story comes out,

[1]Reprinted from *NTS* iv (1958), 263–81.

and, being written backwards, like a good detective story, the Gospels everywhere presuppose this solution. But we who have never expected any other fail to realize how surprising this is. If we did not know this was the way it would work out, we ought to begin by expecting something quite different. And this clue on which I have fastened is, at any rate in St Matthew's Gospel, the first hint that could possibly put us on the right trail.[2]

We assume that all along John has been introduced into the story as Elijah, the forerunner of the Messiah, that he was taken for Elijah and regarded himself as Elijah. But of this, except in Luke, there has been no hint. In the whole of the first half of the Marcan story there is only one person who is taken for Elijah—and that is Jesus!

But did not John think of himself as Elijah, preparing the way for the Christ? John in fact never mentions Elijah, except in one very significant passage to which we shall return. He spoke simply of the one mightier than himself who was to come after him (Mark 1.7 and pars), of the nameless 'one who should come' (Matt. 11.3 = Luke 7.15). Who this was to be we are not told. But to anyone who knew his Old Testament, there was one figure with whom at any rate this expected one corresponded most closely in his prospective *function*—and that ultimately for the Jew was decisive. For what he would *do* would be what the figure in the closing chapters of Malachi was cast to do. This is the one of whom it was written: 'Behold, he is coming, says the Lord of Hosts. But who can endure the day of his coming, and who can stand when he appears?' (Mal. 3.1 f.). And in the prophecy as we now have it, and as the men of the New Testament read it,[3]

[2]This may not be strictly true; for in his initial description of John it is possible that he has dropped a hint which afterwards can be seen for what it is. He has described John as wearing 'a garment of camel's hair, and a leather belt round his waist' (Matt. 3.4 = Mark 1.6). This *could* be an allusion to II Kings 1.8, where Elijah is recognized by his wearing 'a garment of hair cloth (RSV), with a leather belt round his waist'. But the LXX and the previous English versions are almost certainly right in taking the Hebrew to mean simply that Elijah, like Esau, was a hairy man. This is the sort of man a prophet was expected to be, and, according to Zech. 13.4, anyone who wished to be taken for a prophet would put on a hairy mantle. There is no suggestion that its wearer was intended to be identified specifically with Elijah. C. Kraeling, *John the Baptist*, pp. 14 f., agrees that there is no reference to Elijah in John's dress.

[3]The Messenger and Elijah are clearly equated in Matt. 11.10–14.

this coming one is subsequently identified as 'Elijah the prophet' (Mal. 4.5).

In other words, if John saw anyone as Elijah, it was *not* himself but the one coming *after* him. To be sure, this figure remains anonymous, though it is just possible that there may be an allusion to his identity in the fourth Gospel, which preserves, I am persuaded, in the Baptist material some very good independent tradition.[4] Here the Baptist's description of 'the one coming after me' is supplemented by the mysterious words, ἔμπροσθέν μου γέγονεν, ὅτι πρῶτός μου ἦν (1.15; cf. 1.30). In the present purpose of the Evangelist the reference is undoubtedly to the pre-existent Logos. But if these words have any place on the lips of the Baptist himself, they might well indicate, in a deliberately cryptic manner, that the man (1.30) for whose appearing John was waiting was one who had already been before him, namely, Elijah.[5]

But it is the *character* of the coming one which is the real indication that John may have seen him as Elijah *redivivus*. For he is before anything else to be a man of fire. And the man of fire *par excellence* was Elijah. It was he whom Jewish tradition remembered and extolled as the 'prophet like fire, whose word was like a burning furnace' and who 'three times brought down fire from

[4]Whatever the circumstances and the environment in which this Gospel was eventually put out, there is little doubt in my mind that it rests upon oral tradition with a southern Palestinian milieu prior to AD 70, parallel to, and independent of, the Synoptic tradition. It can also be shown, I believe, to have come through an individual or group originally within the Baptist movement. John 1.37 ('the two disciples heard him say this') represents accurately enough the angle from which this material is written (cf. the saying under discussion in this paragraph, which at its first appearance in 1.15 is introduced by the words, 'This is he of whom I *spoke*'). There is indeed little to set against the traditional view that the unnamed disciple of the pair was the actual source of this material—whether or not he was also the author of the Gospel. This assessment of the early chapters of John is, I believe, strengthened, as I shall indicate, by the evidence of the Dead Sea Scrolls.

[5] This suggestion, for what it is worth, has since been accepted by R. E. Brown, 'Three Quotations from John the Baptist in the Gospel of John', *Catholic Biblical Quarterly* XXII (1960), 297 f. Dr C. H. Dodd suggested to me that the saying may originally have meant: 'There is one among my disciples who has gained precedence over me, for he is my superior.' This is very attractive and fits the regular use of ὀπίσω ἔρχεσθαι for being a disciple (e.g. Mark 8.34 and pars; Luke 14.27). But the close Synoptic parallel to the saying in Mark 1.7 f. and pars must have a temporal reference; cf. also Acts 13.25: ἰδοὺ ἔρχεται μετ' ἐμέ.

heaven' (Ecclus. 48.1–3).[6] For the coming one is to baptize not merely in water, like John, but with fire (Matt. 3.11 = Luke 3.16). He is to purge his threshing floor (Matt. 3.12 = Luke 3.17), just as the messenger of Malachi, like a refiner's fire, will purge and purify the sons of Levi (Mal. 3.2 f.). The axe is laid to the root of the trees, ready for them to be cut down and thrown into the fire (Matt. 3.10 = Luke 3.9), and, after the winnowing, the chaff is to be burnt with unquenchable fire (Matt. 3.12 = Luke 3.17)— all of which again is in the programme of Malachi for when 'the day comes, burning like an oven, when all the arrogant and all evildoers will be stubble; and the day that comes shall burn them up, says the Lord of hosts, so that it will leave them neither root nor branch' (Mal. 4.1).

But whether or not John specifically saw the coming one as Elijah, one thing is clear: he could not have thought of *himself* as Elijah. Elijah was not the man to operate with water! As on Carmel, Elijah was the one to appear on the scene when Israel (symbolized deliberately in the twelve stones out of which the altar was made) had already been drenched in water: then *he* could come near and call down fire from the Lord (I Kings 18.30–9). If John did think of the coming one as Elijah, then he may, as Dr G. S. Duncan has suggested,[7] have seen himself rather in the position of Elijah's servant (I Kings 18.43; 19.3), preparing for his master's return in the Jordan valley, unworthy though he was even to take off his shoes.

But perhaps we have allowed ourselves to be obsessed with Elijah as a category in terms of whom somehow John must be interpreted. Elijah is after all introduced only into the coda of the Malachi prophecy, and it would be a mistake to assume that John geared all his thinking to this single figure. John, as we have seen, never speaks of himself or of any one else as Elijah. And the closest background for the activity of John is now, I believe, provided in the scrolls of the Qumran sect,[8] who, as far as we know, did not look specifically for the coming of Elijah at all.

[6] Cf. II Kings 2.9–11, where both spirit and fire are associated with Elijah's assumption; and the gloss on Luke 9.54: 'Shall we bid fire come down from heaven, and consume them, *as Elijah did*?'

[7] *Jesus, Son of Man* (1947), pp. 82–6.

[8] See 'The Baptism of John and the Qumran Community', pp. 11–27 above.

Perhaps the most remarkable effect of this new material has been the vindication it appears to offer of the picture of John and his mission provided by the fourth Gospel.[9] It may, therefore, predispose us to credit that there is after all historical truth, and not merely polemic, when this Gospel makes John answer the question, 'Are you Elijah?' with a laconic and uncompromising 'No' (1.21). That is indeed an astonishing piece of evidence to have survived in a story which clearly states, on the authority of no less than Jesus himself, that this is precisely what he was. But the two statements are not in fact mutually incompatible. Let us see what happens if we assume both to be true. *John* said that he was not Elijah; but *Jesus* said that that is just what he was. In other words, Jesus' judgment exactly reverses what the story has led us so far to expect. That, I believe, is the first thing to grasp if we are to understand the incident from which we started. But even this does not exhaust the full irony of the situation.

John had spoken of a mightier one coming after him. Jesus had in fact come after him. As far as the Synoptic account goes, John never drew the conclusion.[10] But he did pose the question: 'Are you, can you be, the coming one?' I shall suggest later that John's question is provoked because Jesus appeared no longer to be fulfilling the role that John had cast for him. In other words, the question assumes, rather than rules out,[11] the supposition that John had at one time seen Jesus as the fulfiller of his hopes. And this is what the fourth Gospel says. But whether or not *John* had recognized in Jesus 'the coming one', it is evident that others had. Jesus was precisely what, according to the fourth Evangelist, John had said that he himself was not: he was the Prophet that should come into the world (John 6.14; 7.40); he was Elijah (Mark 6.15; 8.28). And it is instructive to observe that this estimate that he was Elijah is, on each occasion, offered as an *alternative* to the supposition that he was John the Baptist raised from the dead, which is further, and from its incidental character very strong,

[9] See the essay just mentioned, and the works there cited, pp. 24–26 above.

[10] The Synoptists never *deny* that John recognized Jesus. Indeed, Matthew clearly presupposes that he did (3.14 f.), though the passage is obviously secondary and cannot be used for interpreting the mind of John. The supposed contradiction with the fourth Gospel rests in fact upon an argument from silence.

[11] As Kraeling maintains, *op. cit.*, p. 127.

evidence that people did not think of identifying *John* with Elijah.[12]

It was in such categories as the Prophet and Elijah that men first sought to understand Jesus. We tend to think that, of these answers, while the former was inadequate, the second was clearly wrong, and could have been given only by those on the fringe. On the contrary, on the basis of all that they had to go upon, it was right, and was, as I shall try to show later, the estimate, not of outsiders, but of disciples.[13] Precisely this was the response of *faith*, to identify Jesus fully and completely with 'the coming one' of John's preaching. And this, once more, is what the fourth Gospel asserts: 'They said, "John did no sign, but everything John said about this man was true." And many *believed* in him there' (10.41 f.).

And so we come to the point from which we started. '*Are* you the one of whom I spoke?', asks John from his cell. The reply he receives throws the question back on him. Exactly what it means we shall consider later. It is deliberately wrapped up; for the identity of the central figure of the mystery cannot be disclosed except to faith. But while we are still looking, as it were, in the other direction, another most important clue is dropped at our very feet. It reads: '*This* (οὗτος) is the one of whom it is written, "Behold, I send my messenger before thy face, who shall prepare thy way before thee"' (Matt. 11.10 = Luke 7.27). In other words, *John* is the messenger of Malachi, the coming mighty one. And, as if this were not enough, it is at once followed, in Matthew, by another statement even more explicit: 'And if you are prepared to accept it, he is himself (αὐτός ἐστιν) Elijah, the one who is to come' (Matt. 11.14). There is nothing so effective as a clue you

---

[12]Cf. T. W. Manson, *The Sayings of Jesus* (1949), p. 69.
[13]In this it contrasts strongly with the view that Jesus was John the Baptist raised from the dead, which, as O. Cullmann points out in an excellent discussion (*The Christology of the New Testament* (ET, 1959), pp. 31–4), could have been entertained only by those who had never known that Jesus was a contemporary of John or had been baptized by him. Mark (6.14–16), followed by Matthew (14.1 f.), introduces this notion, in contrast to the others, as a peculiarity of Herod's. And this could well preserve an historical reminiscence. Against T. W. Manson ('John the Baptist', *BJRL* xxxvi (1953–4), 399), I should accept ἔλεγεν as the original reading. The plural ἔλεγον is readily explained by the tendency (already visible in Luke 9.7) to assimilate this to the other estimates as a general view.

do not need to hide. To us it is so obvious that we miss its significance; to the crowds it must have sounded so fantastic as to find no lodgment. 'Are you the coming one?', asks John of Jesus. 'He is *himself* the coming one', says Jesus of John; 'all that this man said of another is true—but of himself!'

By this time we ought not to know where we are, on our head or our feet. But the trouble is that we know very well. For we have read the last chapter. Moreover, if the edition of the story we are reading is that of Mark, some spoil-sport has actually scribbled it in on the first page. In the very opening line, right underneath the title, we read: 'As it is written in Isaiah the prophet, "Behold, I send my messenger before thy face, who shall prepare thy way; the voice of one crying in the wilderness: Prepare the way of the Lord, make his paths straight" ' (1.2 f.).

Now it does not require Sherlock Holmes to detect that there is something very peculiar here. The words 'Behold, I send my messenger before thy face, who shall prepare thy way' are not written in 'Isaiah the prophet': they are written in Malachi (3.1; cf. Ex. 23.20 (LXX)). Moreover, the phrase to 'prepare *thy* way', which has been deliberately changed from the original, does not agree grammatically with 'make *his* paths straight'. It is all a very botched affair, and I have little doubt that someone wrote in the words from Malachi[14] to supply the clue which he knew was coming later, that the messenger of Malachi (alias Elijah) was none other than the Baptist himself. I called him a spoil-sport; Lagrange, with more scholarly restraint, is content with 'un glossateur très ancien'.[15]

But the real reason why Jesus' disclosure does not perplex us is that like our glossator we already have a neat little framework into which everything fits. It consists of the following formula: 'John was the messenger (alias Elijah), who came to prepare the

[14] The fact that the Malachi quotation agrees neither with the LXX nor with the Hebrew but is verbally identical with its citation in Matt. 11.10 = Luke 7.27 strongly suggests that this is where it came from. It is absent from the parallels to Mark 1.2 in both Matthew and Luke, which may indicate that it was not in their copies of Mark—though they would, of course, have had the same reasons for rejecting it as we have. The common phrase to 'prepare the way', would easily explain how the two quotations from Isaiah and Malachi came to be fused. The fourth Gospel carefully refuses any such assimilation: John *is* the voice of Isaiah (1.23) but he is *not* Elijah (1.21).

[15] *S. Matthieu* (1923), p. cxx. So also V. Taylor, *St Mark* (1952), *ad loc.*

way of "the Lord"; and "the Lord" was Christ.' According to this view, John asks, 'Are you the coming one?', meaning, 'Are you the Christ?' Jesus replies, in effect, 'Yes'. Whereupon Jesus says, 'And John is Elijah'—naturally, since Elijah is by definition the forerunner of Christ. The figure of whom John asks, 'Are you he who is to come?', and the person to whom Jesus refers in his answer as 'Elijah, the one who is to come' are not, on this view, the same (as we should otherwise naturally presume). On the contrary, the latter prepares the way for the former. In this way everyone is neatly cast; and the only mystery is why Jesus should say at the end, 'If you are prepared to receive it'. Why not?

For this solution one simple assumption alone is necessary. It is that the role of Elijah is to be the forerunner of the Christ. For then, if Jesus is the Christ, John must be Elijah. And this assumption is indeed one of the most potent psychological factors in making us think (against all the evidence) that John must have seen *himself* as Elijah. For if he had regarded the one coming *after* him as Elijah, and if, by definition, Elijah is the forerunner of the Messiah, then John must have seen himself as the forerunner of the forerunner—which is getting fantastic. Indeed, it is precisely on these grounds that Professor Jeremias in his article on Elijah in Kittel's *Wörterbuch*[16] denies that John could have thought of himself as preparing for Elijah. For 'Elijah' presupposes yet another figure; and there is no suggestion that John visualized *two* people coming after him.

But let us stop and look at this definition that Elijah is the forerunner of the Messiah. It is one that Albert Schweitzer retained, despite the fact that he recognized the most important clue of all, that it was only Jesus who first thought of calling John Elijah.[17] And thereby he laid himself open to Jeremias' criticism, of a whole regress of forerunners.

I believe we have got to go further and say that it was also Jesus and the Church who between them fixed the notion that 'Elijah' meant 'the forerunner of the Christ'. Jesus himself never says this; but he made the equation inevitable. For he identified

[16]*TWNT* II, 930–43.
[17]*The Mystery of the Kingdom of God* (ET, 1925), pp. 138–56; *The Quest of the Historical Jesus* (ET², 1911), pp. 371–4. M. Dibelius' argument that this identification does not go back to Jesus (*Die urchristliche Überlieferung von Johannes dem Taufer* (1903), pp. 30–32) is to me unconvincing.

John, who had in fact gone before him, with the messenger of
Malachi (alias Elijah) who was to go before 'the Lord'. With the
Church's equation of 'the Lord' of the Old Testament with Jesus
as the Christ, the completion of the formula was bound to follow.
I am not arguing that no one before had ever thought of Elijah
like this: we simply have not the evidence to say. What I am
maintaining is that one cannot assume that Elijah was at that time
by definition or consent the forerunner of the Christ. There was
no such consent. In fact, as far as I can discover, there is no pre-
Christian evidence that he ever was so regarded.

In Malachi, the origin of all the later speculation, Elijah is to
come, not before the Christ, but before 'the great and terrible
day of the Lord'. Again, in Ecclesiasticus, the only other pre-
Christian document to speak specifically of Elijah's return,[18] he
comes 'to still the heart before the fierce anger of *God*' (48.10 f.).
As G. F. Moore recognized,[19] 'Sirach does not connect the return
of Elijah with the appearance of the Messiah, of whom, indeed,
there is no mention in the book'. According to Mark 9.11, 'the
scribes' said that Elijah must come 'first'. By this they may have
meant 'before the Messiah', but we do not know. In the context
of Mark it would most naturally mean before 'the rising from the
dead', that is, for the Jew, the general resurrection at the last day.
The first clear reference to Elijah as the precursor, and indeed
anointer, of the Messiah occurs in Justin Martyr's *Dialogue with
Trypho* (8.4; 49.1). Now Justin may or may not be right in saying
that this was common Jewish belief—it is always perilous to
reconstruct the creed of an opponent from a work of apologetic.
Klausner, the Jew, thinks that he is, but has to admit that 'the
Tannaitic literature has little to say with respect to the activity
of Elijah in his role as the Messiah's forerunner'.[20] Again, I should
not wish to assert dogmatically that this is a purely Christian

[18]There is apparently a reference to Elijah in the 'ram' of I Enoch 90.31
(cf. 89.52), but no suggestion of his return to earth. According to IV Ezra
6.26, 'the men who have been taken up, who have not tasted death from their
birth, shall appear'. They undoubtedly include Elijah, but whether they are
to be regarded as forerunners of the Messiah is much more questionable.
In 7.28 it is said that 'my Son the Messiah shall be revealed, *together with* those
who are with him', and these are likely to be the same as those mentioned
in 6.26.
[19]*Judaism* II (1927), p. 358 n. 2.
[20]J. Klausner, *The Messianic Idea in Israel* (ET, 1956), p. 456.

conception. What I wish to challenge is the opposite dogma, that Elijah was understood, and must have been understood, by John and everyone else, as the forerunner of the Messiah.[21]

On the contrary, all recent evidence points to the fact that there was no such graduated messianic programme. It would probably be nearer the truth to see a considerable number of figures, in various strands of popular expectation, all of whom carried 'messianic' or eschatological overtones—the Coming One, Elijah, Jeremiah, the Prophet like Moses, the Son of David, the Elect One, the Son of Man, the Anointed One, and even (since the evidence of the Dead Sea Scrolls) the Anointed Ones. These might be variously combined, like the Prophet and the Anointed Ones of Aaron and Israel in the Qumran Manual of Discipline (1QS ix.11). Or they might be assimilated to each other.[22] In the current expectations reflected in the Gospels, Elijah, the Prophet, the Christ, and the rest are treated always as *parallel* and alternative hopes (John 1.20 f.; 6.14 f; 7.40 f.; Mark 6.15; 8.28 f.; cf. 13.22). Indeed, according to the fourth Gospel, John says specifically that he *has* been sent before the Christ (3.28) and at the same time that he is *not* Elijah (1.21), which would be sheer contradiction if at the time the two functions were equated.

When therefore John asked whether Jesus were 'the coming one', he was not inquiring whether he were the Christ as opposed to his forerunner (the traditional view) or the forerunner as

---

[21]Cf. Moore, *op. cit.*, II, 357: 'It was the universal belief that shortly before the appearance of the Messiah Elijah should return'; and S. Mowinckel, *He that Cometh* (ET, 1956), p. 299: 'The thought of Elijah as the forerunner of the Messiah seems to have been widespread in Judaism.' But the references they give entirely fail to substantiate this. For what scanty Rabbinic evidence there is, see Strack-Billerbeck IV, 785–9 and Jeremias in *TWNT* II, 933–5. There is in fact equally good Rabbinic evidence for *equating* Elijah with the Messiah (of the priestly line) (Strack-Billerbeck IV, 789–92). But again the earlier documents which specifically mention a priestly Messiah (the Dead Sea Scrolls, the Damascus Document and the Testaments of the Twelve Patriarchs) contain no hint of such an equation. Elijah is simply not mentioned.

Cullmann (*op. cit.*, p. 23) maintains that *both* conceptions of Elijah (or the prophet of the end) were current in the New Testament period—that he was the forerunner of God (the original view) *and* that he was the forerunner of the Messiah. But for the latter he produces no more evidence than the rest.

[22]Thus, the designation 'the coming one', which stands by itself in Matt. 11.3, is attached to Elijah in Matt. 11.14, to the Prophet in John 6.14, and to the Christ, the Son of God, in John 11.27.

opposed to the Christ (Schweitzer's view). That is to read back into his question later distinctions. What he was asking was something much simpler, namely whether Jesus were the 'coming one' of John's own preaching. And John's version of the eschatological figure had, as we have seen, largely been painted from Malachi's palette. Was Jesus *this* figure? is John's question.

And when we see it in this light we can begin to understand Jesus' answer. We take that answer, in effect, to be 'Yes'. It might be as near the truth to say that Jesus said, 'No'. 'No, I cannot see myself in that picture. The "coming one" of Elijah's type is the projection of John's own hopes. In fact, if you can accept it, he is himself the embodiment of Elijah's function. I am the "coming one" viewed in a different relation to the final act of God; and, if you would understand that role, you must look not to Malachi, but to Isaiah.' And this is the reason why the answer is given in the language of Scripture (Isa. 29.18 f.; 35.5 f.; 61.1).

But what caused John to ask his question at this juncture, in the midst of the mighty works of Jesus? Was it merely that the dungeons of Machaerus were proving particularly disillusioning? That is pure speculation. If what I propose to put in its place is still speculation, I hope it is not quite so pure.

I suggest the question came when it did because, even from prison, John could tell that all was not going according to programme—that is, according to his programme. There is no reason to suppose that the early reaction that Jesus was Elijah was either arbitrary or misguided. On the contrary, I believe there is evidence to suggest that Jesus began by accepting the Malachi role which John had prepared for him, but that later he laid it aside: if he was to fulfil the Father's will, he could not be 'the mightier one' of that stamp. It was this change of character that John found inexplicable. Jesus was no longer the man he had taken him to be: as Jesus' reply presupposes (Matt. 11.6 = Luke 7.23), John had come to be 'offended at him'.

Such disillusionment, at the height of the Galilean ministry, implies that earlier John had been satisfied with what he saw in Jesus. That, indeed, is how the fourth Gospel represents him: 'This joy of mine is now full' (3.29). And on the strength of this John had been content to fade from the scene (3.30).

But this presupposes in turn that, outwardly at any rate, Jesus was willing to accept the role that John had cast for him. Is this so? If it were, we should hardly expect traces of it to have survived very markedly in our Gospels. For it was clearly a role that he later repudiated, and the Gospels are written to present him, not as Elijah, but as the Christ, the Son of God. But I believe that beneath the surface there is just that amount of evidence to suggest that at the beginning he was prepared to see his mission a good deal more in John's terms.

Later, indeed, while never ceasing to uphold the Baptist and his work (Mark 11.29–33 and pars; Matt. 11.7–11 = Luke 7.24–8; Matt. 21.32), Jesus was to set their ways of life in marked contrast (Matt. 11.16–19 = Luke 7.31–5). But he began by identifying himself with John and his mission. Whatever else Jesus' baptism at the hands of John may mean, it cannot mean less than that.[23] All the Gospels thus represent Jesus as throwing in his lot with John. But the fourth Gospel, though it omits reference to the actual baptism, goes much further, and records a period in the life of Jesus when he worked in close association with the Baptist. This early Judaean ministry is in no way incompatible with the Synoptic assertion that it was not until John was arrested that Jesus began his ministry of preaching and healing in Galilee. Indeed the linking of the two events, which in Mark is merely temporal (1.14) but in Matthew almost causal (4.12), suggests, what the fourth Gospel alone explains, that there is some connexion between them. The actual arrest and death of John is, again, not chronicled by the fourth Evangelist. But he makes it clear that, whereas Jesus' earlier ministry occurred during the period when 'John had not yet been put in prison' (3.24), it was not long (5.35) before he must be referred to in the past tense: 'He was a burning and a shining lamp, and you were willing to rejoice for a while in his light.'[24]

[23]I have suggested above (pp. 20–22), that if John's baptism had its background in the sort of thinking represented at Qumran, it may explain more easily why Jesus should have felt compelled to identify himself with it. For it enables us to envisage John's mission as having a positive and atoning purpose, requiring repentance not merely, as the Gospels would suggest, to escape the coming judgment, but to create in Israel a pure and purifying remnant.

[24]It is just possible that the phrase ἐκεῖνος ἦν ὁ λύχνος ὁ καιόμενος may contain an echo of Ecclus. 48.1, where it is said of Elijah that his word ὡς λαμπὰς ἐκαίετο. If so, we *could* have the Johannine equivalent of *Jesus'*

What, however, is significant is not that Jesus' early ministry overlapped that of John, nor simply that the two were at first working in the same area. It is the fact that during this ministry Jesus' outlook was still essentially one with John's. As M. Goguel put it, 'When Jesus preached and baptized in Perea, it was as a disciple of John the Baptist that he did it.'[25] This aspect of the early narratives of the fourth Gospel was brought out many years ago by my uncle, Dr Armitage Robinson, in his little book, *The Historical Character of St John's Gospel.*[26] He maintained that during this phase the path that Jesus follows can clearly be seen as that which John had marked out for him.

Thus, he contended for the fourth Gospel's placing of the cleansing of the Temple on the ground that it shows Jesus deliberately starting on the fulfilment of Malachi's programme. For what is this but 'the messenger of the Lord, coming suddenly to his temple?' 'And who can stand when he appears? . . . For he will purify the sons of Levi and refine them like gold and silver, till they present right offerings to the Lord.' 'Will man rob God?', they ask. 'Yet you are robbing me', is the reply, '. . . in your tithes and offerings. You are . . . robbing me, the whole nation of you' (Mal. 3.1–3, 8 f.). And so, consumed with zeal for the house of God, Jesus enacts the first stage of John's programme. The threshing-floor is purged, and the first stroke of the axe is wielded that must end in the destruction of the Temple and nation.

That there is such a connexion between the action of Jesus and the teaching of John is borne out by the association made in the Synoptic account. Jesus, challenged to state the authority by which he purges the Temple court, refers his questioners to the baptism of John: the authority behind the one, he says, is the authority behind the other (Mark 11.27–33 and pars). In the

---

identification of the Baptist with Elijah: '*He* was "the burning lamp" (i.e. Elijah)', even though he was not the Light itself to which he witnessed (John 1.8).

[25] *Jean-Baptiste*, pp. 250 f.; cf. pp. 235–57 as a whole. E. Stauffer goes still further and says: 'This early period of Jesus' ministry is only a chapter in the story of the Baptist's movement' (*Jesus and his Story* (ET, 1960), p. 60). E. Lohmeyer pointed out (*Das Urchristentum*, 1: *Johannes der Taufer* (1932), p. 27 n. 2) that the saying of John 3.30, 'He must increase, but I must decrease', even if it reflects anti-Baptist polemic, witnesses to a previous period when their roles were reversed.

[26] 1908; 2nd ed. 1929, pp. 27–31.

position it occupies in Mark (who, knowing but one visit to the City, had no option but to place it where he did), the reference to John, so long out of the picture, appears strangely artificial.[27] But if the Johannine placing is right, the connexion is at once apparent: Jesus' action can be understood only if the mission of the Baptist is acknowledged; for the one flows directly out of the other.

Again, as Armitage Robinson went on to point out, the conversation with Nicodemus represents Jesus as requiring for entry to the coming Kingdom precisely that baptism, not with water only, but with the Spirit, of which John spoke: 'Truly, truly, I say to you, unless one is born of water and the Spirit, he cannot enter the kingdom of God' (John 3.5). No doubt the Evangelist intends his readers to see here an allusion also to Christian baptism. But the vocabulary of the saying, with its reference to 'the kingdom of God', does not suggest that he created it, and it has parallels in the Synoptic tradition.[28] If the words have a setting in the life of Jesus, then the allusion must be to the teaching of John. In my uncle's words, 'the whole of John's mission lies behind the saying'.[29] It most naturally belongs, where the fourth Gospel places it, in a period when the message of Jesus was still dominated by the preaching of the Baptist.

Subsequently, after a period of independent but parallel missions, their paths divide: John goes to prison and Jesus to Galilee. But Jesus' association with the Baptist is not forgotten. And with him goes, inevitably, his reputation as Elijah (Mark 6.15; 8.28). Indeed, there is one incident, placed by Luke considerably later (9.52–6), where two disciples who had been with him from the early days expect him still to sanction this role.

[27]So also Taylor, *St Mark*, p. 461. Cf. H. E. Edwards, *The Disciple who Wrote these Things* (1953), p. 191: 'Is it likely that if John the Baptist had disappeared from public view *two years before* this incident it would still have been dangerous for any member of the Jerusalem aristocracy to disavow belief in him? . . . In fact, the pendant which St Mark attaches to his own story of the Cleansing is the strongest argument for putting that event back to the time assigned to it in the fourth Gospel.'
[28]With John 3.3 and 5, cf. Matt. 18.3, 'Truly, I say to you, unless you turn and become like children, you will never enter the kingdom of heaven' (which is almost certainly independent of Mark) and Mark 10.15, 23, 25; cf. Jeremias, *Infant Baptism in the First Four Centuries* (ET, 1960), pp. 48 ff.
[29]*Op. cit.*, p. 31.

Being tied to Samaria, the episode has to be placed in the only passage through Samaria of which Luke is aware, namely, on the last journey to Jerusalem; and we cannot say it does not belong there. But it would gain considerable force if it in fact had its setting in an earlier occasion when Jesus 'had to pass through Samaria' (John 4.4), namely, on the journey from Judaea which marked his final break with John. Of the unresponsive Samaritans the disciples ask, 'Lord, do you want us to bid fire come down from heaven and consume them?' And the well-attested gloss, 'as Elijah did', merely draws out what they meant. 'But,' we read, 'he turned and rebuked them.' The words that follow in the received text, though doubtless again the commentary of the Church, describe sufficiently the difference of conception: 'And he said, "You do not know what manner of spirit you are of; for the Son of man came not to destroy men's lives but to save them." '

The 'spirit' has indeed changed; the conception and function of 'the mighty one' has altered. It is this difference above all that the reply to the messengers of John sets forth. Jesus has come as the proclaimer of deliverance rather than judgment, of the acceptable year, rather than the terrible day, of the Lord. So it is that Luke represents the new, Galilean gospel from the beginning (4.16–21); and so, for the fourth Gospel also, it is at this point that the healing miracles commence (John 4.46–54), which are precisely the 'works' that mark off the ministry of Jesus from the 'testimony of John' (5.36; cf. 10.41), a ministry which the context declares is primarily to save rather than to judge (5.19–47; cf. 12.47).

If this change of conception receives its first outward expression in the decisive journey from Judaea to Galilee, then the story of the wilderness Temptations may give dramatic form to the struggle that preceded it. The Synoptists agree in placing these between Jesus' baptism and the arrest of John (Mark 1.13 f.; Matt. 4.1–11 = Luke 4.1–13). If a ministry in Judaea occurred in the interval, the crisis could as well have come after it as before. Mark indeed places the Temptations 'immediately' after the Baptism, but his constant use of the word inspires no confidence in it as a serious indication of time. Moreover, John provides a quite different and much more circumstantial account of the sequel to the Baptist's acknowledgement of Jesus. We must choose between them. But there is one hint which may suggest that the time of crisis is to be located at the end rather than the beginning of this period.[30] The reason given in John 4.1 for Jesus' departure into Galilee is a very curious one to invent if it has not behind it some historical tradition: 'Now when the Lord knew that the Pharisees had heard that Jesus was making and baptizing more disciples than John . . . he left Judaea and departed again to Galilee.'[31] The motive can only be to shun the popularity and notoriety of success; and this could well reflect the same struggle represented in the more mythological categories of the 'Q' Temptation story.[32] If this story does express the decisions of this crisis, it is readily intelligible as Jesus' resolution to model himself henceforth not on the mighty one of John's proclamation but on the servant-Son of the Baptismal voice (Mark 1.11; John 1.34;[33] cf. Isa. 42.1). For this call to be God's Son found its archetypal expression in the wilderness call to Israel, and thus it is that Jesus replies to it in the classic words of Deuteronomy,[34] as later he was to use those of Isaiah to answer John.

If there was this change of function, it is perhaps not altogether fantastic to see in the utterances of Luke 12.49–53 (which, like the rest of that chapter, I believe to belong to good, early tradition) Jesus' subsequent reflection upon it. 'I came', he says, 'to bring fire upon the earth.' That was the role of Elijah. The words that follow—καὶ τί θέλω εἰ ἤδη ἀνήφθη;—are usually taken to mean

[30]The interval involved would not in any case have been very long if there is anything behind the reminiscence of the early preaching that it was not until John was 'finishing his course' that he even referred to the one coming after him (Acts 13.25).

[31]G. H. C. MacGregor's proposed emendation to 'When the Lord realized he was making' ('John the Baptist and the Origins of Christianity', *ExpT* XLVI (1935), 360) is quite arbitrary and unnecessary.

[32]H. Preisker has pointed out how all the three wilderness temptations are paralleled in historical incidents in the Gospel of John (in 4.31–4; 6.14 f.; 7.2–6) without the mythological setting in which the 'Q' narrative had already placed them ('Zum Charakter des Johannesevangeliums', *Luther, Kant, Schleiermacher in Ihrer Bedeutung für den Protestantismus. Forschungen und Abhandlungen Georg Wobbermin dargebracht* (1939), pp. 279–84; quoted by P.-H. Menoud, *L'évangile de Jean d'après les recherches récentes*, 2nd ed., 1947, p. 29).

[33]Even if ὁ ἐκλεκτὸς τοῦ θεοῦ is not the true reading (as Jeremias argues, *The Servant of God*, p. 61), I believe that the παῖς conception here lies behind and interprets the title υἱός, as in Mark 1.11.

[34]8.3; 6.13 f.; 6.16. See 'The Temptations', (pp. 53–60 below).

'And how I wish it were already kindled!' But they could equally
naturally, if not more naturally, be translated 'But what do I care
if it is now kindled?'—for that baptism with fire belongs to
another conception of my work. In any case, goes on Jesus, 'I
have a baptism to undergo (rather a baptism to dispense), and
how I am constricted until it is accomplished!' Moreover what
comes next may perhaps contain a deliberate reference to that
mission of Elijah which still men suppose he is aiming to fulfil.
'Do you think', he says, 'that I have come to bring peace to the
earth?' Now this was, from the beginning, the function of Elijah.
He was to come to 'turn the hearts of fathers to their children
and the hearts of children to their fathers' (Mal. 4.6; Ecclus.
48.10; cf. II Esdras 6.26), which the Rabbis interpreted to mean
to settle all disputes, to 'make peace in the world' (Eduyyoth
8.7).[35] 'That', says Jesus, 'the work of the Restorer prior to the
end, cannot describe what I have come to do. My coming is to
bring not peace but division; its result must be precisely the
opposite, to *divide* father against son and son against father. For
this is the period of the end itself, the time when prophecy has
declared that family strife is bound to come.'[36]

The most fundamental change of all is marked by the recognition that Jesus has a baptism not simply, as John said (Mark 1.8
and pars; John 1.33), to administer but himself to suffer. It is to
this baptism to be endured that he refers the same two disciples
who wish to take the kingdom and the glory, if not by storm,
at any rate by reserved ticket: 'Are you able to be baptized with
the baptism with which I am baptized?' (Mark 10.35–40). And that
painful scene is followed by the classic redefinition of the 'mighty
one', in terms not of the potentate but the slave: 'For the Son of
man came not to be served but to serve, and to give his life as a
ransom for many '(10.41–5).

The full recognition of this change, that as the Son of man Jesus
could fulfil God's purpose only through suffering and death, is
again bound up with the person of the Baptist. Professor Carl
Kraeling has plausibly suggested[37] that the difficult saying in

[35]Quoted by Klausner, *op. cit.*, p. 454; cf. Strack-Billerbeck IV, 796 f.
[36]I Enoch 100.1 f.; II Baruch 70.3–7; II Esdras 5.9; 6.24; cf. Micah
7.6; Isa. 19.2; Ezek. 38.21.
[37]*Op. cit.*, pp. 156 f.

Matt. 11.12, 'From the days of John the Baptist until now the kingdom of heaven has suffered violence, and men of violence take it by force', was born of preoccupation with the fate of John. It acknowledges that there is at present a period of duress, still not finished but one day to reach its term, during which the kingdom must needs be subject to the violence and oppression of its enemies. This violence has already engulfed John: 'They have done to him whatever they pleased' (Mark 9.13). And the same necessity now imposes upon Jesus the constriction of his own baptism: 'So also the Son of man must suffer at their hands' (Matt. 17.20).

These last quotations come from the other crucial passage in which Jesus points to John the Baptist as himself being Elijah. This is the conversation on the descent from the mount of Transfiguration—that vision which has so dramatically represented the figures of Elijah and Moses yielding to the servant-Son (rather than the Prophet)[38] as the one that men must heed. The drift of the talk confessedly baffled the disciples, and the Marcan tradition (9.9–13) has preserved it in a confused state, which Matthew has done his best to sort out (17.9–13). It is clear that the inner disciples were no more prepared for the identification of John with Elijah than were the crowds. But this time there was also a further theme, the deep mystery that a *suffering* Elijah was of a piece with a suffering Son of man. Mark (though not Matthew) says of both that this was 'written' of them; but if so, it is certainly true that the disciples 'knew not the scriptures'—nor, for that matter, do we.[39] In any case, of all the disciples these three, Peter,

[38]Cf. Mark 9.7 and pars with Deut. 18.15.

[39]In his article on Elijah in *TWNT* II, 942 f., Jeremias argues that the conception that the returning Elijah must suffer would not have been strange; for it was 'written' in the apocalyptic tradition, of the kind that W. Bousset brought to light in his *Antichrist Legend* (ET, 1896), pp. 203–10, and which has been preserved most notably in the *Apocalypse of Elijah* (tr. G. Steindorff, TU XVII, 3a, 1899, pp. 163 f.). This latter records a tradition remarkably parallel to Rev. 11.1–12, and is, Jeremias argues, independent of it: both, he thinks, go back to a common *Jewish* legend in which Elijah and Enoch(?) suffer and die. He may be right; but all the documents with which we are dealing are late, and are either Christian or heavily worked over by Christian hands; and this applies strongly to the relevant section of the *Apocalypse of Elijah* (Steindorff, pp. 161–9), which opens with the vision of Christ coming on the clouds of heaven preceded by the sign of the Cross. Jeremias' arguments for a tradition within Judaism of a suffering Moses (*TWNT* IV, 867 f.) are also, I believe, precarious.

James and John, were the ones whose minds were apparently least open to the thought that the man of fire must now pass through it himself (Mark 8.31–3; 10.37 f.; Luke 9.54 f.). The reinterpretation of Malachi by Isaiah, and the passing of the role of Elijah to John himself, were indeed for those who could 'receive it'.

How far did the Church receive it? The very fact that the consciousness of its difficulty survived and the question was still of concern to the first two Evangelists suggests that it was not settled out of hand. The Gospels, as we have them, are, of course, the work of a community that had already accepted the solution that Jesus was the Christ and John his forerunner. This is particularly obvious in the case of the third Gospel. Luke omits both the passages in which Jesus proposes his tentative identification of John with Elijah. For him the person of the Baptist is no longer a mystery: he is Elijah from birth (1.16 f.).[40] And yet, paradoxically, it is Luke's writings, because he is so faithful to his sources, that, once we get beneath the editorial surface, provide the most interesting material for reconstructing the process he ignores.

Thus, in Acts 3.12–26, we have a speech which, I have argued elsewhere,[41] preserves extremely primitive material, and indeed reflects a Christological outlook as primitive as any other in the New Testament. The proclamation it presents appears to run like this: God has sent his servant, Jesus, in fulfilment of the promise of a prophet like Moses, to convey the blessing covenanted to Abraham and to turn Israel from its sins. But, instead, the Jewish people have made away with him. Nevertheless, God has not been defeated. He has raised him up, and in his mercy has extended the period open for repentance. 'Repent, therefore,' says Peter, 'and turn again, that your sins may be blotted out, that times of refreshing may come from the presence of the Lord, and that he may send the Christ appointed for you, even Jesus, whom heaven must receive until the time of the restoration of all things.'

So used are we to reading into this the later doctrine of the

[40]The phrase 'in the spirit and power of Elijah' cannot, in view of the functions predicated of him, be interpreted as a denial that John *is* Elijah. For similar expressions, meaning Elijah *redivivus*, cf. Justin, *Dial.* 49.3–7.
[41]'The Most Primitive Christology of all?' (pp. 139–53 below).

second coming of Christ, that we miss the fact that, according to this speech, the Christ has not yet come at all. Jesus *has been* sent 'first' (Acts 3.26),[42] as Servant and Prophet: he *will be* sent as the appointed Messiah when the time is ready. And the time will be ready when, through repentance, all things have finally been 'restored': then the renewal that will mark the messianic age can occur.

According to this very primitive Christology, Jesus is quite explicitly the Prophet like Moses (as he is also in Stephen's speech in Acts 7.37). It should hardly therefore come as a shock to find that he is equally evidently Elijah in all but the name.[43] For who is it who comes 'first to restore all things' but Elijah? (Mark 9.12). The verb to 'restore' is the one running through the whole Elijah tradition. In the LXX of Malachi (3.23 = EVV 4.6) he is to 'restore' the heart of father to son and the heart of a man to his neighbour, and in Ecclus. 48.10, by turning the heart of father to son he will 'restore' the tribes of Jacob. Just as, in history, Elijah's function was to 'turn back' the people to the Lord their God (cf. I Kings 18.37), so he would come again to turn back Israel from its evil ways by a final preaching of repentance. Now this, according to Acts 3, was precisely what Jesus had been sent to do—'to turn every one of you from your wickedness' (3.26). And it was all in order that God might then be able to send the Christ. For only when Israel was fully repentant, said the tradition, could the Messiah come.[44] All this was pure Judaism. The distinctive feature of this early Christology was that the destined Messiah when he came would be none other than Jesus himself. Jesus was indeed to be the Christ. *But he was also Elijah first.* Such at any rate was one very early accommodation which some followers of Jesus made to the rethinking that he imposed upon them. Yes, they 'received' it; but they could not wholly discard

[42]*For Luke* 'to you first' presumably meant 'to the Jew first' (cf. Acts 13.46), but originally it must have had a different implication.

[43]The two functions are, of course, closely related. Cf. the Samaritan expectation of the *Taëb*, the Restorer, based on the promise of a prophet like Moses in Deut. 18.15.

[44]'If all Israel together repented for a single day, redemption through the Messiah would follow' (Pesikta 163b); 'If Israel practises repentance, it will be redeemed; if not, it will not be redeemed' (Sanh. 97b); 'Israel will not fulfil the great repentance before Elijah comes' (Pirke R. Eliezer 43); cf. Strack-Billerbeck 1, 598.

nor transfer to another the categories in which first they had been taught[45] to see him.

But, perplexing as it evidently remained, Jesus' remembered identification of Elijah with John proved too strong. The parallel title of the Prophet, however inadequate it might later appear, was never transferred to him;[46] but the language of Elijah could attach in future to no one but the Baptist. Despite the tradition that John himself disowned it, the title could come to rest on no one else. And nowhere is it more firmly attached to him than in the Lucan infancy narratives: 'He will turn many of the sons of Israel to the Lord their God, and he will go before him [still, be it noted, God, not Christ] in the spirit and power of Elijah, to turn the hearts of the fathers to the children, and the disobedient to the wisdom of the just, to make ready for the Lord a people prepared' (Luke 1.16 f.).

But, and here I come to the last twist in the tail of the story, did all this apply originally to *John*?

It has often been noted that the language of the Lucan stories of the infant John has, to say the least, remarkably little quality for understatement. Generations have chanted the Benedictus fully persuaded that the child in whom God has visited and redeemed his people is none other than Jesus; and indeed the position it has occupied in Anglican worship, *after* the New Testament lesson, has really left no option. But how has such a 'high' doctrine come to be associated with the son of Zechariah? A prevalent view has been that this canticle, with other material, once formed

[45]I have suggested elsewhere (*Jesus and His Coming* (1957), p. 148) that this Christology was the product of circles that entered Christianity through the movement of John the Baptist. I would go further and guess that it represents as accurately as anything the kind of sermon which Priscilla and Aquila would have heard Apollos preach in the synagogue at Ephesus (Acts 18.24–8). He was evidently a convinced follower of Jesus, though he knew only the baptism of John. If, as I assume, he stood in much the same position as the 'disciples' whom Paul found there subsequently (19.1–7), we may deduce that the two elements which this gospel lacked were the conviction that Jesus was even now the Christ (18.28) and that the Holy Spirit had already been given (19.2), or, in other words, that the messianic age and its renewal had actually begun. It was this conviction that was registered in the reception of the Spirit (19.2) through baptism into the name of Jesus as Lord (19.5).

[46]Both J. Knox (*On the Meaning of Christ* (1947), pp. 53 f.) and Cullmann (*Christology*, pp. 23–8) assert that it was. But the evidence is extremely slender. On Luke 1.76 see below.

part of a Baptist infancy cycle, composed originally by disciples of John to honour him as Messiah, and was then taken over by the Church with suitable adjustments. Professor Kraeling has presented this view with great persuasiveness and sketched a most ingenious outline of alternating rapprochement and alienation between the Baptist and Christian groups.[47] But this whole history rests upon a brilliantly imaginative reconstruction from the Gospels themselves: there is, as he admits, no corroborative evidence.

Perhaps I am not by now the one to cast this particular stone. But I hope at any rate that I am not playing a game of counters with purely hypothetical groups. And that is my trouble with Kraeling's theory. I am far from saying there could not have been these Baptist groups to create all this fine literature and throughout the first century to indulge in this game of hide and seek with the Church. But I cannot find a shred of reliable historical evidence for them at the time—that is, for the mere existence of disciples of John after his death who were not in some way Christians, let alone for those who were actively anti-Christian. There were indeed 'disciples' who knew only the baptism of John, and their understanding of the gospel may have left much to be desired (Acts 18.24–19.7). But I cannot believe that Priscilla and Aquila would have vouched that Apollos 'spoke and taught accurately the things concerning Jesus' if they had found in his pocket a copy of the Benedictus in honour of John as Messiah.[48] First let us find the sect which is supposed to have written this literature.[49]

---

[47]*Op. cit.*, pp. 163–81.

[48]According to Stauffer (*Jerusalem und Rom* (1957), p. 101) what Apollos had in his pocket, and was bringing from Alexandria to Ephesus, was 'the Baptist Logos-hymn' which the fourth Evangelist was to use for his prologue!

[49]The whole question of the existence of this Baptist sect deserves a thorough re-examination, since it is regularly taken for granted and a great deal of what passes for New Testament criticism is built upon it. Not only are half the Lucan infancy narratives attributed to it (for a recent assault on this thesis *vide* P. Benoit, 'L'enfance de Jean-Baptiste selon Luc', *NTS* III (1957), 169–94), but ever since W. Baldensperger's *Der Prolog des vierten Evangeliums* (1898) Johannine criticism has been dogged by the notion that the whole treatment of the Baptist in the fourth Gospel is motivated by polemic against Baptist opposition (cf. earlier J. B. Lightfoot, *Colossians* (1875), pp. 163–5). The denials and disclaimers recorded of John which are supposed to prove this thesis (John 1.8, 15, 20–3, 30 f.; 3.27–30) are in fact

perfectly natural, and in accord with the Synoptic tradition (Mark 1.7 f. and pars; Acts 13.25). Even Cullmann, who argues strongly for the element of polemic, admits that they could well fit the historical situation (*op. cit.*, p. 29). In fact, the relations between John and Jesus are represented as uniformly friendly throughout the Gospel; and there is absolutely no evidence for such a statement as that of Goguel (*op. cit.*, p. 274)—and it is typical—that John regarded Jesus as a renegade. It is very significant that when later Jesus is forced to flee from Judaea he deliberately seeks refuge in Bethany beyond Jordan where John and he were first associated (1.28; 3.26) and there finds a ready following among those who recalled John's teaching (10.39–42). This hardly suggests the groups were at daggers drawn, either then or later. It is much easier to think that the fourth Evangelist had an eye to *persuading* those who, like him, were brought up in the Baptist's teaching to believe in Jesus as the one to whom John pointed.

Frequently the existence of this rival sect is simply deduced, by circular argument, from the supposed signs of polemic within the Gospels themselves (e.g. Goguel, *op. cit.*, p. 104; 'The existence of this literature [viz. the Lucan birth narratives and John 3 and 4] establishes that of a Baptist group'). But after the disciples of John bury their master and tell Jesus (Matt. 14.12) we hear nothing more of them in the New Testament. Even if those in Acts 18 and 19 who knew only the baptism of John were not Christians (and Kraeling himself admits that they were, *op. cit.*, p. 209; cf. B. T. D. Smith, 'Apollos and the Twelve Disciples at Ephesus', *JTS* xvi (1915), 241–6), they certainly do not fulfil the necessary conditions as a rival group preaching John as Messiah. The sole direct evidence that there was such a group at any time is in fact confined to two passages in the *Clementine Recognitions*, namely, 1.54: 'Sed et ex discipulis Ioannis, qui videbantur esse magni, segregaverunt se a populo et magistrum suum veluti Christum praedicarunt'; and 1.60: 'Et ecce unus ex discipulis Ioannis affirmabat Christum Ioannem fuisse et non Iesum; in tantum, inquit, ut et ipse Iesus omnibus hominibus et prophetis maiorem esse pronuntiaverit Ioannem. Si ergo, inquit, maior est omnibus, sine dubio et Moyse et ipsi Iesu maior habendus est. Quod si omnium maior est, ipse est Christus.' Ephrem Syrus (*Ev. expos.* ed. G. Moesinger (1876), p. 288) records the same tradition but evidently from the same source. At best this cannot provide evidence of anything before the second century; and since the information occurs in a list of Jewish sects (classified as the Sadducees, the Samaritans, the Scribes and Pharisees, and the Baptists) in which the Sadducees are said to have originated about the time of John and the Scribes and Pharisees to have been baptized by him, it is evidently not of very notable historical value. In addition, indirect references are claimed to be visible in other passages in the *Clementines* (all the evidence, such as it is, is assembled in J. Thomas, *Le mouvement Baptiste en Palestine et Syrie*, pp. 114–39). But the fact remains, as Thomas admits (p. 132), that none of the Fathers mention the disciples of John in their lists of heretics, just as in the New Testament the Baptists are never among the enemies of Jesus. That there were elements of John's following which did not find their way into the Church is indeed very probable; that these elements constituted a rival group to Christianity in the first century, with a competing Christology, is, I believe, without any foundation whatever.

The attempt to use the Mandaean literature as evidence for a sect founded by John the Baptist must be judged to have collapsed. The references to the Baptist cannot be shown to belong to the earliest strata of this literature.

In the meantime I have a simpler hypothesis to propose. It is that the Church wrote it—but originally in honour, not of John, but of Jesus.[50] And I suggest that Luke picked it up in much the same circles as he found that rather primitive essay in theology now reproduced in Acts 3. For basically they have the same Christology and much the same vocabulary.[51] The Benedictus, like Peter's speech, speaks of 'the prophet', in whom the Lord God has visited his people (Luke 1.76; Acts 3.22). Here also he has been 'raised up', i.e. sent (Luke 1.69; Acts 3.26), in fulfilment of the 'covenant' sworn by God with Abraham (Luke 1.73; Acts 3.25) and 'as he spoke by the mouth of his holy prophets from of old' (Luke 1.70; Acts 3.21), in order that he should 'go before the Lord [i.e. God] to prepare his ways, and to give knowledge of salvation to his people in the forgiveness of their sins' (Luke 1.76 f.; Acts 3.26). Once more we have the traditional role of Elijah. The end of the canticle is not absolutely clear, because of the state of the text; but it almost certainly looks to another still future visitation,[52] when 'the day shall dawn from on high' and the messianic age, as represented in Isa. 9, will break for those who have sat in darkness (Luke 1.78 f.). This is parallel to the promise in Acts 3.20 of the sending of the Messiah and 'the times of refreshment from the presence of the Lord' when repentance is

---

Thomas, while allowing that the Mandaeans may well be ancient and Palestinian, fails to find any connexion between them and John till the Mohammedan era (*op. cit.*, pp. 184–267, especially 256–67). See also H. Lietzmann, *Ein Beitrag zur Mandäerfrage* (1930); Dodd, *The Interpretation of the Fourth Gospel*, pp. 115–30; Menoud, *op. cit.*, pp. 33–50. But cf. Cullmann, *op. cit.*, p. 27 n. 1.

[50]This is argued convincingly by Benoit (*op. cit.*, NTS III, 186–8), but I find no compelling reason for excepting, as he does, Luke 1.76 f. It seems to me no more difficult to believe that the whole canticle was written originally of Jesus and has since been transferred to John than that Luke has added the reference to the child John and thereby made the high Christology of all the rest apply to him.

[51]Some of the common vocabulary must certainly be ascribed to Luke, though the presence of Lucanisms does not demonstrate that he is not using sources, as the Marcan material in his Gospel shows. What is significant is the common phraseology, and above all the common framework, which is *peculiar* to these passages.

[52]Reading ἐπισκέψεται with ℵ* B L W Θ 𝔓⁴ sy³ vg sa bo arm. I see no grounds, with Benoit (*op. cit.*, p. 185), for supposing that the aorist ἐπεσκέψατο is less likely to represent a correction. The tense is, if anything, perhaps more likely to have been assimilated to the ἐπεσκέψατο of *v.* 68 than to the futures of *v.* 76.

achieved. The whole framework is the same, of the Restorer
followed by the Christ. And I suggest the child (the παιδίον)
addressed (Luke 1.76) is one with the servant (the παῖς) of the
Church's early theology (Acts 3.13 and 26) and continuing
liturgical use. Here at least we have an actual milieu, where hymns
are known to have been composed, and a theology which we know
was applied to Jesus. That there was at that date a Baptist Church,
with a Baptist hymnal, and a Baptist theology, not even the most
ardent ecumaniac can demonstrate!

Of course, by the time the Gospels were written, all the
language of the one who 'goes before the face of the Lord' had
long since been applied to him whom Jesus designated as Elijah;
and it is on this basis that Luke or his source apportions the
canticles in his material. But, should the real identity of this
'child' still be in doubt, I have a last resort. It is to the technique
of a late Vicar of Glastonbury, who, when a tourist was ultimately
sceptical that Joseph of Arimathea had come to Glastonbury
and was buried in his church, is reputed to have stooped and
pointed to some letters cut on the bottom of a tomb, and exclaimed
with a gesture of finality: 'Look—"J.A."!' So, if anyone does not
believe that the Benedictus was addressed originally to Jesus, as
out of its context I submit everyone would assume, let him look at
its second verse. For there he will see that the 'horn of salvation'
has been raised up by God *in the house of his servant David* (Luke
1.69), a phrase which indicates, not the nation in general, but
quite specifically the house and lineage of David (1.27; 2.4). And
to this lineage John did not belong; but Jesus did.[53]

[53]The difficulty was clearly recognized by C. R. Bowen, 'John the Baptist in
the New Testament', *American Journal of Theology* xvi (1912), 99: 'The
reference to the house of David suggests plainly that the boy John is somehow
to be credited to the Davidic family, which seems to fit ill the son of a priest
and a "daughter of Aaron". No doubt historically there would be a difficulty,
but that such a tradition could arise seems not impossible.' The tortuous
hypotheses to which he is then compelled (that David's line *was* priestly after
all, and that there *must* have been a genealogy connecting John with David)
reveal only what the judgment 'not impossible' can if necessary include.
The supposition that the reference is not to John at all is on every count the
simpler.
It is possible, and indeed probable, that the first half of the Benedictus
(1.68–75) is modelled on traditional material; but whoever wrote the canticle
as a whole must have meant it for someone in the Davidic line.

III

THE TEMPTATIONS[1]

It is never possible to sustain a rigid distinction between the person and the work of Christ. Our estimate of the one will always be reflected in and tested by our estimate of the other. But which we begin with, whether we deduce the significance of his works from that of his person, or the other way round, makes a considerable difference. The liberal theology began from the acts and teachings of Jesus, and from these concluded to his divinity (or to what other status the conscience of its devotees allowed him). Its preoccupation with what he *was* was, on the whole, secondary to its interest in what he said and did. This general emphasis comes out quite clearly in what is now the most widely accepted interpretation of the Temptation narrative. Without stating it in its extreme liberal form (a very human prelude to the career of a great leader of men), one could represent this interpretation as follows.

With the full consciousness of his destiny as God's Messiah thrust upon him for the first time by the circumstances of his baptism, Jesus retires to adjust himself in prayer to the stupendous reorientation which this realization must have meant for his whole life. What sort of a Messiah was he to be? What was to be his programme, and what the means he should employ to achieve it? As the executant of God's purpose, his end could not be other than that great end God had appointed for the universe—the fashioning of sons to himself in free and loving obedience. This, then, must determine also the means to be employed. For it would avail nothing to win the whole world, if, by the very methods used, men were to be transferred to a submission grounded in something less than the absolutely free dedication of love. In the Temptations, Jesus rejects any definition of the divine omnipotence than that of perfect love. Playing upon the enticing consciousness of his new powers ('If thou art the Son

[1]Reprinted from *Theology* L (1947), 43–8.

of God . . .'), the devil urges upon him the well-tried methods of all human reformers. They had failed only because they were not able to back their programmes with the power to carry them out. But link the irresistibility of the divine omnipotence to the politician's dream of universal plenty, or to the known ability of sheer display to dazzle the human mind, or (taking 'the temple' to represent the Temple party) to the surge of legitimate nationalist aspiration, or to the 'realism' of skilful diplomacy—and with any such programme how could he fail to win the world? But Jesus rejects in turn each of these suggestions, as involving an appeal to something other than the free response of love to love. There could be no short cuts to the kingdom of God.

According to this interpretation, the Temptations presuppose that Jesus had already become convinced that he stood in a unique relationship to God. They are temptations, not to question this status of Sonship, but to abuse it. They are not primarily about his person, but about his work; not about his relation to God, but about his relation to men; not about whether he was the Messiah, but about what kind of a Messiah he should be.

Now, if we turn to a study of the biblical narratives, it is very doubtful whether these statements can in fact be substantiated. Let us go back to the text and examine the three temptations in turn, taking them in the Matthean order.

(1) *Bread.* In this, as in each of the other cases, the key to the meaning of the temptation is to be sought in the quotation from Deuteronomy with which Jesus counters it. For we have a right to assume, until we have evidence to the contrary, that the answerer has at least understood the point of the suggestion made to him. Now the first reply, the conviction that man does not live by bread alone, but by every word that proceeds out of the mouth of God, is presented in its original context (Deut. 8.2 f.) as the lesson which God taught the Israelites in the wilderness by the deliberate policy of 'proving' and 'humbling' them by starvation. It was not a lesson understood or accepted by the people at the time. In fact, they retorted by an attempt to 'prove' or 'tempt' God himself (Ex. 17.2). They forced Moses to require of God a sign, to settle the question once and for all: 'Is the Lord among us, or not?' (Ex. 17.7). Now this act of tempting God, which gave to the place the name of Massah ('that is,

Tempting, or, Proving,' RVm.), became the type of all such behaviour for the Old Testament. 'The day of temptation' of the *Venite* should properly be translated 'the day of Massah' (Ps. 95.8, RV). And when the general commandment became formulated, 'Ye shall not tempt the Lord your God,' the explanatory clause was added, 'as ye tempted him in Massah' (Deut. 6.16). Now this connexion between Jesus' reply to his first temptation and the 'proving' of God, together with the fact that the injunction of Deut. 6.16 is actually quoted in his next answer, suggests that the first temptation has also to do with the sin of tempting God. This becomes the more certain when we recall what this 'type' of Old Testament temptation consisted of. For what happened at Massah was that Moses produced water from the rock. And Satan's suggestion to Jesus was to produce bread from stones (Luke, 'this stone').

What, then, was this first temptation? It was the incitement to Jesus to tempt God, by putting to the proof what must rest on the conviction of faith—namely, that he was the Son of God. We find him struggling with the question: Can it really be that I am the Son of God? It is easy for us to forget that the acceptance of the amazing truth of his person cannot, if he was genuinely human, have come to him except by gradual and hard-won stages. There must have been a period of hesitancy, as the incredible implications of it bore in upon him. This hesitation was not in itself sinful: indeed, the path of sin lay in seeking to bring it to a premature close. 'Why not satisfy yourself once and for all?' tempts Satan. And so, fastening upon his weakest spot (the other interpretation seems to forget that the hunger was genuinely *his* and not that of his hypothetical hearers), the devil presents him with a suggestion whose subtlety lies in the fact that it could be used to satisfy both his physical and his spiritual cravings at once. For the action proposed would, if successful, not only produce bread, but, being a miracle, would demonstrate at the same time beyond any doubt that he was no ordinary man. What was wrong in the suggestion was, not that a man should want bread, nor even, primarily, that a man with divine powers should use them to get bread; it was that he should use the (legitimate) satisfaction of a physical need as a way of obtaining the illegitimate satisfaction of a spiritual need. That was precisely the sin of the Israelites in the desert.

The Lord had tempted the old Israel by leading it forty years in the wilderness and suffering it to hunger (Deut. 8.2 f.). The new Israel was also led by the Spirit into the wilderness to be tempted and to hunger for forty days. The test was the same in each case: Had it enough faith to know that it was the people of God? By deliberate quotation Jesus showed that he could give the answer before required in vain.

(2) *The Temple pinnacle.* This, as the reply specifically indicates, is again a temptation to put God to the test. 'Am I really the Son of God?' meditates Jesus. 'Force God to declare the answer' says the devil. 'Put yourself in a position where, if you are, God cannot fail to act unmistakably. Just as the old Israel, by threatening to stone Moses at Massah, drew from God the act that proved it to be the people of God, so, by threatening to cast yourself against a stone, force God to reply unambiguously. If you will not prove it by a miracle of your own, prove it by impelling God to one. But at all events, *prove* it.' So prompts the devil: prove that you are the people or Son of God by doing something that is a denial of the very relationship which constitutes you such—the relationship of faith. Once more, Jesus deliberately gives the answer that at Massah was demanded but not heard: 'Thou shalt not tempt the Lord thy God.'

(3) *The Mountain-top.* This is the temptation which at first sight lends greatest support to the supposition that the theme throughout is the work or programme of the Messiah rather than his person. For is not the offer by Satan of the kingdoms of the world to become the kingdom of God and his Christ a clear indication that the theme of the temptation is evangelistic, that it concerns how men are to be won? Before, however, accepting this conclusion as final, let us allow ourselves to be guided by the method hitherto adopted, that of beginning with Jesus' answer. 'Thou shalt worship the Lord thy God, and him only shalt thou serve.' This is quoted from the LXX version of Deut. 6.13, a passage immediately prior to the commandment against tempting God. It is independent of it, however, and the fact that the third temptation is not, like the other two, introduced by the words, 'If thou art the Son of God,' suggests that the tenor of it is rather different.

The Book of Deuteronomy sets out ostensibly to present the

guiding principles of life for God's people in their new home, as these are distilled by Moses from the events and experiences of their late wanderings. The various commandments are stated as the lessons of history. Thus, the injunction not to tempt God is, as we saw, specifically traced back to the incident at Massah. Is it possible to point to a similar root in the Exodus story for the contents of Deut. 6.13–15 ? The answer is not far to seek when we note the parallelism between this passage and Ex. 34.11–17 (which was actually *written* first is here irrelevant). In both, there is the strict injunction not to go after the gods of the other peoples round about; for Israel's Lord is a jealous God, and he alone must be the object of his people's worship. But the significant thing for our purposes is that the Exodus passage occurs in the course of the incident in which Moses goes for the second time up to *the top of the mount* to meet God (34.2), where, we read, he was with the Lord *'forty days and forty nights; he did neither eat bread nor drink water'* (34.28).

So, then, the Old Testament context in which the third temptation is to be understood must be the conversation between Moses and God at the top of Mount Sinai. If this is so, what interpretation does it suggest?

On Mount Sinai Moses is told of the heathen peoples who will be driven out to afford the Jews their new home. Israel is to secure its national existence by no covenant with them, no acts of intermarriage, and, above all, no compromise with their gods. The other kingdoms are mentioned, not because they have any place in the divine plan, but purely as factors likely to distract Israel from the singleness of its dedication to the one God. Similarly, therefore, we must suppose that the emphasis in the third temptation is not primarily on the kingdoms of the world and the means of their evangelization. It is rather on the integrity of the people of God. The temptation to Jesus is to repeat the easy path of the old Israel and to establish himself in this world by compromise with the forces that control it. The point at issue, as in the other two tests, is his relationship, not to men, but to God. The temptation is to try to serve God and mammon. The emphasis on the kingdoms of the world is purely secondary, as in Jesus' own saying, 'What shall it profit a man if he shall gain the whole world, and lose his own soul?' (Mark 8.36).

So the devil, foiled in his efforts to play upon Jesus' hesitation whether he really was the Son of God, changes his tack. If he would not deny his status by faithlessness, then like God's people of old he would surely do it by unfaithfulness. But no; to this too Jesus returns the answer that to the old Israel remained a command: 'Thou shalt worship the Lord thy God, and him only shalt thou serve.'

The result of the foregoing exegesis has been to establish that the Temptation narrative as we have it is the record of a struggle, not about the programme of the Messiah, but about his person. This conclusion leads to a reconsideration of a further question. What is the interest which led to the inclusion of the Temptation narrative in the Gospels at all?

The very raising of this question may cause us some surprise. To the modern eye the biographical interest is obvious. What is more reasonable than that the Evangelist should give his readers, as a key to what follows, some sort of a picture of how Jesus himself viewed the ministry upon which he was entering, of how this conception of it formed itself in his mind, and of the other possibilities he entertained only eventually to reject? But the Evangelists were not primarily biographers. Moreover, as we have seen, the temptations they choose to record have in fact nothing directly to do with the nature of Jesus' ministry. That we have found a 'programme' discussed in them, despite the evidence, shows what with our interests we expect to find; but it is also an indication that these interests are not the same as those of the Evangelists. What, then, were their interests?

Confronted as we are by an opposition to the Gospel which is predominantly non-Jewish, we are inclined to forget what an extraordinary claim it was which the first Christians made, in saying that *they*, and not the old body of Judaism, were the true Israel, and the sole heirs of the covenants and promises. To uphold such an assertion, the Church had to be prepared to show that it possessed a continuity with the old even more indisputable than the succession of the scribes and Pharisees—no easy task. At the same time it had to contend that it was not merely a continuation of the old—the age of the new covenant had actually started. To establish these two claims, nothing less than the whole weight of scriptural authority would suffice. A complete reinterpretation of the Old Testament was needed; and for this task the Church relied on three closely connected methods of exegesis. (*a*) It claimed to fulfil all the messianic prophecies. (*b*) It claimed to fulfil the 'Law', and that included not only the moral law (Matt. 5.17) and the ceremonial law (Hebrews *passim*), but the whole of the Pentateuch, which was history before it was commandment. (*c*) It claimed to see Christ as present in the history of Israel and the world from the beginning. For what further proof of continuity could be required if this Christ, recently to be seen walking in Galilee, was in fact the very same person who was the agent of creation (John 1.1–14), who was in the wilderness of old (I Cor. 10.4) and who had instructed the prophets (I Peter 1.11)?

This claim to be the new and true Israel occupied such a decisive place in the Church's first apologetic that the theory has even been advanced that the recording of each of the Gospel incidents is to be accounted for by some Old Testament passage of which it is expounded as the Christian 'fulfilment'. One need not go as far as that to admit the profound influence of this apologetic interest upon the selection and presentation of the Gospel stories. The Temptation narrative is a clear case in point. The Church claimed that, as the new Israel, it was the fulfilment of the Law, in the widest sense (Luke 24.44). All that the old covenant stood for was to be taken up in the new, which was made this time not with the Jews but with the Christians. Now this claim to the new covenant involved the Church in showing that it had entered upon the title of the people of God. To do this it pointed to the fact that there was a definite 'type' (I Cor. 10.6, 11) or historical pattern to which the life of God's true people must conform. The old Israel had passed through it, but had failed to respond in the way required. The world was to be redeemed by the new Israel 'repeating' that divinely ordained pattern, but this time giving the answer it had been chosen to make. In modern terms, we might say that in his attack on the world in sin God had devised a plan of assault which was to be decisive for the issue of the war—Operation 'Salvation', to use the current jargon. For this he selected and trained a special task force. On the first attempt the plan had met with only very partial success, owing to failures and desertions within the ranks of the picked troops themselves. However, the plan of operation was not discarded. What was required was a body of men, or even one man, sufficiently dedicated to sacrifice himself in seeing it through victoriously to the end. The concern of the Church was, first, to proclaim that Jesus, as the true representative of God's people, had in fact carried out and completed that operation without failure, and, secondly, to call its members to repeat the pattern in their own lives.

The details of the pattern need not concern us here. Creation (I Cor. 15.45 ff.), the flood (I Peter 3.20 f.), the descent into Egypt (Matt. 2.13 ff.), the crossing of the Red Sea (I Cor. 10.1 f.) all reappear in the economy of salvation. But none of them occupies such a decisive place as the wilderness journey. The significance for the old Israel of this phase in its history was that here for the first time was pressed upon its consciousness its unique position as the people of God. The object of such a testing time had been to purify it as God's chosen instrument and to bring home to it the meaning, privileges and responsibilities of a relationship which rested on grace and faith alone. So, if Jesus really was the true representative of God's people, he too must be shown to have had his wilderness journey and endured the test which proved his person, only without sin. There is no need to suppose that the withdrawal of Jesus into the desert after his baptism was invented to fit the requirements of the scheme. But the interest which recorded it and which selected the three temptations from the many which must have assailed him is clearly controlled by the overriding apologetic purpose. Here, said the Church, was the decisive issue being fought out afresh. Would Jesus accept for himself the role of the people of God; or would he deny it by faithlessness or unfaithfulness as the people before him? Triumphantly it listens, as he gives the very answers which the old Israel failed to make its own.[2]

[2]G. H. P. Thompson has subsequently, but independently, argued along many of the same lines as this article in his 'Called-Proved-Obedient: A Study in the Baptism and Temptation Narratives of Matthew and Luke', *JTS*, NS XI (1960), 1–12.

IV

THE 'OTHERS' OF JOHN 4.38[1]

A TEST OF EXEGETICAL METHOD

OF all the Evangelists John is most patently looking at the Gospel events through the spectacles of the Church's life. The convictions taught by the Christ of faith mingle indistinguishably with the words of the Jesus of history. But does he create sayings and incidents which had and could have had no place in the historic ministry of Jesus in order to speak the word of the living Christ? Here lies the crux of Johannine interpretation. There comes a point, however hard it may be to define, at which it would be necessary to say, 'These words, this incident, admit of no possible setting within the ministry of Jesus: they must be interpreted solely with reference to the situation of the Church.' This is the point where the Gospel would really cease to be distinctively a Gospel at all, in the sense of being theological history of the life, death and resurrection of Jesus, and become theology pure and simple, such as could equally have been purveyed through the medium of an Epistle.

The question is, Does the fourth Evangelist in fact reach this critical point and go beyond it? This cannot be settled without examining the whole of his work. But I should like to test it at a place where many would argue he clearly does so, namely, in the words of John 4.38: 'I sent you to reap that for which you did not labour; others have laboured, and you have entered into their labour.'

Who are these 'others'? The question has recently been raised again by Professor O. Cullmann in his usual stimulating way in a short study called 'Samaria and the Origins of the Christian

---

[1]Reprinted from *Studia Evangelica* (TU 73, ed. K. Aland, F. L. Cross, J. Daniélou, H. Riesenfeld, and W. C. van Unnik, 1959), pp. 510-15 (originally given as a paper to the conference at Oxford on 'The Four Gospels in 1957').

Mission', reprinted in his collection of essays, *The Early Church*.[2] His answer is that the 'others' here refer to the Hellenists of Acts 8, who under Philip the Evangelist first took the Gospel to Samaria. The Apostles (whom Jesus is at this point conceived as addressing) enter subsequently, in the persons of Peter and John, upon the harvest for which these others have laboured.

This may, on the face of it, appear a surprising answer in the context of John 4, but Professor Cullmann's criterion for the exegesis of this Gospel is that regard must constantly be had to the setting of its words and incidents, not merely in the life of Jesus, but in that of the Church, regarded as the direct expression of the living Lord. The Evangelist's aim, he says, is 'to show that the Christ of the Church corresponds to the Jesus of history, and to trace the connexion between the life of Jesus and the varied expressions of Church life'.[3] Earlier, in *Les sacrements dans l'évangile johannique*,[4] he sought to establish this aim in relation to the Church's worship. Here he tries to show how it is relevant also to another aspect of its life, its mission. One of the purposes of John 4, he argues, is to provide dominical authority for the extension of the Christian preaching to Samaria, in face of the inference that might be drawn, and doubtless was drawn, from the saying recorded in Matt. 10.5 : 'Enter no town of the Samaritans.' The justification for the apostolic mission, which the Evangelist believes to have behind it the authority of the risen Christ, is placed in the mouth of the historic Jesus on the occasion of his own ministry in Samaria. The historical allusion in the words, 'I have sent you to reap that on which you have not laboured: others have laboured, and you have entered into their labour', is therefore to be sought not within the ministry of Jesus but within that of the early Church.

My present purpose is not to criticise Professor Cullmann's own thesis, though I confess to finding it more ingenious than probable. Other considerations apart, it presupposes a familiarity on the part of the fourth Evangelist with the story of Acts 8 for which there would appear to be no evidence—unless, of course,

[2]1956, pp. 185–92. It appeared originally in the *Annuaire de l'Ecole pratique des Hautes Etudes*, Paris, 1953–4, 3–12. Cullmann continues to uphold his thesis in his *Christology of the New Testament*, p. 184.
[3]*The Early Church*, p. 186.
[4]Translated in his *Early Christian Worship* (SBT 10, 1953), pp. 37–119.

one assumes (as Cullmann does not) that the Evangelist was himself involved as John the Apostle.

I am concerned with it rather from the point of view of methodology. Professor Cullmann's own criterion is, as we saw, that any saying or incident in the fourth Gospel must be regarded both from the point of view of its setting in the ministry of Jesus and from the viewpoint of the Church's life. But in fact in this case the *only* intelligible reference of these words, he believes, is to the apostolic age; and he specifically offers his interpretation as an alternative to previous answers, which he dismisses as unsatisfactory, such as that the 'others' are the men of the Old Testament or John the Baptist.[5] In other words, in this instance at least he concedes that the historical allusion, so far as the ministry of Jesus is concerned, is simply a fabrication: Jesus could not have said these words in the situation in which he is represented as saying them, for there had at that time been no 'others' for him to refer to. This admission seems to me of far-reaching importance for the interpretation of the Gospel and for the Evangelist's view of history, though it would, I imagine, be accepted with reasonable equanimity by most recent exegetes.

But before making it—and thereby throwing over Professor Cullmann's own criterion—I should wish to ask very carefully whether there is not in fact an intelligible reference for the words within the historical situation which the Evangelist is purporting to describe.

The words are, indeed, notoriously difficult to place at the stage of the ministry in which the Evangelist puts them. For by then Jesus has not explicitly sent his disciples to anything, nor is it clear that any others have been in the field before them. Indeed, it is not unjust to say that such plausibility as attaches to Professor Cullmann's theory derives very largely from the bankruptcy of any alternative.

I believe, however, that good sense can be made of the words on the assumption that the reference of the 'others' is to the only mission hitherto mentioned in the Gospel, namely, that of John the Baptist and his followers.

This Gospel represents the Baptist and Jesus as operating at

[5] *The Early Church,* p. 189.

any rate for a time in close conjunction, each practising a ministry of baptism and gathering disciples round them. To begin with, they are together at Bethany beyond Jordan (1.28; 3.26). Subsequently John is found working at Aenon near Salim (3.23) and Jesus in Judaea (3.22). Though a controversy is mentioned between the disciples of John and 'a Jew' in 3.25 (where the conjecture, going back to Bentley, that the true text is 'Jesus' is very plausible), the Baptist himself is specifically represented as denying any rivalry between Jesus and himself, and according to the following verses (3.26–30) is well content to see the results of his own work flow into the greater work of Jesus. That this could really represent their historical relation is regularly denied with scornful incredulity. But it is very significant that when later Jesus has to flee from Judaea he deliberately seeks refuge—and finds a ready following—in Perea, precisely at the place where John and he were first associated (10.40–42). This strongly suggests that the two missions remained on friendly terms, and argues against the widely accepted view that this Gospel's treatment of John is directed against rival Baptist groups. There is indeed no actual evidence (though on *a priori* grounds we may judge it probable) that John's followers continued any mission of their own after his imprisonment.[6] His own wish, to judge from 3.26–30, would presumably have been for them to have found their way into the growing movement associated with Jesus. Even the final decision of Jesus to move to Galilee (though I believe that it was associated in Jesus' mind with the recognition that the Father's way for him must be fundamentally different from that marked out for him by John, and that this was reflected in the abandonment of a purificatory rite as the central expression of it (4.2)) was taken, according to this Gospel, not because of any antagonism between the two men, but because the swing of success was drawing upon him in turn the embarrassing attention of the Pharisees (4.1; cf. 1.24).

En route for Galilee Jesus must pass through Samaria (4.4). Now, according to evidence set out by Professor Albright, it appears highly probable that 'Aenon near Salim' is to be located a few miles south-east of Shechem (in Greek, Sychem, of which Sychar is a corruption), 'a town of Samaria' and the site of

[6]See 'Elijah, John and Jesus', pp. 49–51 above.

Jacob's well (4.5).[7] In other words, the conversation of chapter 4 takes place in the immediate vicinity of John's later mission. Other evidence also connects the activity of John the Baptist with Samaria.[8] There is the tradition, preserved in Eusebius, that John himself was buried at Sebaste, the city and capital of Samaria, some ten miles or so from Salim. Moreover, both Dositheus of Shechem and Simon Magus of Gitta (south of Sebaste), whose heresy was from the beginning (Acts 8.14–24) and subsequently associated with Samaria, are stated in the *Clementines*[9] to have been disciples of John the Baptist. Even if this is untrue, it attests a tradition which associates John's activity with this area.

There is therefore some ground for supposing that when Jesus spoke in Samaria of his disciples entering upon the labours of others he may have been alluding to the work of the Baptist groups in that area, which had already made the people receptive to his message.[10]

With this in mind let us look at the passage itself in its context, John 4.35–42.

Jesus arrives in Samaria to find the situation already much further advanced than his disciples, and perhaps he himself, expected. The remark, 'Do you not say, "There are yet four months and then comes the harvest"?', may either refer to an (unknown) proverbial saying, 'There are four months between sowing and reaping'; or, more likely, in view of the 'yet', and since the interval was apparently six months, it means that this is January and that the corn is still four months off harvesting. In any case, says Jesus, spiritually speaking the time of harvest has

---

[7]W. F. Albright, *The Archaeology of Palestine* (rev. ed., 1956), pp. 247 f., and 'Recent Discoveries in Palestine and the Gospel of St John', in *The Background of the New Testament and its Eschatology*, pp. 157 f. The alternative site for Aenon, south of Scythopolis, is also in Samaria.

[8]Cf. B. W. Bacon, 'New and Old in Jesus' Relation to John', *JBL* xlviii (1929), 50–55; E. Lohmeyer, *Das Urchristentum* 1: *Johannes der Taufer*, pp. 37–40.

[9]*Hom.* 2.23 f.; *Recog.* 2.8.

[10]Lohmeyer, *op. cit.*, p. 26 n. 3, and E. Stauffer, *Jerusalem und Rom*, p. 154 n. 108, suggest this possibility. R. Bultmann, *Das Evangelium des Johannes* (1950), *ad loc.*, allows that it may have been the reference if the saying goes back behind the Evangelist: for the Evangelist himself, however, the reference is to the situation of the Church, though in entirely general terms to the predecessors of *any* missionary activity.

come and the reapers have already been engaged. Thus sower and reaper can both enjoy the fruits of their labour (ὁ σπείρων ὁμοῦ χαίρῃ καὶ ὁ θερίζων). This does not mean, I think, that the sowing and reaping are conceived as *coinciding*, without any interval as Cullman[11] and most others argue; rather, that the sower too has seen the fruits of his labours. The saying is indeed still true that 'one sows and another reaps'. But in this case it does not, as usually (Job 31.8; Micah 6.15), indicate frustration. Others, certainly, have laboured and Jesus' disciples have here in Samaria entered into their labours. But there is no rivalry or disappointed hopes. For the sower has himself lived to rejoice in the harvest. As the Baptist is made to say in the previous chapter (3.29), 'This joy of mine is now full.' He had come to point men to the figure who should 'take away the sin of the world' (1.29); it is therefore the fulfilment, not the failure of his mission when, taught by him, the Samaritans come to recognize in Jesus the one who 'really is the Saviour of the world' (4.42).

If this is the most natural interpretation, and the 'others' of v. 38 are in the first instance the Baptist and his disciples, it is still possible, if one wishes, without any distortion of historical perspective to see in the passage a validation of the Church's later mission in Samaria. But to *start* from this latter is by implication to admit a principle of exegesis which does great violence to history. It is, I believe, by taking the historical setting of St John's narrative seriously, and not by playing ducks and drakes with it, that we shall be led to a true appreciation of his profound reverence for the history of Jesus as the indispensable and inexpendable locus for the revelation of the eternal Logos itself.

[11]*Op. cit.,* p. 188.

V

THE PARABLE OF THE SHEPHERD[1]

(JOHN 10.1-5)

IN his notable work on *The Parables of Jesus* Professor Joachim Jeremias has applied a technique of scientific investigation which he believes affords solid grounds for hope that we can still get behind the early Church to the teaching of Jesus himself, and are not compelled to rest content with the formulation of the theology of the early Christian community. In the second half of his book he draws from time to time on Johannine material, with the implication that it can be legitimately used in the total reconstruction of the message of Jesus. The amount of parabolic material in the fourth Gospel, even in the very wide sense in which he rightly uses the term 'parable',[2] is of course very scanty. It is the more remarkable, therefore, that he does not apply his critical analysis to the only piece of Johannine teaching which is specifically called a παροιμία,[3] namely, John 10.1-5.

Now, the supposition that it is even worth while attempting to get beneath the Johannine narrative to an original 'core' in the teaching of Jesus is one that until recently would hardly have been accepted.[4] But the only way to test the worth of such a presupposition is to try. It may be that we shall not get very far.

---

[1]Reprinted from *ZNW* XLVI (1955), 233-40.

[2]*Op. cit.,* pp. 17 f. The references throughout are to the ET by S. H. Hooke (1954).

[3]It is generally agreed among modern commentators that παροιμία and παραβολή are simply variant translations of *mashal* and that there is no difference in their meaning (Jülicher, Lagrange, Bernard, Hoskyns and Davey, Bultmann, etc.). There is exactly the same equivocal relationship between παροιμία and ἐν παροιμίαις (16.25) as Jeremias detects between παραβολή and ἐν παραβολαῖς in Mark 4 (*op. cit.,* pp. 11-16). Cf. L. Cerfaux, 'Le thème littéraire parabolique dans l'évangile de Saint Jean', *Coniectanea Neotestamentica* XI (1949), 15-25.

[4]It is noteworthy that not one of the commentaries I have been able to consult even asks the question of the relation of this *pericope* to the teaching of the historical Jesus.

But the criteria advanced by Professor Jeremias at least provide some tests which it is possible to apply, even when one grants that the transposition in key which the whole Johannine material has undergone makes the operation very much more hazardous and the quest for *ipsissima verba* probably hopeless.

If we consider the whole section, John 10.1–21, we may note first that there is a clear break between the 'parable' and its reception on the one hand (vv. 1–6) and its allegorization on the other.[5] This corresponds exactly to the structure of parable plus allegorical interpretation which we find in the cases of the Sower (Mark 4.2–20) and the Tares (Matt. 13.24–43), except that in John the audience remains the same.[6] The break is remarkably clear, and examination shows that the allegorization has been kept separate and has not affected the parable itself,[7] as it has affected many of the Synoptic parables. This affords good confidence that we may, as it were, remove the first skin 'clean' and confine ourselves to vv. 1–6.

Turning to v. 6, we note that the parable is addressed to Jesus' opponents: ἐκεῖνοι, both from 10.19 and the previous chapter, are clearly the Jews, and in particular the Pharisees (9.40). This is not what we should expect (we think of the Good Shepherd like the True Vine being addressed to the disciples),[8] and it is for Jeremias

[5]This is obscured by the interlarding of parable and allegory which Bultmann's intricate rearrangement of the verses in this chapter produces (contrast J. Schneider, 'Zur Komposition von Joh. 10,' *Coniectanea Neotestamentica* XI, 220–5). The separation of the two is as clear as the separation of miracle and allegory in chapter 6.

[6]In the Synoptists the parables are given to those without, while the interpretation is esoteric. In John Jesus speaks both to the Jews and to the disciples in παροιμίαι (John 10.6; 16.25) and the interpretation does not require a change of audience. For it remains equally hidden to all until 'that day', when Jesus is glorified and the Spirit declares it. Up till then everything can therefore be spoken 'openly' (18.20), without fear of the mystery being disclosed. In the last discourses, where the glorified Lord is to some extent already speaking, the disciples sense an anticipation of the day when the need for παροιμία is past (16.29); but it is at once made clear that it is only an anticipation (16.32).

[7]Lagrange, Strachan and Bultmann agree in insisting that 1–5 is a genuine parable and not allegory. It is remarkable that Jeremias does not distinguish and writes generally: 'The two great parables of the fourth Gospel (John 10.1 ff. and 15.1 ff.) have more of an allegorical character than any of the Synoptic parables' (*op. cit.,* p. 69).

[8]Jeremias himself describes John 10.1–30 as 'esoteric self-revelation', 'after the period of public proclamation' (*op. cit.,* p. 152).

one of the clear marks of authenticity (*op. cit.*, pp. 23–31). It is also, I believe, an important clue to its elucidation.

Confining ourselves now to vv. 1–5, we may detect signs of a suture in v. 3 after the words τούτῳ ὁ θυρωρὸς ἀνοίγει. In 1–3a the parable is concerned with two figures who seek to enter a sheep-fold, a bandit and the shepherd himself, and it is to the latter that the porter opens. In 3b–5 we have a different point, concerning the difference in relationship of the sheep to a stranger and to their own shepherd; and here the picture is of the shepherd driving and leading his sheep *out*, presumably to pasture. It looks as if we have here an instance of the fusion of two parables, such as Jeremias finds in the Synoptists (*op. cit.*, pp. 73 f.). The two are skilfully woven together and run on without even a break in the sentence, and until we analyse them we are scarcely aware of the contrasting situations.

Can we now go further and seek to discover the original setting and point of each half? Continuing to work back, let us examine first vv. 3b–5.

There is nothing in the phraseology of these verses to suggest that we have not here a genuine parable drawn from life in Palestine,[9] and the language is not coloured by the Old Testament in the way that it is in the allegorical sequel. In content, the parable has affinities, though not especially close ones, with the other parabolic or metaphorical sayings of Jesus about the relation between the shepherd and his flock, e.g., Matt. 18.12–14 = Luke 15.4–7, Luke 12.32, Matt. 15.24 and particularly perhaps Mark 14.27 f.: 'You will all fall away; for it is written, "I will strike the shepherd, and the sheep will be scattered." But after I am raised up, I will go before (προάξω) you into Galilee.'

As regards its original setting, it is impossible to be dogmatic. A reasonable supposition might be that it arises out of the claims of Jesus for his own teaching, when his authority is challenged by the scribes and Pharisees. His authority cannot be proved by signs: it is self-authenticating. The true people of God hear his voice, because they recognize in it the authentic note of the shepherd of God's flock. By implication the Jewish leaders, who were meant to be the shepherds of Israel (Ezek. 34; Zech. 11; etc.), are

[9] So Jeremias *op. cit.*, p. 149.

condemned as ἀλλότριοι, foreigners to God's people (cf. Matt. 17.25 f.; Heb. 11.34).

This is in fact very much the setting which it actually occupies in the fourth Gospel; for the whole of chapter 10 is concerned with the authority of Jesus' teaching, and the connexion is made explicit in vv. 24–7: 'The Jews gathered round him and said to him, "How long will you keep us in suspense? If you are the Christ, tell us plainly." Jesus answered them, "I told you, and you do not believe. . . . You do not believe, because you do not belong to my sheep. My sheep hear my voice, and I know them, and they follow me." '

We may conclude, then, that in this case both the parable and its setting are preserved in a form that we have no reason to believe may not be original, though the 'shape' of the parable has suffered by the loss of its opening through fusion.

Going back now finally to the first half of the double parable, we are presented with a more complicated situation. Acting on the principle that the point of the parable is likely to be found at the end, we begin by examining the closing words: τούτῳ ὁ θυρωρὸς ἀνοίγει. Why is the θυρωρός there at all?[10] Perhaps it is a detail introduced in order to be given allegorical significance later. But in fact this is virtually the only detail in either parable which receives no place in the allegory. There is no further mention either of the porter or of opening. The fact then that it is extraneous to the Johannine purpose suggests strongly that the author of the Gospel found it in the tradition and did not himself introduce it. Indeed, his narrative would run on more smoothly without this clause altogether, and any momentary confusion as to whether 'his voice' of 3b refers to the shepherd or to the porter would be eliminated.

If then we may see in the words τούτῳ ὁ θυρωρὸς ἀνοίγει a bit of the bed-rock of the original tradition, we may have struck the clue to the primary meaning of the parable. The parable is built round the contrast between τούτῳ and ἐκεῖνος, the two figures

[10]To us a door-keeper seems out of place at a sheep-fold. The commentators seem generally agreed however that the αὐλή represents either a walled enclosure where a number of shepherds left their flocks for the night under a common guard, or, more probably, the courtyard of the house, which in the country was used as a sheep-pen at night, and whose gate would be controlled by the house porter (as of a town house, in John 18.15–17).

who seek to gain access to the courtyard. If the closing words are original and, as we should independently expect, make the real point of the parable, then the central figure is not the shepherd but the gate-keeper, faced with two aspirants to entry: ὁ μὴ εἰσερχόμενος διὰ τῆς θύρας and ὁ εἰσερχόμενος διὰ τῆς θύρας. The former he has to keep out, the latter he must be ready to let in.

If this is so, then certain connexions at once become apparent with the Synoptic tradition. The figure of the θυρωρός appears as the central figure in the parable of watching in Mark 13.34; that of opening to the master coming to his house in Luke 12.36; that of the thief coming and breaking through in the parable which immediately follows in Luke 12.39; while in Mark 13.29, we have a possible echo in the words that he who is expected 'is near, even at the gates'.

Now it is significant that all these parallels are to be found in the same part of the Synoptic material. They occur in teaching whose setting can, I believe, be shown to be the closing stages of Jesus' ministry, when he is concerned to warn the Jews, and particularly their leaders, of the urgency of the eschatological situation in which they are living and of the short time left before the final crisis comes upon them. While he is still with them the authorities have a last chance to fulfil their role as the watchmen of God's people (cf. Jer. 6.17; Ezek. 3.17; 33.7; Isa. 56.10; 62.6), to recognize and admit the master of the house of Israel and not to allow it to be broken into. Finally, when the day of their visitation arrives [11] and they refuse to open to him that comes to them through the gates, their house is declared left to the assaults and ravages of others.[12]

I suggest that the parable of John 10.1–3a originally belonged to the same context and posed the same challenge to the θυρωροί of Israel. Would they be prepared to recognize and open to him who came to them by the door of the sheep-fold and had the right to entry? That Israel was intended by the sheep-fold needed no more explanation than the similar language of the 'house' or the 'vineyard'. It is not allegory but simply allusion, which makes it clear, or should make it clear, to Jesus' opponents that the parable

---

[11]Cf. Micah 7.4: 'the day of thy watchmen, even thy visitation, is come.'
[12]Cf. Luke 12.39: οὐκ ἂν ἀφῆκεν διορυχθῆναι τὸν οἶκον αὐτοῦ with Luke 13.35: ἰδοὺ ἀφίεται ὑμῖν ὁ οἶκος ὑμῶν.

is told against them (Mark 12.12: ἔγνωσαν; contrast John 10.6: οὐκ ἔγνωσαν).

This setting requires the θυρωρός as the central figure of the parable. As a result of the fusion with the parable of 3b–5, this is no longer the case in the fourth Gospel; the ποιμήν dominates, and the gate-keeper, as we have seen, drops out in the later narrative. There is however a possible indication that the original setting is not so far beneath the surface, and indeed that the parable suggested itself to the Evangelist at this point precisely because its original application to the θυρωροί of Israel still clung to it in the tradition as he received it. In Isa. 56.9–12 we have the only instance in the Old Testament of the ideas of 'watchmen' and 'shepherds' applied *together* to the leaders of God's people, and there alone the watchmen are thought of as posted, not on a city wall, but like watchdogs, to guard the flock against devouring beasts. It is therefore the more significant to find that they are described as 'blind' and 'without knowledge', which is precisely the condemnation of the Pharisees in the Johannine context (9.40 f.; 10.6).[13] Thus, though the 'watchman' theme is entirely subordinated in the Evangelist's treatment, it may still have been strong enough to suggest the link, perhaps by unconscious association, between 9.40 f. and 10.1–6.

It is noteworthy that this parable contains another mark which Jeremias (*op. cit.*, p. 40) claims to recognize as primitive, namely, the identification of the figure of the κλέπτης not with the Lord (as at the end of the tradition in Rev. 3.3; 16.15), but with an enemy one must guard against. In Luke 12.33 men are told to have their treasure ὅπου κλέπτης οὐκ ἐγγίζει, and a few verses later in 12.39 the thief is pictured as coming to 'break through', διορύσσειν, the same word that is used in the Matthean parallel of Luke 12.33 (Matt. 6.19 f.). In John 10 the contrast between the coming of the legitimate one and the coming of the thief is quite explicit and is made still more pointed in the allegory: 'The thief comes only to steal and kill and destroy; I came that they might have life, and have it abundantly' (v. 10). Thus the Johannine use of the 'thief' motif may be a further indication that we are dealing with an early stage of the tradition.

[13]It is remarkable that this passage does not appear to have been noticed by the commentators, even by Hoskyns and Davey.

The Parable of the Shepherd (John 10.1-5)

It is worth noticing, in passing, how the equivalent in the fourth Gospel of the Q parable of the Thief compares favourably with the version of it both in the Synoptists and in I Thessalonians. In I Thess. 5.2-5 Paul applies to 'the Day of the Lord' the words ὡς κλέπτης ἐν νυκτὶ ἔρχεται. The thief is here still an image of destruction, which should *not* overtake those who are 'sons of light'. But as a result of his allegorization the metaphor breaks in his hands, and what begins as a symbol of darkness ends inconsequentially as a figure for 'the Day': 'You are not in darkness ἵνα ἡ ἡμέρα ὑμᾶς ὡς κλέπτης καταλάβῃ.' In John 12.35 f. we have the same contrast as in Thessalonians between 'the sons of light' and those who walk 'in darkness', but with the injunction: 'Walk while you have the light, ἵνα μὴ σκοτία ὑμᾶς καταλάβῃ.' This is precisely what Paul should have said, and what has every probability of representing the tradition before it suffered allegorization. And not only is the fourth Gospel more likely to have preserved the original form of the saying; it may well give us its original setting. Both in the Synoptists and in Paul the parable is applied to the Parousia. In the former case, there are good grounds[14] for thinking this application to be secondary, and in the latter we have already seen that precisely this is the source of the dislocation. In John the reference of the saying is not to the Parousia but to the imminent climax of the ministry in the lifting up of the Son of man and the judgment which that will bring (vv. 31-4). And it is in view of this that Jesus says: 'The light is with you (only) for a little longer. Walk while you have the light, lest the darkness overtake you.' This I believe is exactly the situation to which the parable of the Thief in Luke 12, like that of the Watchman in Mark 13, is likely to have been spoken; and it again confirms the historical value of the Johannine tradition at this point, which here appears to preserve elements more primitive even than our earliest Epistle and our earliest Synoptic source.

Further, the emphasis that the parable of John 10 lays on the fact that the owner is to be recognized by his coming in διὰ τῆς θύρας (on which it is implied that he knocks[15]) may well provide the background in the teaching of Jesus, absent from the Synoptists, for the idea which enters strangely in Mark 13.29 that Jesus

[14]Cf. Jeremias, *op. cit.,* pp. 39-41.
[15]Cf. Luke 12.36.

73

himself comes ἐπὶ θύραις, or, as in James 5.9, stands πρὸ τῶν θυρῶν. It also strengthens the possibility that in Rev. 3.20 we have a genuine ἄγραφον of Jesus. The language bears striking resemblance to our passage: ἰδοὺ ἕστηκα ἐπὶ τὴν θύραν καὶ κρούω· ἐάν τίς ἀκούσῃ τῆς φωνῆς μου καὶ ἀνοίξῃ τὴν θύραν, εἰσελεύσομαι πρὸς αὐτόν. The similarity may be due, not to an interrelationship between the fourth Gospel and the Apocalypse, but to a tradition of a parabolic saying of Jesus lying behind them both.[16]

In this first half-parable, then, we again have good indication that we are dealing with authentic and early tradition of the teaching of Jesus. In this case, the setting and emphasis have undergone modification. But the form and shape of the parable are remarkably unaffected; and again there are no signs of allegorization. One may say that the parable has been emptied of its eschatological urgency, though it is still set under the imminent shadow of the Passion, which the fourth Gospel is concerned to depict as the eschatological event in very much the manner in which I believe Jesus himself saw it. Moreover, there is no doubt that for John the advent of the Good Shepherd is the fulfilment of the eschatological prophecy of Ezek. 34 and Zech. 11, concerning the supersession of the false shepherds of Israel by a true Shepherd, who shall act for God himself. At any rate, what is much more significant is that in this parable, in marked contrast with the comparable ones in the Synoptic tradition, there is no trace at all of the tendency to transfer the application of the eschatological teaching from the contemporaries of Jesus to *the Church,* to prepare it for a second coming. The absence of this may be put down to a deliberate 'correction' by the fourth Evangelist in favour of a 'realized eschatology'. I confess to finding remarkably few signs that this is in fact the process at work in the Gospel. I hold it much more convincing to believe that in the fourth Gospel we have preserved a stream of tradition of the life and teaching of Jesus which never seriously underwent[17] what Jeremias and others have recognized as a potent factor of distortion, namely the tendency towards apocalyptic and the reference of Jesus' eschatological teaching to a second moment of glorifica-

[16]Rev. 3.20b–21 also has interesting affinities with the tradition behind Luke 22.29 f.
[17]Cf. C. H. Dodd, *The Interpretation of the Fourth Gospel,* p. 447.

tion beyond his own death. The fact that this parable shows so few marks of Johannine re-casting confirms the impression that we have here material in a state which the most searching tests suggest is early and authentic.

One could sum up by listing the various influences which Jeremias sees at work upon the parabolic teaching of Jesus, and noting how the parable of John 10.1-5 survives them. These are:

(1) Embellishment
(2) Change of audience
(3) Hortatory use by the Church
(4) The influence of the Church's situation
    (a) in the Hellenistic world
    (b) in its world mission
    (c) in the delay of the Parousia
(5) Allegorization
(6) Collection and conflation of parables
(7) Change of setting.

In respect of (1), (2), (3), and, most importantly, of all three sections of (4), the parable is 'clean'. Allegorization (5) occurs indeed round the parable, but not in it. There is, I believe, (6) a fusion of two parables; and (7) the emphasis and setting of the former has been affected by this fusion.

This is a record which compares favourably with that of any of the Synoptic material. Its significance for the historical value of the fourth Gospel as a whole lies in the fact that this should be true of a section which is typically Johannine and which cannot possibly be attributed to any kind of dependence on the Synoptists.

VI

THE 'PARABLE' OF THE SHEEP
AND THE GOATS[1]

THE vision of the Last Judgment with which St Matthew concludes so magnificently the teaching ministry of Jesus stands out from the Gospel pages with a unique and snow-capped majesty. It is a literary *tour de force* never quite approached elsewhere in the first Gospel, and it possesses that grandeur of simplicity which removes it *toto coelo* from the lurid and melodramatic scenes of the End which Jewish apocalyptic, like subsequent Christian thought, found it necessary to paint.[2] As Professor T. W. Manson says,[3] and Professor J. Jeremias agrees,[4] 'It contains features of such startling originality that it is difficult to credit them to anyone but the Master himself'; or, again, in the more recent words of Théo Preiss,[5] it evinces 'a sobriety of feature and colour, a reserve, a bareness which can come from hardly any other source but that of Jesus himself'.

Yet by its very isolation it poses the question of its own authenticity. In form it is unique. It is usually known as the 'parable' of the Sheep and the Goats: yet the parabolic element is confined to two verses (Matt. 25.32 f.). Nor is it marked by the same structure of a simple parable followed by an allegorical interpretation such as we find in the other two parables of separation (the Tares, Matt. 13.24–30 and 36–43; and the Drag-net, Matt. 13.47–50) and in those of the Sower (Mark 4.1–9 and 13–20) and the Shepherd (John 10.1–18). It is a combination of parabolic, apocalyptic and ethical teaching which is yet woven almost without seam into an incomparable literary whole.

But if it has proved intractable to form criticism, the source critics have got no further. It is significant, for instance, that the

[1]Reprinted from *NTS* II (1956), 225–37.
[2]Cf. and contrast Enoch 90.20–27 and *Orac. Sib.* III 663–97.
[3]*The Sayings of Jesus*, p. 249.
[4]*The Parables of Jesus*, p. 144.
[5]*Life in Christ* (ET, SBT 13, 1954), p. 47.

passage is never once mentioned either in J. C. Hawkins' *Horae Synopticae* or in B. H. Streeter's *The Four Gospels*. It stands, without Synoptic parallels, in the Matthean tradition; but whether it is late or early, composed by the Evangelist or derived from his source, integral or composite, or, if composite, what are its ingredients, does not seem to have been successfully analysed. The commentators have been content to leave it where W. O. E. Oesterley leaves it, with the words: 'Though it is impossible to indicate precisely what the original form of our "parable" may have been, that does not affect the wonderful beauty of its teaching: "one of the noblest passages in the entire Gospel" (Montefiore).'[6]

Even the acid bath into which Professor Jeremias plunges the parables leaves it relatively unaffected.[7] There are certain points that he notes which afford hints for discrimination between earlier and later strata, and these will receive attention in due course. But as a whole the passage eludes the tests which serve him so well on the other material. Thus, one could not point to any of the seven influences, with all their sub-headings, which he sees at work on the parables of Jesus and say that Matt. 25.31–46 affords a good example. Yet at the end he is left with a discourse of Jesus which, if it is not composite, is extraordinarily unlike the short *pericopae* in which the authentic teaching of Jesus seems elsewhere to have been preserved. Moreover, he like others admits that the transition from 'the Son of man' in v. 31 to 'the King' in vv. 34 and 40 is suspicious. And further it puts into the mouth of Jesus a clear allusion to the Parousia, which Jeremias, again with others, does not believe to have formed the original reference of the other parables of Jesus.

In this situation it might seem rash to make a further attempt on what appears to have proved an Everest of Synoptic criticism. Yet it remains 'there'—a sufficient reason in itself, we are told, for the assault. Moreover, the unsuccessful attempts call in

---

[6] *The Gospel Parables in the Light of their Jewish Background* (1936), p. 153.

[7] *Op.cit.*, pp. 142–4. C. H. Dodd, earlier, contented himself with a reference to the 'parable' in a footnote, in which he says: 'The climax of the passage is to be found in the two sayings 25.40 and 45, which are parallel to Matt. 10.40–2, Mark 9.37. The judgment scene was probably composed to give a vivid, dramatic setting to these sayings' (*The Parables of the Kingdom* (1935), p. 85).

question the adequacy of conclusions in other fields—in particular, our reconstruction of the eschatology of Jesus and our ability, technically, to assess the value of the special Matthean material, upon which so much turns.

Relying, therefore, almost wholly on the tools which previous workers have put into our hands, we may set out again, without any confidence of final success. For our method we are forced back well-nigh completely on the slow painstaking application of linguistic tests. Where there are no parallels in the other Gospels and the techniques of form-criticism fail us, there is little else left. By this method we must try, if we can, to analyse out the work of the Evangelist himself and to peel away different layers in the tradition, as and if they become apparent.

The opening sentence, v. 31, provides our first, and in many ways our easiest, problem. This verse supplies, as it were, the stage directions and backcloth of the scene which follows. Not only is it separable in content from what follows, it also bears traces, in a degree unparalleled in any succeeding verses, of the editorial style of the Evangelist himself. This is shown most simply by setting it alongside two other verses from the Gospel:

25.31	16.27
When the Son of man comes in his glory, and all the angels with him, then he will sit on his glorious throne.	For the Son of man is to come with his angels in the glory of his Father.
	19.28
	When the Son of man shall sit on his glorious throne. . . .

Now in both these other verses it can be demonstrated with reasonable confidence that Matthew's phrasing represents an editorial modification, in the first instance of Mark and in the second of Q.

Matt. 16.27 indeed represents the end term of a considerable development. The most original version of the tradition seems to be the Q passage in Luke 12.8 f.:

Everyone who acknowledges me before men, the Son of man also will acknowledge before the angels of God; but he who denies me before men will be denied before the angels of God.[8]

[8]The reasons for regarding the Matthean version (10.32 f.) as secondary are given on p. 90 below.

In Mark 8.38 we have:

Whoever is ashamed of me and of my words in this adulterous and sinful generation, of him will the Son of man also be ashamed, when he comes in the glory of his Father with the holy angels.[9]

In the Matthean parallel at this point (16.27), the final clause about the Parousia, added in Mark, becomes a main sentence, and, with embellishments, completely supersedes the original logion:

The Son of man is to come with his angels in the glory of his Father, and then he will repay every man for what he has done.

The eschatological reference, which attaches originally to the final significance of the response to Jesus in the here and now, becomes directed with progressive emphasis to a second coming. It is no longer in the ministry of Jesus that men are in the presence of the eschatological event, reaction to which has eternal consequences: the event by which they are judged is still awaited.

Moreover, this series of parallels reveals two other tendencies reaching their end term in Matthew, which also feature in 25.31. The first is the association of the note of retribution with the Parousia, which indeed within the Gospels is exclusively Matthean. It is added by Matthew to Marcan material in 24.30 as well as in 16.27, and is found in the allegorization of the parable of the Tares (13.40–2), which Jeremias has clearly shown to be Matthean in style.[10] When we find the idea of eternal punishment again associated with the Parousia in 25.31–46, it is reasonable to assume that the connexion here also is the work of Matthew himself.

Secondly, there is to be seen in these same passages a progressive detachment alike of the glory and of the angels from the Father to the Son. In Q (Luke 12.8 f.) it is 'before the angels of God' that the Son of man will be the advocate, and in Mark (8.38) he is to come 'in the glory of his Father with the holy angels'. The Lucan parallel of Mark 8.38 has 'in *his* glory and the glory of the Father and of the holy angels' (9.26), and the Matthean 'with *his* angels in the glory of his Father' (16.27). That this last

---

[9]Luke 9.26 follows Mark without significant variation, except at one point to be noted below.

[10]*Op. cit.*, pp. 65–7.

at any rate is not a fortuitous change[11] is shown by the fact that in the following verse Matthew alters Mark's 'see that the kingdom of God has come with power' to 'see the Son of man coming in *his* kingdom'. Moreover, in the Matthean allegory of the parable of the Tares we read, 'The Son of man will send out *his* angels, and they will gather out of *his* kingdom all causes of sin and all evildoers' (13.41); and in 24.31 Matthew again introduces a 'his' into the Marcan narrative, giving the angels of the Parousia unequivocally to the Son of man. So when in 25.31 we read: 'When the Son of man comes in *his* glory, and all the angels *with him*, then he will sit on *his* glorious throne', it is legitimate to detect once more the marks of the same hand.

This brings us to the second half of our verse, the session of the Son of man on his throne of glory, whose only parallel is in Matt. 19.28. Here we have what may be a Q passage, though the wording is very disparate:

Matt. 19.28	Luke 22.28–30
In the regeneration, when the Son of man shall sit on his glorious throne, you who have followed me will also sit on twelve thrones, judging the twelve tribes of Israel.	You are those who have continued with me in my trials; as my Father appointed a kingdom for me, so do I appoint for you that you may eat and drink at my table in my kingdom, and sit on thrones judging the twelve tribes of Israel.

There is nothing to suggest that the words we are concerned with ('when the Son of man shall sit on his glorious throne') were represented in the Q tradition. Indeed, the only common phrasing is 'sit on . . . thrones judging the twelve tribes of Israel', and this may well have suggested to Matthew an initial throne scene similar to that in 25.31. The fact that these two passages alone in the Old Testament or in the Gospels depict anyone but *God* on the throne of judgment suggests strongly that they belong together and are due, as every other trait would suggest, to

[11]I do not believe it is fortuitous in Luke 9.26, but he appears to have a different motive confined to this passage. He seems deliberately to be making connexion with the words with which he supplements the Marcan Transfiguration narrative in v. 32: 'And they saw his glory and the two men who stood with him.' The glory of Jesus, of the Father revealed in the *Shekinah*, and of the two celestial figures corresponds in anticipation to the triad of v. 26.

Matthew. Both in Q (Luke 12.8 f.) and in Mark (8.38) the Son of man is not the judge but the advocate at the court of heaven.

If we ask where Matthew derived the scene he depicts in 16.27; 19.28 and 25.31, the answer may well be the vision of the judgment given in the Similitudes of Enoch, the only pre-Christian source (if indeed it is pre-Christian) to represent a Messianic figure as occupying the throne of God's judgment. This idea is found in Enoch 45.3; 51.3; 55.4; 61.8; 62.2 f. (of the Elect One); 62.5; 69.27, 29 (of the Son of man).[12] The closest parallel in wording is in 62.5: 'And they shall be downcast of countenance, and pain shall seize them, when they see that Son of man, sitting on the throne of his glory.' Nowhere in Enoch, nor indeed anywhere else,[13] do we find the angels associated with this figure;[14] but their connexion with the 'coming' of Jesus is doubtless due to their Old Testament association with the 'coming' of 'the Lord'. Indeed, the 'coming' of the Son of man and 'all his angels with him' may be an adaptation of Zech. 14.5, 'Then the Lord your God will come, and all the holy ones with him', which is also quoted of 'the coming of our Lord Jesus Christ' in I Thess. 3.13.[15]

We may conclude then that the evidence points strongly in the direction of v. 31 being supplied by the Evangelist himself as a setting to the scene which follows. What follows is still a picture of the final judgment; but we cannot assume that the apocalyptic framework or the link with the Parousia is integral to it. Furthermore, the figure of the Son of man must provisionally be regarded as part of this framework. What connexion he has, if any, with the tradition or traditions behind the rest of the material must be considered. But the present position of this figure, which makes him identical by an unexplained transition with 'the King' of v. 34, must remain suspect as part of the editorial construction of the Evangelist.

[12]Contrast 47.3, where 'the Head of Days' 'seated himself upon the throne of his glory'.

[13]Cf. Strack-Billerbeck I, 973.

[14]The nearest parallel is Enoch 61.10, where the Lord of Spirits summons to the judgment 'all the angels of power, and all the angels of principalities, and the Elect One'.

[15]The association of the coming of *God* with his angels also forms part of the Enoch vision: 'Behold, he comes with ten thousand of his holy ones to execute judgment upon all, and to destroy all the ungodly' (1.9). This is cited in Jude 14 f.

It will be convenient now to pass straight to v. 34 and examine the person of 'the King'. The words, 'Come, ye blessed *of my Father*', clearly designate 'the King' as Jesus, and therefore identify him with 'the Son of man'. But this phrase, 'of my Father', at once draws suspicion to itself. It upsets the balance between the εὐλογημένοι and the simple κατηραμένοι of v. 41. This would not be decisive (despite the deliberate symmetry of the entire structure), were it not for the actual phrase itself. The term πατήρ μου is used of God by Matthew sixteen times, never by Mark, and four times by Luke. Of these sixteen times, fifteen are either clear editorial changes or occur in special Matthean material.[16] Among these the nearest parallels to Matt. 25.34 ('Come, O blessed of my Father, inherit the kingdom prepared for you from the foundation of the world') are:

Matt. 13.43: 'Then the righteous will shine like the sun in the kingdom of their Father' (in the Matthean allegorization of the parable of the Tares).
Matt. 20.23: 'To sit at my right hand and at my left is not mine to grant, but it is for those for whom it has been prepared by my Father'[17] (Mark omits 'by my Father').
Matt. 26.29: '. . . until that day when I drink it new with you in the kingdom of my Father' (Mark: 'the kingdom of God').

There is therefore a strong presumption that the phrase 'of my Father' in 25.34 is similarly a Matthean editorial addition. We must therefore be prepared to examine the figure of 'the King' without assuming necessarily that the title applied originally to Jesus.

But what of the title itself? Apart from the present passage, there are four others in the Gospels where the figure of a king appears in a parabolic setting. One is the special Lucan parable of the king contemplating war with another king (Luke 14.31). Here the figure of the king is entirely in keeping with and integral to the situation depicted.

The other three are parables where Matthew alone introduces the figure and where the fact that the character is a king is fortuitous, if not otiose. Thus in the parable of the Unmerciful Servant, the kingdom of heaven is 'compared to a king who wished to settle

[16]The remaining one is in the famous Q passage of Matt. 11.27 = Luke 10.22.
[17]Cf. the D text of Matt. 25.41: ὃ ἡτοίμασεν ὁ πατήρ μου.

accounts with his servants' (Matt. 18.23). But this is the only suggestion that the central figure is a royal personage and the rest of the parable speaks of a 'master' in relation to his 'slaves'. If the sums involved seem to require the scale of an imperial exchequer, this is not necessarily to say more than that Matthew felt the appropriateness of adding such a touch. For this is certainly what he seems to have done in the parable of the Great Supper. Here again he compares the kingdom of heaven ἀνθρώπῳ βασιλεῖ (22.2), where Luke has simply ἄνθρωπός τις (Luke 14.16). The introduction of the king with his armies in 22.7 is highly inconsequential and is generally regarded as secondary.[18] With this parable Matthew has fused[19] another, that of the Wedding Garment, to which the figure of the king may originally belong, though even here it is by no means indispensable. In each of these cases, moreover, it is to be noted that the figure of the king stands implicitly for the action of *God*, and in one case explicitly so: 'So also will my heavenly Father do to every one of you, if you do not forgive your brother from your heart' (18.35).

The conclusion appears to be that Matthew has a partiality for parables featuring a king, and we cannot therefore be sure that he has not introduced the figure also in 25.34 and 40. Moreover, we should independently expect it to describe the action not of Christ but of God. And this would seem to be borne out by the fact that 'the kingdom' (v. 34), to which 'the king' would naturally be correlative, is evidently the kingdom of the Father (as it is specifically in 13.43).

Having detached v. 31 and looked at the figure of the King, we must now examine the passage as a whole for traces of peculiarly Matthean style. This is inevitably a tentative and precarious procedure and its results must be accepted with great caution.

In v. 32 συνάγω is listed by Hawkins,[20] as a characteristic word of Matthew, and the figures are impressive (Mark 5, Luke 6, Matthew 24). The idea of assembly is, however a familiar feature of the End (cf., for example, Mark 13.27) and nothing certain can therefore be built upon it. Moreover, in the comparable parables of the Tares and the Drag-net it occurs in each case not

---

[18]Luke has the much more appropriate οἰκοδεσπότης (14.21).
[19]Cf. Jeremias, *op. cit.*, pp. 37 f.
[20]*Horae Synopticae* (2nd ed., 1909), p. 7.

in the allegorization, which may definitely be shown to be editorial, but in the parable itself (13.30 and 47).[21] It is, however, noteworthy that whereas in this verse it is used in the regular Matthean sense, in vv. 35, 38 and 43 it has the meaning, found only here in the New Testament, of 'take in' or 'show hospitality to', which is generally recognized as a Semitism.[22]

In this same verse ὥσπερ is also listed by Hawkins[23] as Matthean (Matt. 10, Mark 0, Luke 2), though the word is difficult to avoid in any comparison.

In v. 34 we have the first of five occurrences of τότε (apart from one in v. 31, already analysed as typically Matthean in style). The figures for Matthew's use of this little word (particularly as a simple conjunction) are indeed remarkable. Hawkins[24] gives them as Mark 6, Luke 15, Matt. 90. This can therefore confidently be regarded as a small but significant indication of where Matthew is editing and not simply reproducing his sources.

In the same verse, the invitation δεῦτε may also be considered a Matthean trait, though the figures here are not decisive (Mark 3, Luke 0, Matt. 6). We may compare the invitation to the marriage feast in Matt. 22.4: δεῦτε εἰς τοὺς γάμους.

Also in this verse, Jeremias sees the word κόσμος as a favourite of Matthew (the figures are Mark 2, Luke 3, Matt. 8); but this cannot be regarded as evidence in the case of such a stock phrase as ἀπὸ (or πρὸ) καταβολῆς κόσμου, which also occurs in Luke 11.50 and seven other times in the New Testament (cf. also Matt. 13.35).

In vv. 37 and 46 οἱ δίκαιοι is used as a designation for the saved at the Last Judgment. Except in the traditional phrase 'the resurrection of the just' (Luke 14.14; Acts 24.15), this is found elsewhere in the New Testament only in Matt. 13.43 and 49, where it occurs in a similar context in the Matthean interpretations of the Tares and the Drag-net. Moreover, in chapter 25 it is not a designation that grows out of the story itself. Commentators, taking the title seriously, have been much stretched to prove that

---

[21]The same conclusion must also hold for ἀφορίζω which Jeremias (*op. cit.*, p. 67) regards, with insufficient evidence, as a characteristically Matthean word.

[22]So W. C. Allen and A. H. McNeile (*ad loc.*), Jeremias (*op. cit.*, p. 143), Preiss (*op. cit.*, p. 45).

[23]*Op. cit.*, p. 8.

[24]*Ibid.*

it does not teach a doctrine of justification by works! It looks like a bit of stylization from the same editorial hand at work in chapter 13.

In v. 40 Jeremias suspects τῶν ἀδελφῶν μου as a Matthean explanation of τούτων τῶν ἐλαχίστων in terms of members of the Christian Church ('the brethren'), which is here inappropriate. This tendency is certainly at work in Matthew (and also to a lesser degree in Luke)[25] and he may well be right, for again it destroys the parallelism with v. 45, and the words are in fact absent from B* etc., arm., Clement, the Latin version of Origen, Ambrose and Cyril. But in view of Mark 3.33–5, 'Behold . . . my brethren! Whoever does the will of God, this is my brother', it is not impossible that Jesus could have used the word ἀδελφός in a general sense, even though Matthew in his version of that saying (12.49) does deliberately limit its reference to the disciples.

In vv. 41 and 46 the word αἰώνιος is applied to retribution; and this, within the Gospels, is a peculiarly Matthean feature (though cf. Mark 3.29). Its association with 'punishment' is unique, but 'the eternal fire' occurs also in 18.8. 'Fire' for punishment is again a favourite symbol of Matthew's. Apart from the fire of judgment which features in Q in the preaching of John the Baptist, Mark uses πῦρ of final retribution twice (9.43 and 48), Luke never, and Matthew seven times. 'The oven of fire' is used in the allegorization both of the Tares and the Drag-net (13.42 and 50), though in the latter it is inappropriate to the parable and represents, like 'the eternal fire' of 25.41, a purely stylized picture of damnation, derived perhaps from Enoch 98.3.

Also in v. 41, 'the devil and his angels' may be a mythological embellishment by the Evangelist. It upsets the parallelism with ἡτοιμασμένην ὑμῖν in v. 34, and Jeremias[26] argues that διάβολος belongs to a later stratum of the Gospel tradition than σατανᾶς; but the evidence is not overwhelming. ὁ διάβολος also features in the allegorization of the Tares (13.39), and the *angels* of the Devil may derive from the same stock of apocalyptic imagery which has coloured v. 31.[27]

[25]Cf. Jeremias, *op cit.,* p. 84, note 96.
[26]*Op. cit.,* p. 65, n. 94.
[27]Cf. (for example), Enoch 10.13, where the fallen angels are 'led off to the abyss of fire, to the torment and the prison in which they shall be confined for ever'.

We have now examined all the traces of what could be regarded as peculiarly or characteristically Matthean traits. Some must be dismissed as evidence, and others accepted with caution. But if we now separate out those verses in which these influences may be detected from those from which they are absent, the result is significant.

(*a*) v. 31 stands by itself as a purely Matthean introduction.

(*b*) vv. 32 f., the actual parable of the Shepherd, are free from editorial traces, except perhaps in the non-parabolic phrase (καὶ συναχθήσονται ἔμπροσθεν αὐτοῦ πάντα τὰ ἔθνη) which links them with v. 31, and possibly in the use of ὥσπερ.

(*c*) v. 34 (τότε ... ὁ βασιλεύς ... δεῦτε ... τοῦ πατρός μου ...), v. 41 (τότε ... τὸ πῦρ τὸ αἰώνιον ... τῷ διαβόλῳ καὶ τοῖς ἀγγέλοις αὐτοῦ), v. 46 (εἰς κόλασιν αἰώνιον ... οἱ δίκαιοι), and the *narrative parts* of v. 37 (τότε ... οἱ δίκαιοι), v. 40 (ὁ βασιλεύς), vv. 44 and 45 (τότε) contain all the remaining Matthean traits,[28] with the exception of the possible interpolation of τῶν ἀδελφῶν μου in v. 40.

(*d*) vv. 35–40 (with the exception just noted) and vv. 42–5 are *in their dialogue* free of all editorial traces.

Taking now first the latter half of the passage where (*c*) and (*d*) are intertwined, we observe that all the references to division, separation and punishment, and to the whole court setting, occur in section (*c*), that with the Matthean colouring. This may be set out as follows:

Then the King will say to those at his right hand, 'Come, O blessed of my Father, inherit the kingdom prepared for you from the foundation of the world. . . .' Then the righteous will answer him. . . . And the King will answer them. . . . Then he will say to those at his left hand, 'Depart from me, you cursed, into the eternal fire prepared for the devil and his angels. . . .' Then they also will answer. . . . Then he will answer them. . . . And they will go away into eternal punishment, but the righteous into eternal life.

[28] A. Schlatter (*Der Evangelist Matthäus*, 1929, pp. 16 f.) sees the use of the participial λέγων (which also appears in these same verses, 37, 44 and 45) as characteristically Matthean. In a comparison with Mark, which is his point of reference, he probably establishes his case; but this is only to say that Matthew, like Luke, writes smooth Greek in contrast with Mark's reiterated καὶ ἔλεγεν. It requires more to establish the usage as 'a stylistic *peculiarity* of Matthew' (Jeremias, *op. cit.*, p. 66 n. 3). Nevertheless, the fact that it occurs in verses which are already indicated as Matthean may be regarded as some confirmation.

Next let us set alongside this the parable (*b*) which immediately precedes it:

> Before him will be gathered all the nations, and he will separate them one from another as a shepherd separates the sheep from the goats, and he will place the sheep at his right hand, but the goats at the left.

With the exception of τὰ ἔθνη, where the application is already made (and which may belong with the whole opening phrase to the preceding verse), this is a simple parable without allegorical traits. In content it is closely parallel with Matt. 13.24–30 and 13.47 f. All three are parables of division, one from agriculture, one from fishing, and one from sheep-farming. Perhaps we may reconstruct the beginning of our parable on similar lines:

> The kingdom of heaven is like a flock, which a shepherd gathers in; and he separates the sheep from the goats, placing the sheep at his right hand, but the goats on the left.[29]

What is more plausible than that the judgment scene of section (*c*) should be the Matthean allegorization of this parable? If we excise the editorial connexions necessary to introduce the conversation that forms the ground of the judgment, this runs as follows:

> Then the King will say to those at his right hand, 'Come, O blessed of my Father, inherit the kingdom prepared for you from the foundation of the world.' Then he will say to those at his left hand, 'Depart from me, you cursed, into the eternal fire prepared for the devil and his angels.' And they will go away into eternal punishment, but the righteous into eternal life.

This scene would then perform precisely the same function as the allegorization of the other two parables of separation, making specific the application to the Last Judgment. The parallels of language are striking:

> Just as the weeds are gathered and burned with fire, so will it be at the close of the age. The Son of man will send his angels, and they will gather out of his kingdom all causes of sin and all evil-doers, and throw them into the furnace of fire; there men will weep and gnash their teeth. Then the righteous will shine like the sun in the kingdom of their Father (13.40–3).

[29]It will be noted that this reconstruction avoids the use of ὥσπερ, which may have been introduced by Matthew when making the comparison with the Last Judgment, exactly as in 13.40.

87

So will it be at the close of the age. The angels will come out and separate the evil from the righteous, and throw them into the furnace of fire; there men will weep and gnash their teeth (13.49 f.).

In the parable of the Flock (as 25.32 f. should perhaps be called) the formula introducing the allegory ('So will it be at the close of the age') is expanded and placed *before* the parable itself (section (*a*)); and the whole is then further filled out by the insertion of section (*d*).

Now this last material, in contrast with the scene into which it is introduced, is stylistically entirely free of Matthean touches (with the possible exception of τῶν ἀδελφῶν μου). If we set it out without the editorial additions necessary to register the change of speakers, it reads as follows:

'I was hungry and you gave me food, I was thirsty and you gave me drink, I was a stranger and you welcomed me, I was naked and you clothed me, I was sick and you visited me, I was in prison and you came to me.' 'Lord, when did we see thee hungry and fed thee, or thirsty and gave thee drink? And when did we see thee a stranger and welcome thee, or naked and clothe thee? And when did we see thee sick or in prison and visit thee?' 'Truly, I say to you, as you did it to one of the least of these (my brethren), you did it to me.'
'I was hungry and you gave me no food, I was thirsty and you gave me no drink, I was a stranger, and you did not welcome me, naked and you did not clothe me, sick and in prison and you did not visit me.' 'Lord, when did we see thee hungry or thirsty or a stranger or naked or sick or in prison, and did not minister to thee?' 'Truly, I say to you, as you did it not to one of the least of these, you did it not to me.'

When commentators find in Matt. 25.31–46 the authentic touch of the Master, it is pre-eminently to these words that they refer. And this is no subjective judgment. For the words reflect very closely three other sets of sayings, two at least of which are represented both in Mark and in Q, and have therefore very high authenticity value. These sayings are recorded thus:

(i) Matt. 18.5	**Mark 9.37**	Luke 9.48
Whoever receives one such child in my name receives me.	Whoever receives one such child in my name receives me; and whoever receives me, receives not me but him who sent me.	Whoever receives this child in my name receives me, and whoever receives me receives him who sent me.

Matt. 10.40			Luke 10.16
He who receives you receives me, and he who receives me receives him who sent me.			He who hears you hears me, and he who rejects you rejects me, and he who rejects me rejects him who sent me.

(ii) **Matt. 10.42**	Mark 9.41		
Whoever gives to one of these little ones even a cup of cold water because he is a disciple, truly, I say to you, he shall not lose his reward.	Truly, I say to you, whoever gives you a cup of cold water to drink because you bear the name of Christ, will by no means lose his reward.		

(iii) Matt. 10.32 f.			**Luke 12.8 f.**
Everyone who acknowledges me before men, I also will acknowledge before my Father who is in heaven; but whoever denies me before men, I also will deny before my Father who is in heaven.			I tell you, every one who acknowledges me before men, the Son of man also will acknowledge before the angels of God; but he who denies me before men will be denied before the angels of God.

	Mark 8.38	Luke 9.26	
	For whoever is ashamed of me and of mine[30] in this adulterous and sinful generation, of him will the Son of man also be ashamed, when he comes in the glory of his Father with the holy angels.	For whoever is ashamed of me and of my words, of him will the Son of man be ashamed when he comes in his glory and the glory of the Father and of the holy angels.	

Without going into a full argument of the different cases, we may judge the most original forms of these sayings to be those in heavy type above, namely:

[30]Omitting λόγους with W and k and C. H. Turner (*JTS* xxix, 1928, 2 f.), T. W. Manson (*The Sayings of Jesus*, p. 78), C. H. Dodd (*The Parables of the Kingdom*, p. 93).

(i) **Mark 9.37** (on the general priority of Mark) and, in the Q tradition, Luke 10.16 (because of the antithetical parallelism). These are probably versions of the same saying, and the 'one such child' of Mark is likely to be more original than the 'you' of Q.[31]

(ii) **Matt. 10.42.** This appears to be from a non-Marcan source (Matthew has no parallel to Mark 9.38–41). Mark's ὅτι Χριστοῦ ἐστε is generally recognized as secondary, and Jeremias points out[32] the probability that the recipient of the cup was originally in Mark also 'one of these little ones' (and not 'you') and that this was the catchword making the connexion with the following verse, 9.42. Manson[33] argues in the same direction.

(iii) **Luke 12.8 f.**, in comparison with Matt. 10.32 f., because Matthew has obliterated the reference to the Son of man (common to both the Marcan and Q versions), as appearing to throw doubt on his identity with Jesus;[34] and, in comparison with Mark 8.38, by reason of its antithetical parallelism and because of the secondary reference to the Parousia in Mark.

If then we place together Mark 9.37, Matt. 10.42, and Luke 12.8 f., we have close parallels for all the essential elements in the verses of Matt. 25 we labelled (*d*) (cf. p. 88 above):

'Whoever receives one such child in my name receives me; and whoever receives me, receives not me but him who sent me.' 'Whoever gives to one of these little ones even a cup of cold water because he is a disciple, truly, I say to you, he shall not lose his reward.' 'I tell you, every one who acknowledges me before men, the Son of man also will acknowledge before the angels of God; but he who denies me before men will be denied before the angels of God.'

We are now in a position to draw conclusions about the construction of Matt. 25.31–46 as a whole. The original core is (*b*) and (*d*), that is to say, a parable about a shepherd separating his flock and a set of antithetical sayings concerning the eschatological consequences of accepting or rejecting Jesus in the outcast and helpless. There is no reason to doubt on linguistic grounds that these are both pre-Matthean.[35] The former, like the com-

[31]Cf. T. W. Manson, *op. cit.*, p. 78, and (ii) immediately below.
[32]*Op. cit.*, p. 144.
[33]*Op. cit.*, pp. 138 f.
[34]Cf. also Matthew's characteristic phrase: 'my Father who is in heaven'.
[35]The sense of συνάγω in vv. 35, 38 and 43 may argue for an Aramaic background for (*d*). Théo Preiss also detects an Aramaism in the use of ποιῶ in vv. 40 and 45 (*op. cit.*, pp. 45 f.).

parable parables of the Tares and Drag-net, may come from the Evangelist's special source. The latter perhaps derives from Q. Nor, from the parallels to both elsewhere (particularly strong in the case of the second), have we any reason for thinking that they do not go back substantially to Jesus himself.

Matthew's artistry consists in having fused the parable with an allegory of the Last Judgment, and then with great skill introduced the sayings of Jesus as the ground upon which the judgment is given. At the same time the whole is linked with the Parousia of the Son of man in a manner suggested perhaps by the connexion already made in Mark 8.38: 'Whoever is ashamed of me and of mine . . . of him will the Son of man also be ashamed when he comes in the glory of the Father with the holy angels.' In his own Gospel Matthew does not retain this connexion at this place (16.26 f.), reserving it perhaps deliberately for the climax of chapter 25.

Finally, we may look again at the characters in the different strands of the story and at the way in which the Evangelist has brought them together. The figure of the original parable is the shepherd. Upon this Matthew or the tradition he represents may already have constructed an allegory of the Last Judgment, in which the shepherd is replaced by God, represented as a King on his royal throne[36] dividing the nations of the world, and dispensing eternal rewards and punishments. When, however, this is combined with the sayings section, a difficulty arises. For the speaker in these is, and must be, Christ: it is only Jesus who can refer to actions done to men as actions done to himself, or, if it is original, to 'my brethren'. Matthew now therefore makes 'the King' represent not God but Christ, by the simple addition of his characteristic τοῦ πατρός μου—despite the fact that the kingdom is still evidently that of the Father. The Son and not the Father is thus the judge; and this unexpected fact is then made clear to the reader by the introduction, which sets the stage and describes how and when it is that Christ comes to occupy the throne.

[36]There is no parallel in the Gospels for 'the King' used allegorically, and not merely parabolically, for God. But the metaphor of the King is so familiar in this connexion as to be little more than a reverential periphrasis (cf. Matt. 5.35: 'the city of the great King'). In *The Assumption of Moses* 10.3 God arises to judgment from his *royal* throne.

Lastly, what of 'the Son of man'? The transition to 'the King' is exceedingly awkward, and we could be required to accept T. W. Manson's ingenious theory[37] that the Son of man is a corporate figure embracing both the King and the little ones only if we were compelled to regard the passage as a unitary whole. On the analysis here given, however, there is an easier explanation. The figure of the Son of man comes from the sayings we labelled (*d*). Both in Q and in Mark it is 'the Son of man' who is to acknowledge or deny before God those who have accepted or refused Jesus and his own. He is not the judge, but he is the advocate and accuser at the court of heaven. It is therefore no great step to make him the subject, not only of the sayings, but of the entire judgment scene. For, as we have seen, these sayings were already linked with the Parousia in Mark; and the Parousia itself was already associated with the session of the Son of man[38] and, by Matthew, with eternal retribution.

Thus, with superb artistry, Matthew uses the lull before the Passion breaks to draw together, out of the rich treasury of his Gospel, those themes that are to come to such ironic expression in what follows, as the royal Son of man,[39] rejected and unreceived, goes to his own trial, the trial which is to inaugurate, from that moment on (Matt. 26.64), his coming and his session in glory. For anything comparable we must turn to the majestic and studied effect of John 13.1–20, where, with the hour now come for the Son of man to be glorified (12.23) and for the judgment of this world (12.31), 'Jesus, knowing that the Father had given all things into his hands, and that he had come from God and was going to God . . . girded himself with a towel', and, after enjoining such menial service as the mark of the disciple and as the only true blessedness, closes with the words, 'He who receives anyone whom I send receives me; and he who receives me receives him who sent me.'[40] In position and power too it has its parallel in John 17, where, as the Passion is about to begin, a door is opened in heaven, and the Son is seen in glory, the advocate of those for

[37]*The Teaching of Jesus* (2nd ed., 1935), p. 265; *The Sayings of Jesus*, pp. 249 f.
[38]In Mark, at the right hand of God (14.62); in Matthew, on his own throne also (19.28).
[39]Cf. the editorial and hardly fortuitous ὁ υἱὸς τοῦ ἀνθρώπου of 26.2, immediately following.
[40]Cf. also John 12.44 and 48.

whom the kingdom of his Father has been prepared before the foundation of the world. Matthew's construction stands the comparison. In its careful and composite grandeur, which yet destroys nothing of its piercing simplicity, it continues to convey the judgment it records, which, not only 'in his glorious majesty', but also 'in great humility', the Son of man brings by his presence in our midst.

VII

THE NEW LOOK ON THE FOURTH GOSPEL[1]

I SHOULD like to say, first of all, that I put forward these observations with the very greatest diffidence. This is not simply due to modesty, false or genuine, but to the fact that I am not finally convinced whether there is a 'new look' on the fourth Gospel or not; but I *think* there is. The reason for my diffidence is that I am really doing no more than trying to assess straws in the wind: the ground of my conviction, such as it is, is that all the straws seem to be blowing in much the same direction. But I am only too well aware that this may be an optical illusion and that it is I who am being carried along by the wind, and that the new look may represent no more than my look.[2] But with this qualification —and I mean it to be taken seriously—let me come at once to explaining what I mean by this 'new look'.

Obviously it can be understood only with reference to the 'old look'; and by the 'old look' I do not here mean the precritical assessment of the Gospel which served the Church for seventeen centuries and which indeed still serves most of its members today. I mean what might be called the 'critical orthodoxy' which has taken shape over the last fifty years and which is still represented in the most recent commentaries and textbooks. Now this is clearly a vast and inclusive term. In fact, one has only to glance at the swings and roundabouts of Johannine criticism in this period[3] to question whether it means anything at all; and indeed for positive definition it is far too wide a classification to

[1]Reprinted from *Studia Evangelica* (TU 73, ed. K. Aland, etc., 1959), pp. 338–50 (originally given as a paper to the conference at Oxford on 'The Four Gospels in 1957').

[2]Since this was written, two subsequent surveys have come to very similar conclusions: A. M. Hunter, 'Recent Trends in Johannine Studies', *ExpT* LXXI (1960), 164–7, 219–22; A. J. B. Higgins, 'Recent Trends in the Study of the Fourth Gospel', *Religion in Education* XXVIII (1961), 121–6.

[3]See W. F. Howard, *The Fourth Gospel in Recent Criticism and Interpretation* (1931; revised by C. K. Barrett, 1955); P.-H. Menoud, *L'évangile de Jean d'après les recherches récentes.*

be useful. But negatively, I think, it may serve some purpose. For the 'new look', if I discern it aright, may best be understood as a questioning of certain presuppositions that have underlain this approach in all its multifarious manifestations. These presuppositions do not, of course, apply equally to all its representatives, and anyone will be able to single out exceptions to whom perhaps they do not apply at all. But for our purposes we may say broadly that current critical orthodoxy on the fourth Gospel rests on five generally agreed presuppositions.

In passing, it is worth noting that the very title 'the fourth Gospel' itself reflects these presuppositions, and I cannot refrain from quoting some rather naughty words from James Montgomery's little book, *The Origin of the Gospel According to St John,* published in Philadelphia as long ago as 1923. 'I may', he wrote, 'have academically "declassed" myself by using the name "Gospel of St John" in the title . . . I frankly think that "Fourth Gospel" is a scholastic affectation. Why not the First, Second, and Third Gospels? Are we any surer of their authors? Any tyro knows that Deuteronomy is not "the Second Giving of the Law", but are we obliged to make constant profession of our critical attainments by calling that document the Fifth Book of Pseudo-Moses?'

But let us return to the five presuppositions I mentioned. These are:

(1) That the fourth Evangelist is dependent on sources, including (normally) one or more of the Synoptic Gospels.

(2) That his own background is other than that of the events and teaching he is purporting to record.

(3) That he is not to be regarded, seriously, as a witness to the Jesus of history, but simply to the Christ of faith.

(4) That he represents the end-term of theological development in first-century Christianity.

(5) That he is not himself the Apostle John nor a direct eye-witness.

Now the effect of each of these presuppositions is to place the Evangelist at one remove or more from the events he is narrating. This may be no loss—it may even provide a gain in perspective— but it does determine the sort of questions which it is worth asking of the Gospel. The 'new look', if I may use the term, is characterized by a certain impertinence, which insists that it may be worth asking other, often apparently naïve, questions, which these presuppositions would rule out as ones that the Gospel was never meant to answer. This is partly because if one does ask them one frequently seems to get what look like astonishingly sensible answers, and partly because the foundations of these presuppositions themselves are beginning to appear a good deal less certain than they did.

Let us consider them each in turn.

(1) The first is that the fourth Evangelist is dependent on sources, including (normally) one or more of the Synoptic Gospels.

That John is dependent on the Synoptists, or at any rate on Mark, is perhaps the presupposition into which the acids of criticism have themselves eaten most deeply. It is indeed a pre-supposition shared, like all the rest, by the most recent critical edition of the Gospel, that of Dr C. K. Barrett,[4] as well as by the late Professor R. H. Lightfoot's posthumous commentary.[5] But the work of Mr P. Gardner-Smith[6] and others has had its effect, and I notice a widespread tendency today, which I fully endorse, to regard the case for literary dependence as quite unproven and indeed quite improbable.[7]

The effect of this has been to emphasize the independence of the Johannine tradition, which in the nineteenth century was the main count *against* its authenticity. How could John be reliable when his was so different a picture from that of the 'Jesus of history' given by the Synoptists? While in the twentieth, paradoxically, it has been its dependence that has discredited it in the eyes of the critics as an original witness: how could John represent a first-hand tradition if he needed to rely on Mark and Luke? But if the Johannine stream is independent of the Synoptists, then potenti-ally it is as near the source as any of the other independent streams of tradition—Mark, Q, special Luke or special Matthew. I do not say that it is as near; and in each case one has to test the waters as critically as one can to assess how far they have flowed before

---

[4] *The Gospel according to St John* (1955).
[5] *St John's Gospel* (1956).
[6] *St John and the Synoptic Gospels* (1938).
[7] It was abandoned by W. F. Howard before his death, as it has also been by Dr C. H. Dodd. Dodd introduced a recent paper to the Cambridge Theological Society with the words: 'The presumption of literary dependence of John on the Synoptists no longer holds.'

they have reached one and how much they have picked up on the way. But potentially one can put the same questions, with the expectation of comparable results, to the Johannine tradition as one can to the Synoptic. This places it on all fours with the Synoptic tradition from the point of view of its relation to source —or, in plain language, its historicity. That, again, is not to say that it is equally historical, but simply that one can approach it with the supposition that it equally might be. We should, according to this 'new look', be prepared to approach both the traditions —or rather all the traditions, since the Synoptic tradition is not homogeneous—impartially, with an open mind as to which, at any given point, may be the most primitive. We shall still give priority to material that is confirmed by two independent traditions, for instance, by Q and Mark, or by Mark and John. And when it comes to material peculiar to one source, be it special Matthew or John, we must be prepared to scrutinize it very carefully. But we should not adopt different criteria just because it is Johannine.

Then there is the further question of the non-Gospel sources upon which the fourth Evangelist has been said to draw—for instance, the *Offenbarungsreden* (revelatory discourses) and the σημεῖα-*Quelle* (signs source) of Professor R. Bultmann.[8] Again, I notice an increasing reluctance to admit any really objective evidence for such sources. As a recent writer has put it, 'It looks as though, if the author of the fourth Gospel used documentary sources, he wrote them all himself.'[9] The detailed examination of the Johannine characteristics undertaken by Professor E. Schweizer[10] and others[11] has told heavily in favour of a unity of style throughout the Gospel, including the last, additional chapter. Professors P.-H. Menoud,[12] E. Ruckstuhl[13] and B. Noack[14] have examined Bultmann's source criticism most carefully and conclude that it cannot stand. In John we are dealing

---

[8]*Das Evangelium des Johannes.*

[9]P. Parker, 'Two Editions of John', *JBL* LXXV (1956), 304.

[10]*Ego Eimi* (1939).

[11]E.g. J. Jeremias, 'Johanneische Literarkritik', *Theologische Blätter* XX (1941), 33–46; E. Ruckstuhl, *Die literarische Einheit des Johannes-evangeliums* (1951).

[12]*Op. cit.*, pp. 17–21.

[13]*Op. cit.*, pp. 20–179.

[14]*Zur johanneischen Tradition* (1954), pp. 9–42.

with a man who is not piecing together written sources but placing his stamp upon the oral tradition of his community with a sovereign freedom. Indeed, he *is* his own tradition. As Menoud[15] puts it, it is as if he is saying to us from beginning to end: 'La tradition, c'est moi!'

(2) The second presupposition which is being re-examined is that the background of the Evangelist himself is different from that of the events and teaching which he is purporting to record.

I have deliberately put this as generally as I can since the proposed 'backgrounds' for the fourth Evangelist are legion.[16] But they all have this in common that they locate him, whether in time or place or mental environment, at a distance from the milieu and thought-forms of Palestine prior to the Jewish war of AD 66–70. Now the kind of reaction that I am describing would not deny that in a real sense this was true. It is perfectly clear that the Evangelist is writing for a non-Palestinian situation in which even the simplest Aramaic words, like *Rabbi* (1.38) and *Rabboni* (20.16), which Mark (9.5; 10.51) does not bother to translate for his Roman public, need to be made plain. Nor, I imagine, could any responsible person deny that his language has echoes and overtones which would evoke a response, and were intended to evoke a response, in circles far wider than those within which the words and works of Jesus himself were circumscribed. It is essentially the Gospel for those who have not seen, because they were not there to see.

And yet, though this may be true of the environment in and for which the Gospel was published, that is not to say that the Evangelist or the tradition he represents was native to that environment. When we look to the *background* of the Evangelist and his tradition, that is, to what actually lay behind him and shaped his thinking, rather than to the environment for which he was writing, I detect a growing readiness to recognize that this is not to be sought at the end of the first century or the beginning of the second, in Ephesus or Alexandria, among the Gnostics or the Greeks. Rather, there is no compelling need to let our gaze

[15]*Op. cit.*, p. 77.
[16]For a survey of the most important, see C. H. Dodd, *The Interpretation of the Fourth Gospel*, pp. 1–130; also Menoud, *op. cit.*, pp. 30–50.

wander very far, either in space or in time, beyond a fairly limited area of southern Palestine in the fairly limited interval between the Crucifixion and the fall of Jerusalem. This area and this interval will not tell the whole story: but I suspect they will be found to tell us a great deal more than we had previously imagined.

This judgment has, of course, received considerable stimulus and support from the evidence of the Dead Sea Scrolls. Their connexions with the thought-forms of the fourth Evangelist have been widely noticed[17] and need not be repeated here. Let me simply say why I think they are significant in this respect. They are important for Johannine study not because they offer closer or more numerous parallels with the language of the fourth Gospel than any other literature. I doubt really if they do. They are decisive, in my judgment, because *for the first time they present us with a body of thought which in date and place (southern Palestine in the first century* BC—AD), *as well as in fundamental, and not merely verbal, theological affinity, may really represent an actual background, and not merely a possible environment, for the distinctive categories of the Gospel.* And when this is combined with the evidence connecting the Johannine tradition with circles that entered Christianity through the Baptist movement, and with the hypothesis, which I believe to be strong, that the Baptist himself had had associations with Qumran,[18] then the sort of thinking represented in that Community becomes a very probable and not merely a very possible background for the Gospel. This does not mean that other suggested backgrounds are ruled out. Indeed, I believe that what Professor B. Reicke[19] has aptly called these 'pre-Gnostic' thought-forms will help us to fill in other connexions,[20] and in particular to understand more clearly why later this Gospel was to have such an appeal for the Gnostics. The new evidence has not changed the whole picture; but it has changed

[17]See the bibliography on p. 26 above, especially the articles by W. Groussow, F. M. Braun and R. E. Brown.

[18]See 'The Baptism of John and the Qumran Community', pp. 11–27 above.

[19]'Traces of Gnosticism in the Dead Sea Scrolls?', *NTS* I (1955), 137–41.

[20]Cf. R. McL. Wilson, 'Gnostic Origins', *Vigiliae Christianae* IX (1955), 193 ff.; 'Gnostic Origins Again', *ib.*, XI (1957), 93 ff.; 'Simon, Dositheus and the Dead Sea Scrolls', *Zeitschrift für Religions- und Geistesgeschichte* IX (1957), 21 ff.; *The Gnostic Problem* (1958).

the perspective. The other influences fall into a different place, and many of them will, I believe, be seen to be more important for understanding the *reception* of the Gospel than for interpreting its background or assessing its purpose.

(3) Now both these first two considerations, that the Evangelist represents an independent tradition and has his background, as it were, on the spot, have naturally affected the third presupposition, namely, that he is not to be regarded seriously as a witness to the Jesus of history, but only to the Christ of faith.

That he is primarily, and indeed all the time, a witness to the Christ of faith is, of course, not to be questioned. 'These things are written that you may believe that Jesus is the Christ, the Son of God' (20.31). That is his purpose—as it is also Mark's purpose —and his sole theological concern. But for him the Christ of faith includes the Jesus of history; and the notion that the former can be had apart from, or at the expense of, the latter was exactly the error which, to judge from the Prologue and the Epistles, he was most concerned to combat.

However, concern for the 'flesh' of Christ as a theological truth and reliability as a historical witness are not the same thing—though it is astonishing how readily critics have assumed that our Evangelist attached the greatest importance to historicity in general and had but the lightest regard for it in particular.

But what marks the newer approach is, as I said, an openness to recognize that in the Johannine tradition we may at points be as near to the Jesus of history as in the Synoptic Gospels. This is not to deny that a good deal of peeling and paring away may be necessary in both, as Professor J. Jeremias has shown in his book, *The Parables of Jesus*. But recent studies indicate that when sayings and incidents in the fourth Gospel are subjected to this process the results are often such as to uncover tradition at least as primitive as in comparable Synoptic material, and sometimes more so.[21]

From another side, it is becoming clear that the Dead Sea Scrolls may force us to think again about the Johannine picture

[21]Cf. 'The Parable of the Shepherd (John 10.1–5)', pp. 67–75 above, and C. H. Dodd, 'Some Johannine "Herrnworte" with Parallels in the Synoptic Gospels', *NTS* II (1955–6), 75–86.

of John the Baptist. Professor W. H. Brownlee[22] and others[23] have claimed, and I would agree with them, that one of the most remarkable effects of the Scrolls has been the surprising vindication they appear to offer of ideas and categories attributed to John by the fourth Evangelist which recent criticism would never have allowed as remotely historical. Indeed, nothing, I prophesy, is likely to undergo so complete a reversal in the criticism of the Gospel as our estimate of its treatment of the Baptist, and therefore of the whole Judaean ministry of Jesus with which it opens. This treatment has almost universally been assumed to spring from purely theological motives of a polemical nature and thus to provide evidence for a very minimum of historical foundation —about as much in fact as I should be prepared to allow to the Baptist group claiming John as Messiah against which the whole construction is supposed to be directed.[24] On the contrary, I believe that the fourth Evangelist is remarkably well informed on the Baptist, because he, or at least the witness behind that part of his tradition, once belonged to John's movement and, like the nameless disciple of 1.37, 'heard him say this, and followed Jesus'.

It is for this same reason that he appears also to be being vindicated in his knowledge of the topography and institutions of Palestine prior to the Jewish war. This is not to imply that he is flawless; but it is equally ridiculous to believe that he is as clueless as some recent criticism has made him. The one thing he is not is vague—as Luke, the historian, is frequently vague about Palestine (compare the 'certain village' of Luke 10.38 where Mary and Martha lived, which in its Lucan setting might be anywhere from Galilee to Judaea, with John's 'Bethany', 'fifteen furlongs from Jerusalem', John 11.18). And his details of name and place certainly seem to be being borne out, as far as I can judge, by such findings as those of Professor W. F. Albright in his *Archaeology of Palestine*[25] and in his article for the Dodd *Festschrift*[26] and of

[22]'John the Baptist in the New Light of Ancient Scrolls', *Interpretation* IX (1955), 71–90.
[23]E.g. B. Reicke, 'Nytt ljus över Johannes döparens förkunnelse', *Religion och Bibel* XI (1952), 5–18. For a fuller bibliography see pp. 11 and 26 above.
[24]Cf. 'Elijah, John and Jesus', pp. 49–51 above.
[25]Pp. 243–9.
[26]'Recent Discoveries in Palestine and the Gospel of St John', in *The Background of the New Testament and its Eschatology*, pp. 153–71.

Professor Jeremias in his monograph on the rediscovery of Bethesda.[27]

I would repeat that the fourth Evangelist is not interested in historical accuracy for its own sake. Indeed, it is precisely because his detail is often so incidental and irrelevant to his overriding theological purpose that it is the more impressive. But, however impossible it may be to draw the line, he would, I think, subscribe to the dictum of C. P. Scott of *The Manchester Guardian* that 'fact is sacred, comment is free'. If only because he is the New Testament writer who, theologically speaking, takes history more seriously than any other, he has at least the right to be heard—on the history as well as on the theology.

(4) And so we come to the fourth presupposition, that the fourth Evangelist represents the end-term of theological development in first-century Christianity. That is to say, even as regards the Christ of faith he stands at the furthest remove from the primitive witness.

Again, this is not to be disputed—in so far as he bestrides the whole development of New Testament thinking like a colossus. But so also does Paul; and, like Paul, he will be seen, I believe, to represent its *Alpha* as much as its *Omega*.

At points where his tradition has been tested he is, as I said, often remarkably primitive in his witness. And this is coming to be recognized also of his theology. Again, no one is saying that it is not an extraordinarily mature theology, the more extraordinary if, as I believe (in substantial agreement with Professor E. R. Goodenough[28]), it had reached its essential, if not its formal, maturity by about the same time as St Paul's, at a date, that is, before any of the Synoptic Gospels were written.[29] But while it is mature, it also stands very near to the primitive apostolic witness.

I will illustrate this from the point above all at which the fourth Evangelist is normally regarded as standing at the end of a line of doctrinal development and administering a 'supreme and final

[27] *Die Wiederentdeckung von Bethesda* (1949); cf., from an earlier period, K. Kündsin, *Topologische Überlieferungsstoffe im Johannes-Evangelium* (1925).

[28] 'John a Primitive Gospel', *JBL* LXIV (1945), 145–82.

[29] I am not saying that the fourth Gospel was written before any of the other three, but that the fundamental theological categories of the Johannine tradition were hammered out in the missionary conflict with Palestinian Judaism prior to the Jewish War.

corrective'[30]—namely, in his eschatology. The primitive eschatology is taken to be what John came to see as 'the apocalyptic
faux pas', and in his writings this crude adventism is held to be
quite—or almost quite—refined away in favour of a more 'mystical'
or 'timeless' or 'realized' understanding of the gospel of the
Kingdom or 'eternal life'. This reconstruction I believe to be
correct at one point, namely, that the path into apocalyptic was
a *faux pas*. It was not, I am persuaded,[31] the original eschatology
of Jesus, which was much more in the line of the prophets than of
the apocalyptists, nor was it that of the most primitive Church.
The Synoptists witness to a progressive apocalypticization of the
message of Jesus, as recent study has shown, and as the Gospel
of Matthew most forcibly illustrates. The fourth Gospel does not,
I believe, stand at the end of this progress, as a reaction against it,
for which I think there is no internal evidence. Rather, as Dr Dodd
in his later work has hinted,[32] it represents a form of the tradition
which has never seriously undergone this process at all. While, in
the Synoptists, elements in the eschatological teaching of Jesus were
gradually detached from the supreme crisis in which he stood to
his own generation and referred to a second separate moment, in
the fourth Gospel the original unity is not broken: its picture of the
vindication and the visitation of the Son of man is still essentially
that, I believe, of Jesus himself and of the most primitive tradition,
however immeasurably it may have been deepened by the recognition that it was in the Cross and not merely in the Resurrection
that, in the terminology also of the earliest preaching, God
'glorified' and 'lifted up' his Son.

What I think we detect in the history of the Johannine tradition
is an increasing rather than a decreasing contact with the more
apocalyptic stream of interpretation. The so-called traditional
concept of the Parousia which makes its appearance in the epilogue
to the Gospel and in the Epistles is not the trace of an earlier
eschatology not wholly refined away. It points rather to the contact
of the Johannine tradition with this stream of thought after it had
been thrown by events from the relative isolation of its Palestinian
milieu into the more cosmopolitan world of Asia Minor. By then,

[30] J. E. Fison, *The Christian Hope* (1954), p. 145.
[31] Cf. my book, *Jesus and His Coming*, particularly the final chapter.
[32] *The Interpretation of the Fourth Gospel*, p. 447.

I believe, the material of the Gospel, whether in oral or written shape, had essentially come to formulation, though it may have been edited and published for its present public, and the Epistles written, perhaps considerably later. The last term of this process is represented by the complete merger of the Johannine tradition with the world-view of apocalyptic in the book of the Revelation.

(5) This reconstruction, which is inevitably very tentative, brings us inescapably to the fifth and final question, that of authorship.

That the Evangelist is not himself the Apostle John nor a direct eye-witness is, Dr Barrett says,[33] a 'moral certainty'. It is naturally impossible here to go into the evidence, which has been so worked over that there would seem perhaps to be nothing more to be said. Again, I think that any change we see—and so far the question has not really been reopened—is likely to be reflected not so much in a flat denial of the answer just given as in a shift in the questions asked.

It is clear to anyone observing the protagonists on each side of the debate—and the conservative position, still presented so monumentally in J. B. Lightfoot's *Biblical Essays*,[34] continues to have protagonists who are no fools[35]—that it is the presuppositions they bring to the evidence which are decisive. Indeed, the combination of the four preceding theses, all of which have the effect of setting the Evangelist at a distance from the events, makes the fifth conclusion of the reigning critics well-nigh inevitable. Long before they train their guns on the hapless Papias and Irenaeus and the ignorant Galilean fisherman we know what the result will be.

Incidentally the particular argument that runs, 'This couldn't have been written by a Galilean fisherman', always seems to me singularly inept. You might have said of Ernest Bevin's speeches as Foreign Secretary, 'These couldn't have been written by a barrow-boy in east Bristol'—to which, of course, the answer is that they weren't: they were written by a man who *had been* a barrow-boy in east Bristol.

[33]*Op. cit.*, p. 112.
[34](1893), pp. 1–198.
[35]E.g. recently in England: A. C. Headlam, *The Fourth Gospel as History* (1948); A. H. N. Green-Armytage, *John who Saw* (1952); H. E. Edwards, *The Disciple who Wrote these Things* (1953); R. A. Edwards, *The Gospel according to St John* (1954).

But my object here is not to argue the case for apostolic authorship. What I want to do is to indicate, in conclusion, how the form of the question is now being changed.

Let me make a further comparison with Synoptic criticism. Until lately the question that dominated the study of the first three Gospels was, to quote the title of Professor Bultmann's book,[36] 'the history of the Synoptic tradition'. That is to say, the centre of interest was not the Evangelist, who was little more than an editor, but the tradition and the community behind the tradition. In the fourth Gospel, however, the Evangelist filled the eye. He may indeed have used sources, but for the most part the discussion ranged round what he made of them, what was the Johannine purpose, the Johannine theology. The difference corresponds, of course, to a real difference in the material; but it is now recognized as exaggerated. There is a great deal more interest in the purpose and theology of the Synoptic Evangelists themselves. And there are now signs of a corresponding interest in the Johannine *tradition* as such and in the community behind it—as witness, for example, the title of Bent Noack's recent book, *Zur johanneischen Tradition,* or of the article by the Finnish professor, Rafael Gyllenberg, in the latest Bultmann *Festschrift,*[37] 'Die Anfänge der johanneischen Tradition'.

Until now the discussion of the fourth Gospel has been dominated by the person of the Evangelist, and therefore by the question of individual authorship. The conservatives maintained that the author was John son of Zebedee, and they thus preserved the link with the Jesus of history—through one man. Their opponents found this link too weak to sustain. But having, as they felt, broken it, they tended to assume that there was no link: any statement in the Gospel belonged to the last decade of the first century or to the first of the second, and could therefore show no serious claim to be considered as history.

The question of authorship is still important, if only because the narrative is patently *presented* as that of an eye-witness and if that claim is groundless it affects our total assessment of it, and also because in this case the dominance of a single mind is so powerful that we have the impression, as we said earlier, that

[36] *Die Geschichte der synoptischen Tradition* (1921; ET in preparation).
[37] *Neutestamentliche Studien für Rudolf Bultmann,* pp. 144–7.

'la tradition—c'est moi'.[38] But the question of authorship is not, I believe, the decisive one for the valuation of the Gospel as history. The decisive question is the status and origin of the Johannine tradition. Did this come out of the blue round about the year AD 100? Or is there a real continuity, not merely in the memory of one old man, but in the life of an on-going community, with the earliest days of Christianity? What, I think, fundamentally distinguishes the 'new look' on the fourth Gospel is that it answers that question in the affirmative. But if we do assert this continuity, it is obviously going at one and the same time to reduce the necessity for making everything depend upon apostolic authorship *and* to make us very much more open to its possibility.

[38]Menoud continues: 'Au terme de l'âge apostolique il ne restait qu'un homme qui ait pu parler ainsi' (*op. cit.,* p. 77).

VIII

THE DESTINATION AND PURPOSE
OF ST JOHN'S GOSPEL[1]

FOR whom and for what, to what audience and to what purpose, were the four Gospels written? This is one of the most elementary questions of New Testament study, and one might think that by now the answers could be given with some degree of certainty and consent. And of the first three Gospels I think this is broadly true. Naturally there will always be room for fresh lines of development and approach, but they are unlikely to modify very radically the conclusions which can be found set out in any text-book. If one had to reduce these conclusions to their barest summary, one could say, without immediate fear of contradiction, that St Matthew's Gospel was evidently written for a Jewish-Christian community, and that its overall purpose was broadly speaking *catechetical*; that St Mark's Gospel was composed for a predominantly Gentile community and that its primary purpose was *kerygmatic,* setting out, for the use of the Church, a summary of its proclamation; and that St Luke's Gospel, as he himself indicates, was again addressed, though more generally, to the Graeco-Roman world, and that its purpose was *instructional*, with the defence and confirmation of the Gospel as a dominant motif.[2]

But when we come to the Gospel according to St John there is no such broad agreement. On almost every question connected with this Gospel it is still possible for the most divergent views to command serious and scholarly assent. And after all this time the question of the destination and purpose of the Gospel is as wide open as it ever was. Was it addressed to a Jewish or a Gentile audience, or indeed to the inquiring individual whatever his background?[3] Again, was it intended primarily for a Christian or

[1]Reprinted from *NTS* vi (1960), 117–31.
[2]Cf., more fully, C. F. D. Moule, 'The Intention of the Evangelists', *New Testament Essays,* ed. A. J. B. Higgins, pp. 165–79.
[3]It has even been doubted recently whether it was consciously addressed to *any* audience. Cf. C. K. Barrett, *The Gospel According to St John,* p. 115: 'It is

for a non-Christian public? Was its motive in the first instance to win the faithless, to establish the faithful, or to counter the gainsayers? And if John's primary purpose was to *defend* the Gospel, was the opposition Jewish, or Gnostic, or Baptist, or even Christian? All these opinions have been canvassed and seriously sustained, before one even reaches the questions that have most divided scholars, and which I must here leave on one side, questions namely about the cultural and intellectual milieu to which the author and his readers belonged, whether they were Jew, Gentile or Christian.

The mere fact that none of these views has succeeded in establishing itself over the others shows that the evidence does not point decisively in any one direction. Nevertheless, I am persuaded that there is one solution that can be stated a good deal more compellingly than it has been and merits the most serious consideration. What I shall advocate is, of course, no new position—it would almost certainly be wrong if it were—and indeed it is substantially that to which Professor W. C. van Unnik of Utrecht gave the not inconsiderable weight of his support at the Oxford conference on 'The Four Gospels in 1957'.[4]

Let us start from the statement which is constantly made, that St John's Gospel is the most anti-Jewish of the four. In a very real sense this is true: the Jews' responsibility for the rejection and death of Christ is in this of all the Gospels the most solid and unrelieved: 'He who delivered me to you', says Jesus to Pilate, 'has the greater sin' (19.11). But there is no need to underline this. The term 'the Jews' is found overwhelmingly in polemical contexts: they are the representatives of darkness and opposition throughout the Gospel.

But it is easy to assume without further discussion that because it is anti-Jewish it is therefore pro-Gentile. We jump to the conclusion that the logic underlying its appeal is that of St Paul's speech to the Jews in Pisidian Antioch: 'It was necessary that the word of God should be spoken first to you. Since you thrust it

---

easy, when we read the Gospel, to believe that John, though doubtless aware of the necessity of strengthening Christians and converting the heathen, wrote primarily to satisfy himself. His gospel must be written: it was no concern of his whether it was also read.'

[4]'The Purpose of St John's Gospel', *Studia Evangelica*, pp. 382–411.

from you, and judge yourselves unworthy of eternal life, behold, we turn to the Gentiles.' 'And', we read, 'as many as were ordained to eternal life believed' (Acts 13.46, 48). 'These things are written that you may believe that Jesus is the Christ, the Son of God, and that believing you may have life in his name' (John 20.31). The purpose of the two seems to be the same.

But this is going altogether too fast for the evidence. For nowhere in St John is there any trace of this transition: the Jews have rejected, therefore we turn to the Gentiles. The remarkable fact is that there is not a single reference to 'the Gentiles' in the entire book. The fourth Gospel, with the Johannine Epistles, is the only major work in the New Testament in which the term τὰ ἔθνη never occurs. Moreover, so far from being anti-Semitic, that is, racially anti-Jewish,[5] it is, I believe, in the words of J. B. Lightfoot's magisterial but far too little known lectures on St John, 'the most Hebraic book in the New Testament, except perhaps the Apocalypse'.[6] If Judaism is condemned, it is always from within and not from without. Such phrases as 'your law' (8.17; (10.34)) and 'their law' (15.25) cannot be interpreted, as they often are, to imply that John wishes to dissociate Jesus from Judaism. For it is fundamental to the Gospel that Jesus himself is 'a Jew' (4.9), that he should distinguish Jews from Samaritans as 'we' (4.22). Indeed the heart of the whole tragic drama is that it is 'his own' to whom he comes (1.11) and 'his own nation' by whom he is delivered up (18.35, τὸ ἔθνος τὸ σόν — ἔθνος in John being reserved always for the Jewish nation, not for the Gentiles).

And not only is Jesus very much a Jew, but the world of the Gospel narrative is wholly a Jewish world. While 'the Jews' occurs nearly seventy times in John (compared with five times in Matthew, six in Mark and five in Luke), the Gentiles as a group receive, as we have seen, no mention. Moreover, from the beginning to the end of the story there is only one individual Gentile—and he is Pilate, hardly the figure by whom to commend the Gospel to the Gentiles. Pilate with his soldiers is necessary because otherwise Jesus could not be sentenced to death (18.31) or 'lifted up from the earth' by the Roman penalty of crucifixion (12.32 f.; cf. 18.32). But Pilate makes it clear that he is a complete

[5]So J. Knox, *Criticism and Faith* (1952), pp. 75-7.
[6]*Biblical Essays*, p. 135.

outsider to the world within which the drama moves: 'Am I a Jew?' (18.35).

The extent indeed to which the drama revolves exclusively round the crisis of Judaism is remarkable—and it stands in noticeable contrast with the Synoptists. In the Synoptic Gospels the centre of the stage is also occupied by the Jews. But we are conscious always of the Gentiles pressing in on the wings. At the very beginning of the Gospel of Matthew, the most Jewish of the Synoptists, come the Magi from the east, to make it clear that Jesus is not the king of the Jews alone (Matt. 2.1 ff.). In Luke too he is hailed from the start not only as 'the glory of God's people Israel' but as 'a light for revelation to the Gentiles' (Luke 2.32). Then, within the ministry, there is the centurion whose faith is held up as an example and reproof to Israel (Matt. 8.10 = Luke 7.9). There is the Syro-Phoenician woman whose claim to eat of the crumbs that fall from the children's table is allowed (Mark 7.28). There is the other centurion's testimony at the Cross, standing as the climax to the Marcan narrative (Mark 15.39). There are the excursions of Jesus to non-Jewish territory, to the region of Tyre and Sidon (Mark 7.24), to Caesarea Philippi (8.27). There is the damning comparison of the Jewish towns with these cities of Tyre and Sidon and 'the land of Sodom and Gomorrah' (Matt. 10.15; 11.20–4). There is the example of God's preference in the past for the widow of Zarephath in Sidon and for Naaman the Syrian (Luke 4.25–7). There is the warning that foreigners like the Ninevites and the Queen of the South, a negress, will stand up in the judgment with this generation and condemn it (Matt. 12.41 f. = Luke 11.31 f.). Many, again, are to come from the east and the west and sit down with Abraham, Isaac and Jacob in the kingdom of heaven, while the sons of the kingdom will be thrown out (Matt 8.11 f.; Luke 13.29 f.). There is the recurrent threat which echoes through the later teaching of Jesus that the vineyard will be taken away and given to others (Mark 12.9 and pars). The Temple is cleared so as to perform its true function as 'a house of prayer for all nations' (Mark 11.17). Above all there is always the sense that, while the immediate ministry of Jesus and his disciples may of necessity be confined to 'the lost sheep of the house of Israel' (Matt. 10.6; 15.24), yet ultimately the Gospel must be proclaimed in the whole world (Mark 14.9).

Released by the Resurrection, the apostles are to go to the ends of the earth (Acts 1.8), making disciples of all nations (Matt. 28.19; Luke 24.47). They will also have to make their defence before Gentiles (Matt. 10.18)—but this too can be turned into an opportunity for witness to them (Luke 21.12 f.). For ultimately the End cannot come till the Gospel has been preached to the entire Gentile world (Mark 13.10; Matt. 24.14).

But in John there is none of this. Jesus is not presented as a revelation to the Gentiles. The purpose of the Baptist's mission is simply that 'he might be revealed to Israel' (1.31). Instead of the Syro-Phoenician woman we have the Samaritan woman, who, though the Jews may refuse dealings with her (4.9), can still speak of 'our father Jacob' (4.12), just as later the Jews speak of 'our father Abraham' (8.53). In the story corresponding to that of the centurion's servant, the healing of the court official's son (4.46–54), there is no commendation of his faith as a Gentile, nor indeed any suggestion that he was a Gentile. (As a βασιλικός in Galilee he was presumably a Herodian.) Again, for all the piling up of witnesses, there is no Gentile witness to Jesus in the entire Gospel—not even the final testimony of the centurion to him as the Son of God, the very title round which the Gospel is written and which many have supposed to be chosen because it could come so easily to Gentile lips. Nowhere are Gentiles held up for favourable comparison with the Jews; nor is there any reference to them in the cleansing of the Temple, which is inspired solely by zeal for true Judaism (2.17). The Romans will indeed come and destroy the Jewish nation and its holy place (11.48), but there is no suggestion of the heritage of Israel being given to the Gentiles. There is nothing about the disciples' having to appear before Gentiles—only of their being expelled from the synagogues of Judaism (16.2). Again, Jesus never leaves Jewish soil; there is no reference to a Gentile mission, nor anything about their coming in, even after his glorification. The 'Greeks' do indeed ask to see Jesus—and this, as we shall see, is a point of decisive significance for the Evangelist. But it is important to insist that these Greeks are *not* Gentiles. They are Greek-speaking Jews, of whom it is specifically stated that they had 'come up to worship at the feast' (12.20)— and there is no suggestion that they are merely 'God-fearers' or even that they had once been Gentiles. All that we can deduce with

certainty is that they spoke Greek rather than Aramaic (and hence
presumably the approach through Philip, with his Hellenistic
name and place of origin (12.21)), and that they were in Jerusalem
for a specifically Jewish reason. In fact, the Evangelist has already
at an earlier point (7.35) equated the term 'the Greeks' with 'the
Dispersion among the Greeks', that is, Greek-speaking Diaspora
Judaism.[7]

Now to stress this unremitting concentration on Judaism is far
from saying that John is narrowly nationalistic or religiously
exclusivist. On the contrary, there is a cosmic perspective to the
Gospel, which is introduced from the very first verse. Jesus is
'the . . . light that enlightens every man' (1.9), 'the Lamb of
God who takes away the sin of the *world*' (1.29); and the purpose
of his being sent is that 'the world might be saved through him'
(3.17). There are no more universalistic sayings in the New
Testament than in the fourth Gospel: 'I, when I am lifted up from
the earth, will draw all men to myself' (12.32). Yet for all this
there is no mention of, nor appeal to, the Gentiles as such. When
Jesus is pressed to 'show himself to the world' (7.4), it is not an
urge to missionary expansion but to public demonstration—and
that to 'the Jews'. The κόσμος is not the world outside Judaism,
but the world which God loves and the world which fails to
respond, be it Jew or Gentile. If as a whole the Jews are hopelessly
blind and walk on in darkness, those who come to the light and
hear Jesus' voice are still Jews, not Gentiles—both in general
(there are repeated references to the Jews who believe in him:
2.33; 7.31; 8.31; 10.42; 11.45; 12.11) and as represented by
particular individuals: Nathanael, the ideal Israelite (1.47),
Nicodemus, 'the ruler of the Jews' and 'teacher of Israel' (3.1, 10),
Joseph of Arimathea (19.38) and the man born blind (9.1–39),

[7]The words μὴ εἰς τὴν Διασπορὰν τῶν Ἑλλήνων μέλλει πορεύεσθαι καὶ
διδάσκειν τοὺς Ἕλληνας; are unfortunately ambiguous. 'The Diaspora of
the Greeks' could mean 'the Greek-speaking Diaspora' (i.e. Jews) and 'the
Greeks' be an abbreviated way of referring to the same group. Or it could
mean 'the Diaspora resident among the Greeks', in which case 'the Greeks'
would be Gentiles. H. Windisch comes down in favour of the latter in
TWNT (art. Ἕλλην) II, 506. But K. L. Schmidt, *ibid.* (art. διασπορά) II, 102,
insists on leaving both possibilities open (cf. H. J. Cadbury in *The Beginnings
of Christianity* v (1933), 72 f.). The decision between them can in fact only be
made in the light of the Johannine context as a whole. As there is no other
reference in the Gospel or the Epistles to a Gentile mission, the probability
would seem to be in favour of the first interpretation.

representing respectively the governing class and the common people.

The contrast for John is always between light and darkness, not between Jew and Gentile. There is no agony, as there is for Paul, about the relation between these latter as groups (as in Rom. 9–11), no middle wall of partition to be broken down between them (as in Eph. 2). For John the question is not how Jews and Gentiles can become one, nor even how the Gentiles *as such* can come in. In this respect, it is instructive to compare their use of the figures of the vine (John 15) and the olive (Rom. 11), recognized Old Testament symbols for Israel. For both branches must be cut off (John 15.2; Rom. 11.17)—but for John there is no grafting in of alien branches. For him the simple question is the relation of *Judaism* to the true Israel, the true vine—and that means, for him, to Jesus as the Christ. For to John the only true Judaism is one that acknowledges Jesus as its Messiah. Becoming a true Jew and becoming a Christian are one and the same thing.

But John is clear that this does not mean what the Judaizers meant, with whom Paul had to fight. It does not mean retaining the whole empirical system of Judaism and fitting Jesus into it. For Judaism to accept Jesus as its truth is no mere reformation, but a complete rebirth (3.3). In him its entire existing structure is challenged and transcended—its *torah* (1.17), its ritual (2.6), its temple (2.19), its localized worship (4.20 f.), its sabbath regulations (5.9–18). And yet John is insisting throughout that there is nothing in Jesus alien to Judaism truly understood. He is the true *shekinah* (1.14), the true temple (2.21). Though Jerusalem is to be transcended as the place God chooses for his 'name' to dwell in (Deut. 12.11)—for that place is occupied by Jesus (John 17.11 f.) —yet still 'salvation is from the Jews' (4.20–2). And that is why the Old Testament plays such a vital part in the Gospel. The truth about Jesus is already present in the witness of Moses (1.45; 5.39–47; 7.19–24), Abraham (8.39, 56) and Isaiah (12.41), who condemn their own children because they do not listen to him of whom their scriptures speak. For he is the crown of everything in Judaism. It is as 'the king of the Jews' that Jesus goes to his death (esp. 19.19–22), and from the beginning he is hailed as 'the king of Israel' (1.49; cf. 12.13), 'the holy one of God' (6.69), 'the prophet who should come into the world', that is, as the context implies,[8] the prophet like Moses (6.14; 7.40; cf. Deut. 18.15).

But above all he is 'the Messiah', 'the Christ'.[9] And this for John is not just a proper name, as it has become for Paul in his Gentile environment. Except in two instances, in the combination 'Jesus Christ' (1.17; 17.3), it is always a title, ὁ χριστός, retaining its full etymological force, as John insists by being the only New Testament writer to preserve it in its Aramaic form, ὁ Μεσσίας (1.41; 4.25 f.). We all recognize that Matthew is above all concerned to present Jesus as the Christ of Judaism. But it comes as a surprise to most to be told that John uses the title more frequently than Matthew (twenty-one times to seventeen), and more often than Mark (seven) and Luke (thirteen) put together. This, rather than 'the Logos', is the category which controls his Christology in the body of the Gospel. This is obvious from a concordance. But the way of thinking reflected, for instance, in E. F. Scott's dictum that 'in the fourth Gospel the Messianic idea is replaced by that of the Logos'[10] has exercised a mesmeric effect.

Moreover, the understanding of St John's other main category, 'the Son of God', must start from the fact that it stands as epexegetic of 'the Christ', especially in the crucial passage that explains the purpose of his writing (20.31). Indeed, I believe there is no other New Testament document more important for studying the Jewish sources of the term 'Son of God' than the fourth Gospel. Nor should it be forgotten that John sides decisively with the Synoptic Gospels in retaining on Jesus' lips the title 'Son of man', which evidently served no purpose in the Gentile mission of the Pauline churches.

Furthermore, the distinctive images which Jesus is made to use of himself in this Gospel—the Manna (6.32–5), the Light (8.1), the Shepherd (10.11–16), the Vine (15.1–6)—all by their associations in the Old Testament and later Judaism represent him in his person as *the true Israel of God*. And the primary contrast implied in the epithet ἀληθινός is with 'Israel according to the flesh'. The true Jew, whose 'praise is not from men but from God', to use a Pauline distinction also made by John (Rom. 2.29; cf. John 5.44),

[8]For he too provides manna from heaven and water from the rock.
[9]For a fuller discussion of this neglected Johannine category, see van Unnik, *op. cit.*, pp. 389–405.
[10]*The Fourth Gospel, its Purpose and Theology* (1920), p. 6.

is the one who recognizes in Jesus the true Light (1.9), abides in him as the true Vine (15.1), and follows him as the true Shepherd of God's flock (10.27). The others may say that they are Jews, but are not: they are children not of Abraham but of the devil (8.30–47; cf. Rev. 2.9; 3.9).

But for the Jew who would remain loyal to his traditional faith, 'How can this be?' (3.9). That is the question put by Nicodemus, the ruler of the Jews and the teacher of Israel. And Nicodemus, the person he is and the question he poses, represents the problem to which the fourth Gospel is addressed. Or, in the terms of the man born blind, how can a man say to Jesus, 'Lord, I believe', without ceasing to be a Jew, even though he may be thrown out of the Synagogue (9.35–8)?

That is the problem which John sets himself to answer. There is not even a side-glance at the problem of the man who is not a Jew but wants to become a Christian, let alone at the problem of the Gentile who wants to become a Christian *without having* to become a Jew. John is not saying, and would not say, that such a man must first become a Jew—that was the answer of the Judaizers. His problem is not even considered. John is not a Judaizer; nor, like Paul, is he an anti-Judaizer: that whole issue never comes within his purview.

But again, how can this be? It is possible only if John is not involved, like Paul, in the Gentile problem as such. All the controversies in the fourth Gospel take place within the body of Judaism. The issues raised by the Judaizers are essentially *frontier* problems—of whether, in a frontier situation like that of Antioch, one lived as a Jew or as a Gentile (Gal. 2.14). But John is not faced with this problem.[11] Consequently circumcision and law have a

[11]In saying this I must dissent from the very interesting suggestions made by C. H. Dodd in his article 'A l'arrière-plan d'un dialogue Johannique', *Revue d'Histoire et de Philosophie Religieuses* xxxvii (1957), 5–17. Dodd would see the background of John 8.35–58 in the Jewish-Christian controversy of the early Church, and he points out a number of parallels with the Epistle to the Galatians. But in the Judaizing controversy the crucial question was 'Who is the true Christian?' (Need he observe the whole law to qualify?) In the Johannine controversy the question is rather 'Who is the true Jew?' (Is sonship of Abraham automatic by race?) This latter is the question posed also by John the Baptist (Matt. 3.7–10; Luke 3.7–9) in a purely Jewish context; and the Pauline parallels to John would appear rather to be Rom. 2.17–29 ('Who is the true Jew?') and 4.9–22 ('Who is the true son of Abraham?'), where the Apostle is addressing himself to the Jews rather than to Judaizers. For the Judaizer the

different significance for him and for Paul. For Paul they represent the fence between Judaism and the Gentile world, barriers of exclusivism to be broken down. For John they are what must be transcended by Judaism within its own life, because they belong to the level of flesh and not spirit, *whether a single Gentile wanted to enter the Church or not.*

This fits with the many other indications that the *Heimat* of the Johannine tradition, and the milieu in which it took shape, was the heart of southern Palestinian Judaism. There is nothing, as far as I can see, to suggest that the great controversies of chapters 5–12, which comprise the hard core of the Evangelist's tradition, were not the product of discussion and debate with Jewish opposition in a purely Palestinian situation. The Gentile world, except as represented by the Romans, is miles away—as it is, incidentally, in the Qumran literature, where the sons of darkness and deceit are in the first instance not Gentiles (who are the Kittim) but faithless Israel. In this lack of contact with the Gentiles John differs from the Hellenists and the group round Stephen. John's is essentially an Aramaic-speaking background.

And yet quite patently his Gospel is in Greek and for a Greek-speaking public. Who are these Greeks? Precisely, I believe, the Greeks who appear in the Gospel. Again, it is necessary to emphasize who these are. For Paul, as for Luke, the distinction between Jew and Greek is the distinction between Jew and Gentile, the Circumcision and the Uncircumcision (cf. e.g. Rom. 2.9–14; 3.9, 29). But for John, the distinction is between the Jews of Palestine (and more particularly of Judaea) and the Jews of the Greek (as opposed, e.g., to the Babylonian) Diaspora.[12] The

___

underlying question is: 'What does it involve for the Gentile to become a Christian?' For John it is always: 'What does it involve for the Jew?' And his answer is: 'Birth, not from Abraham (nor anything "of the earth"), but from above.' There is a close parallel between ch. 8 and ch. 3. Both recount the approach of Jews who believed in some way that Jesus came from God and that God was with him (cf. 8.29 f. with 3.2); and 8.23 shows the issue to be the same as in that of the conversation with Nicodemus. Neither dialogue has any apparent connexion with the Gentile controversy.

[12]Cf. the letter of R. Gamaliel I (Jer. Sanh. 18d) 'to our brethren, the sons of the diaspora of Babylon, the sons of the diaspora of Media, the sons of the diaspora of the Greeks, and all the rest of the dispersed of Israel' (quoted A. Schlatter, *Der Evangelist Johannes* (1930), p. 198). It is to be observed that the phrase 'the diaspora of the Greeks' (where the parallels would lead us to expect 'the diaspora of Greece') is exactly that which John also uses in 7.35.

Ἕλληνες are for him the Greek-speaking Jews living outside Palestine—in distinction again from the Ἑλληνισταί of Acts 6.1 and 9.29, who are Greek-speaking Jews resident in Palestine (cf. Acts 6.9). Naturally the word Ἕλληνες itself draws attention to them as non-Palestinians rather than as Jews, and indeed it is only from a Palestinian point of view that Jews could conceivably be described as Greeks—but then it is from that point of view that I believe the story of St John's Gospel is written. The Hellenistic viewpoint which we have accepted as normative, as indeed it is in the rest of the New Testament, is clearly represented in Acts 21.27 f., where 'the Jews from Asia' stirred up the Jerusalem crowd against Paul on the charge that he brought 'Greeks' into the temple. In Johannine terms this would read: '*The Greeks* stirred up *the Jews* against Paul because he had introduced *Gentiles*.'

Now this division within Israel between Jews and Greeks, thus defined, is of the greatest importance to John and contains, I believe, the clue to his purpose in writing the Gospel. If the tension between Jew and Gentile is never felt (except in the purely external antagonism of the Jews' refusal to enter the Praetorium (18.28)), the tensions within Judaism are never far from the surface. Nothing could be more false than to suppose, as has often been suggested, that 'the Jews' is a blanket-term covering John's ignorance of or indifference to the divisions of Judaism. Indeed, it looks as though a deliberate part of his purpose was to show Judaism, faced with the claims of Jesus, as hopelessly divided against itself.

There is, first, the constant tension between the common people and the Jerusalem authorities (e.g. 7.13, 25–32, 48 f.; 9.22; 12.19), who are themselves sometimes designated 'the Jews' even against their own people (5.10–15; 7.13; 9.18, 22).[13] And there is the more subtle division within these authorities between members of the Sanhedrin (the ἄρχοντες) and the Pharisees (12.42; cf. 7.45–52; 19.38 f.). Moreover, the various groupings—the Pharisees (9.16), the common people (7.12, 43), the Jews who believed on him (6.66), and the Jews who did not (6.52; 10.19–21) —are split among themselves.

[13]Contrariwise, in 11. 45 f. and 12.9–11 'the Jews' are the common people as distinct from the authorities.

Then there are the geographical divisions. Apart from the standing feud between the Jews and the Samaritans (4.9), there is a recurrent and bitter altercation between Judaea and Galilee (1.46; 4.44 f.; 7.41, 52). 'The Jews' for this Gospel are not merely the Jews of Palestine, but, with two exceptions only (6.41 and 52), the Jews of Judaea. Indeed, 'Ιουδαῖος often appears to keep its strict meaning of Judaean (as in the adjective, τὴν 'Ιουδαίαν γῆν, in 3.22). Thus, in 7.1 we read, 'After this Jesus went about in Galilee; he would not go about in Judaea because the Jews sought to kill him', where the RSV margin reads 'the Judaeans' (cf. also 11.7, 54). And there is a sense, important for the Evangelist, in which Jesus himself is 'a Jew' in the narrower sense. According to this Gospel, it is not Galilee but Judaea which is Jesus' πατρίς (contrast John 4.44 f. with Mark 6.1–6 and pars). Though he may come from Nazareth, it is to Judaea that he really belongs, and 7.42 probably presupposes that John knows the tradition of his birth at Bethlehem. In the strictest sense he comes to 'his own', even though his own may not receive him (1.11), but disown him as a Galilean (1.46; 7.41) and even as a Samaritan (8.48).

But behind these tensions within Palestine lies the still more far-reaching division between metropolitan Judaism and the Diaspora. We can hear the disgust and contempt behind the words of 7.35: 'The Jews said to one another, "Where does this man intend to go that we shall not find him? Does he intend to go to the Dispersion among the Greeks and teach the Greeks?"'

But as well as disdain there is also here surely strong irony. For this is precisely where Jesus' teaching is now going through the words of the Gospel. The Gospel has a strong and reiterated evangelistic motive: it is written 'that you may *believe*'[14] (20.31), and almost every incident ends on that note. But as we have seen, there is no indication that it is to Gentiles that John is primarily addressing his message. On the contrary, everything points to his appeal being to Diaspora Judaism,[15] that *it* may come to accept

[14]It is, of course, true that linguistically this could mean either to bring to faith or to deepen in faith. Cf. C. H. Dodd, *The Interpretation of the Fourth Gospel,* p. 9; C. K. Barrett, *op. cit.,* p. 114; C. F. D. Moule, *op. cit.,* p. 168.

[15]K. Bornhäuser, *Das Johannesevangelium eine Missionsschrift für Israel* (1928), saw very clearly that the Gospel is an evangelistic appeal to Israel, but his failure to isolate the particular section of Judaism which John has in mind made much of his argument very vulnerable.

Jesus as its true Messiah, even though, to quote Paul's speech at Antioch, 'those who live in Jerusalem and their rulers . . . did not recognize him' (Acts 13.27). This speech is in fact addressed to precisely such an audience as that for which I am arguing John is writing: 'Men of Israel and you that fear God' (Acts 13.16), that is to say, Greek-speaking Judaism with its God-fearing adherents. In other words, the real situation is the exact opposite of that which was suggested at the beginning. John is writing for the Jews who thrust aside Paul's appeal, not for the Gentiles to whom he subsequently turns.

That John's primary concern is with the Jews is perhaps confirmed by Paul himself in a striking way. In the course of what is unquestionably our best piece of first-hand evidence about the history of the early Church, Paul speaks in Gal. 2.9 of the division of apostolic labour between Barnabas, Titus and himself, on the one hand, and James, Cephas and John, on the other. It was agreed, he says, 'that we should go to the Gentiles and they to the circumcised'. Attention has been so concentrated on the division between Paul and Peter, which is the occasion of the whole narration, that the significance of John's name appears to have been overlooked. James is associated in any case with the Circumcision; but the passage tells us, on the highest authority, two things that we should not otherwise know about John: first, that he was alive and in Jerusalem at least fourteen, and more probably seventeen, years after Paul's conversion, which is surely the most decisive disproof, though it is seldom adduced,[16] of the tradition that he was executed with his brother James before the death of Herod in 44; and, secondly, that at that time at any rate he was committed to evangelism among the Jews. This fits exactly with what I believe to have been the milieu of the Johannine tradition *during this period*, namely, the Christian mission among the Jews of Judaea. This of course will not impress anyone who does not think that John son of Zebedee was in some way connected with the tradition of the fourth Gospel, nor does it prove anything for a later period. But it does not seem to me entirely coincidental that the only three occurrences of the term διασπορά in the New Testament should be in the writings associated with

[16]Though cf. B. P. W. Stather Hunt, *Some Johannine Problems* (1958), pp. 118 f.

the three persons specifically mentioned by Paul as concentrating on the Jewish mission, namely the Gospel of John (7.35), the First Epistle of Peter (1.1), and the Epistle of James (1.1). Even if traditional ascriptions of these writings cannot be sustained (and in no case do I regard this as proved), it is surely significant that this was the field of evangelism with which these particular figures were associated in the mind of the Church.

But the case for St John's Gospel being addressed to Diaspora Judaism stands on its own merits. And once we are prepared to take this hypothesis seriously, it is surprising what light it throws upon many passages in the Gospel.

The Evangelist's peculiar understanding of the work of Christ at once becomes perspicuous. The purpose of this is carefully defined (again in a context of heavy irony) in 11.51 f. In an editorial comment on Caiaphas' words John writes: 'He did not say this of his own accord, but being high priest that year he prophesied that Jesus should die for the nation, and not for the nation only, but to gather into one the children of God who are scattered abroad.' 'The nation' is, as we have seen, for this writer metropolitan Judaism. Who are 'the children of God who are scattered abroad'? As in the case of 'the Greeks', the reference is almost universally taken to be to the Gentiles.[17] But this is quite arbitrary. There is nothing in the Gospel to suggest it, and every reason, from the wealth of Old Testament parallels, to identify them with those of God's people, the Jews, at present in dispersion.[18] In the prophetic words of her own high priest, the purpose of Jesus' death, as Israel's Messiah, is to bring about the final ingathering of which her prophets so constantly spoke. And it is when Diaspora Judaism, in the persons of the Greeks at Passover, comes seeking him, that Jesus knows 'the hour has come for the Son of man to be glorified' (12.23). Hitherto he has been confined to 'his own' to whom he came; but once the seed falls into the ground and dies it will bear much fruit (12.24).

The supreme purpose of the laying down of Jesus' life is that all Israel should be one flock under its one shepherd (10.15 f.).

[17]Most recently J. Jeremias, *Jesus' Promise to the Nations* (ET, SBT 24, 1958), pp. 37 f. and 64–6.
[18]See C. K. Barrett, *op. cit., ad loc.,* who, however, declines to accept what he admits 'in a Jewish work this would naturally mean'.

And once more this pastoral imagery in chapter 10 is clearly modelled upon passages in Ezekiel (especially 34 and 37.21–8) and Jeremiah (23.1–8; 31.1–10) whose whole theme is the ingathering of the scattered people of Israel. The 'other sheep, that are not of this fold', whom also Jesus must bring in (10.16) are not the Gentiles—again there is nothing to suggest this—but the Jews of the Dispersion. And the purpose, that 'there shall be one flock, one shepherd', is reflected again in the repeated prayer of chapter 17 'that they may all be one', the chapter above all which interprets the purpose of Jesus' going to the Father. Here once more we have the same distinction as that between 'this fold' and the 'other sheep', the 'nation' and 'the children of God who are scattered abroad'. The prayer is not 'for these only', that is, for those already faithful to Jesus in Palestine, but 'for those also who shall believe in me through their word', that is (in terms of the same distinction again from chapter 20), for those who believe without having seen (20.29), for whom clearly the Gospel is being written. The prayer 'that they may all be one' is, on Jesus' lips, not a prayer for broken Christendom but for scattered and disrupted Judaism, viewed as the true Israel of God.

'Brethren, my heart's desire and prayer to God for them is that they may be saved' (Rom. 10.1). That could be John speaking. His consuming concern is for the whole Jewish people, that they should find the life which is their birthright. Throughout the Gospel we can trace the anxiety of the pastor and evangelist that none of those should be lost for whom this life is intended (6.39; 10.28 f.; 17.12; 18.9). This theme is first introduced in 6.12 f., where great importance is attached to the care with which the fragments must be gathered up after the feeding—'that nothing may be lost'. Filling as they do twelve baskets, they symbolize the fullness of Israel still to be gathered in after 'the Jews' have eaten their fill.

Again we must insist that John, with Paul, is the least exclusivist or nationalistic writer in the New Testament. The right to become the 'children of God' is given to all who believe, exactly as in the Epistle to the Romans (John 1.12; cf. Rom. 3.22). John is certainly not suggesting that Christianity is for the Jews only: it is for the whole world. Indeed, it is explicitly stated in 17.21 that the bringing in of 'those who shall believe in me through their word' (those for whom the Gospel is written) is itself in order 'that *the world* may believe'. Nevertheless, he is directing his appeal in the first instance to a specific audience, and like a good evangelist is defining salvation in the terms of their own heritage. In the same way Paul, when he wants to, can so identify Christianity with the true Judaism as to say of the Church, '*We* are the circumcision' (Phil. 3.3), and equate being 'outside Christ' with being 'alienated from the commonwealth of Israel' (Eph. 2.12).

But, unlike Paul, John is not fighting on two fronts. He is not all things to all men, but limits himself voluntarily as an apostle to the Circumcision. Always he speaks as a Jew, and indeed, like Jesus, as a Jew of Palestine. In the course of his work he writes damningly of 'the Jews'—yet never perhaps with quite the animosity that shows through Paul's words in I Thess. 2.14–16. This passage indeed provides an instructive comparison with John.[19] It is constantly said that John's use of the term 'the Jews' could come only from a man who stands outside Judaism and from a date when the break between the Church and the Synagogue was bitter and complete. Yet here in Thessalonians, in the early 50's, we see Paul, a Hebrew of the Hebrews, writing in exactly the same vein (though with a personal animus that John does not show) and actually differentiating 'the Jews' from Christians in Judaea exactly as John does. 'For you, brethren', he says to the Thessalonians, 'became imitators of the churches of God which are in Judaea; for you suffered the same things from your own countrymen as they did from *the Jews*, who killed both the Lord Jesus and the prophets, and drove us out, and displease God and oppose all men . . . so as always to fill up the measure of their sins. But God's wrath has come upon them finally and for ever (εἰς τέλος)'. If John also speaks thus of 'the Jews', it is always with the chastisement that comes from within, drawn out of him by the tragedy of his own people.

Sometimes too he speaks of them with a terrible objectivity, explaining their customs as though he did not belong to them, and indeed as though he were not writing to fellow-Jews at all. But should this seem a decisive objection to our thesis, we should remember two things.

[19]Its relevance was first brought to my attention by H. E. Edwards, *The Disciple who Wrote these Things*, p. 115.

(*a*) In the majority of such passages John is interpreting *Aramaic-speaking* Judaism to those who know nothing of its language and ethos. And by the very regularity with which he renders into Greek the most obvious words, like Μεσσίας (1.41; 4.25), or ʿΡαββεί (1.39) and ʿΡαββουνεί (20.16), which Mark never even bothers to translate for his Gentile public (Mark 9.5; 10.51, etc.), we know that he is not a man who fears being redundant. Indeed, his whole style bears this out: he would rather give superfluous explanations than fail to make his meaning clear.

(*b*) His explanations are frequently not as redundant as they sound. The fact, for instance, that he regularly designates the feasts as feasts 'of the Jews' (as if anyone did not know it, let alone a Jewish audience) becomes intelligible when we observe that, in every case but one (6.4), this is put in in order to explain why it is that Jesus must go up to Judea (2.13; 5.1; 7.1–3; 11.55). It is precisely because they are feasts of 'the Jews' that Jesus, a Galilean, must travel into the country of the Jews, and this is of great significance for the unfolding of the drama (cf., especially, 7.1–9; 11.7–16). Again, John's explanation of the customs of purification (2.6) and burial (19.40), on the face of it so unnecessary for an audience of fellow-Jews, is not given simply for its own sake—because otherwise they might not know (though doubtless the water-pots were distinctively Palestinian)—but because every detail is seen by him as supremely significant for the sign and its interpretation. He is concerned that nothing shall be missed which reveals Jesus as the true fulfilment of Judaism.

To say that the Gospel belongs to the world of Hellenistic Judaism is still, of course, to leave undefined what sort of level of Hellenistic Judaism. That must be settled by examination of its literary and cultural background, into which it has not been my purpose to go. But since the term 'Hellenistic Judaism' immediately connotes for most Johannine commentators the world of thought most signally represented by Philo of Alexandria, I should like to dissociate my own conclusion from that inference. Mr W. D. Stacey, in his valuable book *The Pauline View of Man*, uses these words: 'Philo found in the Pentateuch . . . the wisdom after which Greek thinkers had been striving, and he tried to present the Pentateuch in such a way that Greeks would see in it their journey's end.'[20] It is a widely held view that we should need only to alter that very little to have a perfect description of the fourth Gospel: 'John found in Jesus as the Logos the wisdom after which Greek thinkers had been striving, and he tried to present Jesus as the Logos in such a way that Greeks would see in him their journey's end.' I am convinced that this is in fact a serious misrepresentation of his purpose. Philo was commending Judaism to Greek-speaking paganism: John was commending Christianity to Greek-speaking Judaism. And between those two aims there is a world of difference.

Nor am I convinced (though this again rests on detailed considerations of language for which this is not the occasion) that the world he addressed was the world of speculative philosophy in which Philo was at home. He stood, I believe, much more in what has aptly been called the 'pre-Gnostic'[21] stream of Jewish wisdom-mysticism, new light on which is constantly coming before us. I confess, moreover, to seeing less and less evidence of a polemical motive in the Gospel, whether against Baptist, Jewish or Gnostic groups. There is undoubtedly such a motive in the Johannine Epistles. But these were written specifically for the stablishing of those who had already accepted the faith (I John 2.21), to the converts of his Gospel message, which is constantly presupposed in what they are stated to have 'heard from the beginning' (I John 2.24). The difference of aim between the Gospel and the Epistles is in fact summarized in the clearly connected statements which set out their respective purposes. Of the Gospel it is said: 'These [things] are written that *you may believe* that Jesus is the Christ the Son of God, and that believing *you may have life* in his name' (20.31); while of the first Epistle the author says: 'I write this to you *who believe* in the name of the Son of God, that *you may know that you have* eternal life' (5.13). Professor E. C. Colwell's title *John Defends the Gospel* would be appropriate enough for the Epistles; but the Gospel itself has an evangelistic purpose. It is composed, no doubt, of material which took shape as teaching *within* a Christian community *in Judaea* and under the pressure of controversy with 'the Jews' of that area. But in its

[20]*Op. cit.* (1956), p. 215.
[21]The term was used originally of the Qumran literature by B. Reicke, *NTS* 1 (1954-5), 141.

present form it is, I believe, an appeal to those *outside* the Church, to win to the faith that Greek-speaking *Diaspora Judaism* to which the author now finds himself belonging as a result (we may surmise) of the greatest dispersion of all, which has swept from Judaea Church and Synagogue alike. His overmastering concern is that 'the great refusal' made by his countrymen at home should not be repeated by those other sheep of God's flock among whom he has now found refuge.

IX

THE DESTINATION AND PURPOSE
OF THE JOHANNINE EPISTLES[1]

In the previous essay I argued that the fourth Gospel may best be understood as an evangelistic appeal addressed to Greek-speaking Diaspora Judaism to accept as the Christ him whom 'the inhabitants of Jerusalem and their rulers' ('the Jews' of this Gospel) refused to acknowledge. If this thesis is to establish itself it must be prepared to account for the evidence of the Johannine Epistles. For, whether or not they come from the same hand as the Gospel, the milieu they presuppose is so similar that any theory about the nature of the community for which the Gospel was written which will not fit the evidence of the Epistles is bound to be precarious.

It is not the purpose of this article, any more than it was of the previous one, to enter into the question of authorship. But since any discrepancies are obviously *eased* if one can postulate a difference of hand, it will be well to say at the beginning that I am persuaded that the Gospel and the three Epistles all come from the same pen and are addressed to the same community, though in a different situation.

The difference of situation is sufficiently indicated in the consciously similar statements that set out the respective purposes of the Gospel and the first Epistle:

These [things] are written that you may believe that Jesus is the Christ, the Son of God, and that believing you may have life in his name (John 20.31).
I write this to you who believe in the name of the Son of God, that you may know that you have eternal life (I John 5.13).

While the Gospel is addressed to those who do not believe in order that they may have life, the Epistles are written to those who do believe in order that they may know that they have it. In other words, the purpose of the latter is reassurance of the faithful, in a

[1]Reprinted from *NTS* vii (1960–61), 56–65.

situation where they are in grave danger of being shaken from their belief in what they had accepted. Nine times in the first Epistle the writer offers his readers tests by which they may assure themselves of the truth of the Christian position, each beginning with the words: 'By this we know' or 'By this we may be sure' (2.3, 5; 3.16, 19, 24; 4.2, 6, 13; 5.2). And the occasion of this reassurance is clear from the internal evidence—the heretical and schismatic influence of a number of false teachers in the churches which formed the pastoral cure of the writer. The appeal to the readers is to remember and return to what they had 'heard from the beginning' (I John 2.7, 24; 3.11; II John 6); and it is made by one who, from the way he speaks, had evidently been their evangelist and pastor from the earliest days. He is too well known to them to need to declare his identity, and there is no hint that any other Christian missionary has been in the field either before him or since. He is the one man they have known who could speak to them as he does. Indeed, the intimate form of address 'my little children' (I John 2.1) carries the presumption that he had himself begotten them in the Faith, as it does when Paul uses it to the Galatians (Gal. 4.19).

Moreover, the references to *what* they had 'heard from the beginning', and much else that is alluded to or presupposed in the Epistles, make it clear that 'the type of teaching to which they had been delivered' (Rom. 6.17) was that which comes to expression in the fourth Gospel. This was evidently the form of Christianity to which they had been won, though it does not, of course, follow that they had been converted through the Gospel itself or even that they knew it in written form.

The evidence, indeed, would seem to favour the supposition that the Gospel was written before the Epistles, and that the recipients of the Epistles are presumed to be familiar with it. It is impossible to establish this with any certainty. If a man has been teaching and preaching to a congregation over the years, he will naturally echo themes and turns of phrase, and we cannot argue that their recurrence in a letter presupposes that his readers knew them in written form. Particularly is this true of isolated phrases, which need not presuppose more than oral teaching. Thus, the theme of the 'new commandment' in I John 2.7 or the description of Christianity as a state of having 'passed from death to life' in

I John 3.14 could be commonplaces of Johannine preaching and need not necessarily assume knowledge of John 13.34 and 5.24. On the other hand, where one finds paralleled in the Gospel and the Epistles sequences and combinations of ideas, then the natural assumption is that the writer is presupposing both for himself and his readers a document in which these connexions have already been made. A striking example of this is in I John 3.8–15, where there recurs a series of themes presented in the highly individual dialogue of John 8.40–7 (the difference between being 'born of God' and not; the sinner being a child of the devil, who has always been the same 'from the beginning'; and the only two occurrences of ἀνθρωποκτόνος in the New Testament).

The priority of the Gospel to the Epistles must fall short of proof. But if the Gospel is primarily an evangelistic tool and the Epistles are pastoral letters, then it is at least very natural to suppose that the former preceded the latter. We are not bound to assume that the Gospel was composed at the very beginning of the missionary activity which the author and his community began in their new dispersion surroundings. Indeed, missionary experience suggests that the need for literature occurs at the second stage (though frequently after no great interval), when the very success of the spoken word and personal contact introduces the need for some written evangelistic medium, for the purposes of consolidation and for use by others in places to which the evangelist himself cannot go. Nevertheless, a preaching weapon presupposes a situation where the prime need is still to work among the un-converted; and I believe it is on *a priori* grounds likely, apart from such evidence as we can glean from the Epistles, that at any rate the first draft of the Gospel belongs somewhere near to the time which the writer recalls, obviously with some emotion, as 'the beginning'. This, and the beginning of it all in the historic events to which he himself and those who have come with him from Palestine (the 'we' of I John 1.1–3 ?) can bear eye-witness, are the points to which he desires to recall his wavering children; and of both the Gospel stands written as the reminder and guarantee.

But since those first years much water has passed under the bridges—and this lapse of time is very relevant in assessing the undeniable difference of perspective between the Gospel and the Epistles. One does not in any case remind one's converts of what they heard at 'the beginning' if this was only the day before yesterday. And now it is nearer the end than the beginning: it is already 'the last hour' (I John 2.18). Of that there was no sense in the Gospel—except perhaps in the 'waiting till I come' of the epilogue (John 21.22). Indeed, the last chapter of the Gospel bears all the marks of having been added at about the stage when the Epistles were written. It is clearly the work of an old man, of whom some thought that he would never die (John 21.23). It has the same conception of the Parousia as the first Epistle (John 21.22; I John 2.28), which is not that of the body of the Gospel; it shows the same concern with the pastoral authority of the Church's ministry (John 21.15–17); and the 'we know that his witness is true' of its penultimate verse (John 21.24) echoes both the 'we' of the first Epistle and the 'you know that our witness is true' of III John 12.

But to return to the interval which the Epistles presuppose, if not from the writing of the Gospel, at any rate from the preaching of its message. Considerable evangelistic labour has been put in. 'Take care', pleads the writer in II John 8, 'that you do not destroy all that we have achieved.' II John presupposes at least two churches (in the elect lady and her sister of its opening and closing verses); III John probably another one, and in any case a number of Christian centres visited by travelling missionaries, who have no need to live off the heathen (III John 6 f.). I John is a general pastoral letter without a specific address, presupposing perhaps a group of Johannine churches. III John witnesses to a stage of considerable local autonomy, where the leadership is already in dispute, and I John 2.12–14 to an established Christian community where there is a full range of age-groups in the congregation. But above all sufficient time has elapsed for both heresy and schism to have assumed alarming proportions. The secession referred to in I John 2.19 is clearly no mere local quarrel. It is evidence of the many antichrists (2.18), the many false prophets (4.1) and deceivers (II John 7) that have arisen. And the stress on orthodoxy and sound doctrine (especially in II John 9 f.) argues a development which, to judge from the analogy of the Pauline churches, must have taken some time, though doubtless the process was accelerated towards the close of the century.

None of these points, taken alone, may be decisive; but

together they point to an interval of at least a decade, and more probably two, between the teaching (and perhaps also the writing) of the Gospel and of the Epistles. There is no reason, of course, why the Epistles themselves should not have been written over a period—though II John seems to presuppose the same situation as I John, and the concluding reference in both II and III John to pen and ink as a temporary substitute for a personal visit suggests that they may have been written closely together.

But if the Gospel and the Epistles were composed—though at different stages—for the same group of people, who were these people? Does the evidence of the Epistles confirm or contradict the view we derived from the Gospel that Greek-speaking *Judaism* was the main object of John's appeal and therefore presumably the heart of his Christian congregation?

Unfortunately it does neither very obviously. It is not easy to identify anyone with certainty. Robert Law remarks that I John is the only writing in the New Testament which does not contain a proper name.[2] Nor for that matter does II John, and in its address and greetings there is a studied anonymity. III John has three names—Gaius, Diotrephes and Demetrius—and, for what it is worth, they are all Graeco-Roman. But so, too, are those of Andrew and Philip and the seven of Acts 6, all of whom were clearly Jews. We must look further for other indications in the Epistles themselves.

In fact, it is not strictly true that I John contains no proper name. It contains that of Cain (3.12), and this may serve as our starting-point.

It is often remarked—and it is remarkable—that there is not a single Old Testament quotation in the Johannine Epistles: never once does Nestle,s text require the use of heavy type. In this these Epistles stand apart not only from all the other writings in the New Testament but from the fourth Gospel itself. But it would be very precarious to draw the conclusion that the author was neither interested in the Old Testament nor writing to people who were. Clearly a man's use of the Old Testament will differ if he is seeking to commend Christianity to Jews as the true Judaism, and if he is writing to Christians whose danger is, not that they will relapse into Judaism (the situation in Galatians and Hebrews,

[2] R. Law, *The Tests of Life* (1909), p. 39.

which are full of Old Testament quotations), but that they will 'go ahead' (II John 9) and become so progressive that they end up outside the pale both of Judaism and of Christianity.

But, though the writer does not in these circumstances quote the Old Testament, he does, as we have seen, allude to an Old Testament character and dwell on his story as a warning example. This is very much in the manner of the Epistles of James and of Jude,[3] which are among the most Jewish writings in the New Testament. Only a community grounded in the Old Testament would take such a reference.

There are other indications also that the writer is counting on familiarity with Jewish categories. As in the Gospel, the question is still whether Jesus is 'the Messiah' (ὁ χριστός) (I John 2.22; 5.1). In the Gentile mission of the Pauline Churches χριστός has become a proper name, and the test formula is rather whether Jesus is 'Lord'—a title not to be found in the Johannine Epistles. Again, as in the fourth Gospel, the confession of Jesus as the Christ is interchangeable with the confession of him as the Son of God (4.15; 5.5). The insistence that it is necessary to have the Son in order to have the Father (2.22 f.; II John 9) evidently pre-supposes that the heretics claimed to have the Father without the Son. They claimed, that is, to believe in the same God without confessing the messiahship or sonship of Jesus—in other words, to be orthodox Jews. The categories, moreover, in which the heresy is condemned are all Jewish categories—those of idolatry (I John 5.21), false prophecy (4.1), and, above all, of antichrist (2.18; 4.3; II John 7).

In morals, too, the strictures passed presuppose that the readers acknowledge Jewish standards. It is often said rather freely that the heretics were antinomians, repudiating and sitting loose to any kind of legal morality. In this case, the writer would have needed to insist that ἀνομία is sin. But in fact he says: 'Sin is ἀνομία' and 'everyone who commits sin is guilty of lawlessness' (I John 3.4). This implies that his opponents admitted that contravention of the Law was wrong, but refused to see that what they were doing did contravene it. Furthermore, as E. K. Lee observes, the 'sin unto death' in I John 5.16 'refers primarily to

[3]The only other New Testament writer apart from the Author to the Hebrews to refer to Cain.

131

the Jewish discrimination between those sins for which the legal penalty was death, and those that admitted of ritual atonement'.[4]

Above all, there is still no reference, any more than in the Gospel, to the Gentiles (τὰ ἔθνη). There is no mention of their possessing, as such, any place or promise within the Church. The only allusion is to the ἐθνικοί in III John 7, where the word is used in its typically Jewish contemptuous sense of 'the heathen'. And it is interesting to observe that in this passage (III John 6 f.) there is precisely the same *contrast* between the ἐκκλησία and the ἐθνικοί as in Matt. 18.17: 'If he refuses to listen even to the church, let him be to you an ἐθνικός.'

It is notable too that the differences in doctrinal expression which Dr C. H. Dodd[5] seizes on as distinguishing the Epistles from the Gospel are all on the side of giving the Epistles more rather than less of a Jewish ring. (1) Their eschatology is more apocalyptic—and *ipso facto* more Jewish. Categories like the antichrist, the last hour, the Parousia, the day of judgment (none of which occurs in the Gospel) clearly belong to the apocalyptic stream of Jewish eschatology. (2) The efficacy of the death of Christ is formulated in the Epistles much more explicitly in terms of the Jewish sacrificial system. Phrases like 'The blood of Jesus his Son cleanses us from all sin' (I John 1.7), 'We have an advocate with the Father, Jesus Christ the righteous, and he is the expiation for our sins' (2.1 f.), and 'God sent his Son to be the expiation for our sins' (4.10), are all more distinctively Jewish than the dominant soteriology of the Gospel, of the Son of man who descends in order to be lifted up and draw all men to himself. (3) The doctrine of the Spirit in the Epistles is said by Dodd to 'remain within the limits of primitive or popular belief'. This is only another way of saying that it stands nearer to Judaism. Indeed, one of the most striking parallels with Qumran in the whole Johannine literature is in the passage in I John 4.1–6, where the writer distinguishes between the two spirits[6] of truth and of error (cf. 1QS iii.13–iv.26).[7]

[4]*The Religious Thought of St John* (1950), p. 168.
[5]*The Johannine Epistles* (Moffatt New Testament Commentary, 1932), pp. liii–liv.
[6]The fourth Gospel never uses πνεῦμα in the plural.
[7]On the fundamental affinities between the theological dualism of the Johannine Epistles and Qumran, see W. Nauck, *Die Tradition und der Charakter des ersten Johannesbriefes* (1957), pp. 100–22.

This greater Jewishness would doubtless be recognized readily enough were it not for another set of evidence that has seemed to argue in the opposite direction. The danger in the community, as we have already said, was not of relapse into Judaism, but of becoming so 'advanced' as to leave both Judaism and Christianity behind altogether. It was part of a movement that Harnack described as the 'acute Hellenizing' of Christianity; and it has been generally assumed (*a*) that this is a correct description; (*b*) that naturally such a growth would spring from Gentile rather than Jewish soil within the Church; and (*c*) that our author is prepared to move a long way in combating it in the direction of what Dodd has called 'the higher religion of Hellenism'. If this is so, it is not surprising that it has proved so difficult to frame a consistent hypothesis to do justice to the various aspects of the Johannine Epistles.[8]

It is not in dispute that in this heresy we are dealing with some form of incipient Gnosticism—incipient, if only because there is no trace of the idea of the Gnostic redeemer.[9] There is not even trouble, as in the Colossian heresy, with numerous angelic mediators usurping the role of Christ. John's opponents would seem to have denied the need of *any* mediator: they claimed direct knowledge of God, to have the Father without the Son.

But all the presuppositions of Gnosticism appear to be present —above all the influence of a metaphysical dualism which locates evil in matter rather than in moral choice. It is this distortion of the Johannine dualism, where the conflict between light and darkness is viewed in ethical and eschatological terms, into a dualism which denies the reality and goodness of the material world and evacuates sin of its moral seriousness that John views as the antichrist. For, from whichever end one starts, it reaches the same conclusion. Because it denies the reality of sin it denies that anything has to be done about sin which takes sin seriously; it denies the necessity of expiation through the blood of Christ as

[8]Immediately before listing the doctrinal points which, as we have seen, indicate the more Jewish character of the Epistles, Dodd writes: 'The Epistle is not only less Hebraic and Jewish; it is also more free in its adoption of Hellenistic modes of thought and expression' (*op. cit.*, p.liii).

[9]*Pace* Bultmann, this looks increasingly to be a late, post-Christian element in Gnosticism, and is absent even from *The Gospel of Truth* in the middle of the second century.

the only way to become pure as he is pure; and hence it denies the need for the Incarnation. Alternatively, because it denies the reality and goodness of matter, it denies the fact that Christ came in the flesh; and if one denies the Incarnation one denies the Atonement: Christ did not come 'with the blood'.

This last mysterious allusion in I John 5.6 cries aloud for explanation and provides, I believe, the clue to the closer definition of the heresy and its background. 'This is he who came by water and blood, Jesus Christ, not with the water only but with the water and the blood.' As is well known, Irenaeus, in describing the views of the heretic Cerinthus, summarizes a form of teaching to which this looks very much like the orthodox reply. According to Irenaeus,[10] Cerinthus held that the divine Christ descended upon the human Jesus at his baptism but left him before his crucifixion: Jesus suffered and rose, but the Christ was preserved impassible. John, on the contrary, is insisting that Jesus is the Christ, not only by virtue of his baptism (the water), but also in his atoning death (the blood). 'Jesus Christ in the flesh' (I John 4.2) is his watchword: Jesus is fully the Christ, in the deepest sense of his being the pre-existent Son of God (which again Cerinthus explicitly denied),[11] and he is completely man at every point.

The fact that the cap fits the teaching of Cerinthus at this point is bound to make us look more carefully at this figure.[12] Nor is it a matter of guesswork that he comes into the picture. Irenaeus locates him, with the Johannine literature, in Asia Minor,[13] and the well-known story of the encounter between John and

[10] *Adv. Haer.* 1, 26.1: 'Post baptismum descendisse in eum ab ea principalitate quae est super omnia Christum figura columbae, et tunc annuntiasse incognitum patrem et virtutes perfecisse; in fine autem revolasse iterum Christum de Iesu, et Iesum passum esse et resurrexisse; Christum autem impassibilem perseverasse existentem spiritalem.'

[11] *Ibid.*: 'Iesum autem subiecit non ex virgine natum (impossibile enim hoc ei visum est); fuisse autem eum Ioseph et Mariae filium, similiter ut reliqui omnes homines.'

[12] It would be a mistake to assume that there was a 1:1 correspondence between the views of Cerinthus and John's opponents. Indeed, he never suggests he is attacking an individual person. But, *pace* R. Schnackenburg, *Die Johannesbriefe* (1953), pp. 17 f., I am convinced with A. E. Brooke, *The Johannine Epistles* (1912), pp. xlv–xlix, that the heresy of the Johannine Epistles is better explained by what we know of Cerinthus than by any other known system.

[13] *Op. cit., ibid.*

Cerinthus at the public baths at Ephesus was told to Irenaeus by persons who had heard it direct from Polycarp.[14] As Gustave Bardy says in his very judicious article on Cerinthus in the *Revue Biblique*,[15] 'Nous tenons donc ici un chaînon solide, et nous pouvons affirmer qu'un homme du nom de Cérinthe a enseigné à Ephèse au temps où s'y trouvait saint Jean, et que celui-ci le tenait pour un hérétique dangereux.'[16] Even if we do not accept Irenaeus' statement that St John wrote his Gospel directly to combat the views of Cerinthus,[17] there is sufficient ground for the hypothesis that the teaching associated with this man is highly relevant to the heresies attacked in the Johannine Epistles.

The background, therefore, of Cerinthus is in its turn relevant for determining the milieu in which this teaching arose. Cerinthus is listed by Irenaeus as a direct precursor of the Gnostics, and his docetic Christology and his views on creation bear this out. But though, like the Gnostics generally, he seems to have regarded creation as the work of a power far removed from the supreme God,[18] or at any rate as the work of angelic intermediaries[19] (which was, after all, a common enough view in late Judaism),[20] there is no doubt that Cerinthus was a Jew, and indeed a Judaizer. He is linked very closely by Irenaeus with the Ebionites; but, in Bardy's view, the decisive evidence is furnished by a statement of Hippolytus preserved in the commentary on the Apocalypse by Dionysius bar Salibi.[21] According to this, Cerinthus insisted on circumcision and attacked Paul for not having circumcised Titus. Besides denying the virgin birth and attributing creation to angels, he is also said in this passage to have stressed the importance of (Jewish) food-laws. By the time of Epiphanius[22] and

[14]*Op. cit.*, III, 3.4. It is repeated by Eusebius, *H.E.* III, 28.6; IV, 14.6.
[15]xxx (1921), 344–73.
[16]*Op. cit.*, p. 349.
[17]*Op. cit.*, III, 11.1.
[18]Iren. *op. cit., ibid.*
[19]Pseud. Tert. *Adv. omn. haer.* 3.
[20]It is presented as a Jewish heresy in Justin, *Dial.* 62.3. Cf. the passage in the *Treatise on the Three Natures* quoted by G. Quispel in *The Jung Codex,* ed. F. L. Cross (1955), p. 62: 'They [the Jews] have founded numerous heresies which exist down to the present day among the Jews. . . . Some say that he [God] is the creator of what exists; others say that he created through angels.'
[21]Ed. I. Sedlacek, CSCO, Scriptores syri: series II, vol. CI, versio (1910) p. 1, lines 30 ff. The text is quoted by Bardy, *op. cit.*, p. 353.
[22]*Haer.* XXVIII.

Filastrius[23] Cerinthus is held responsible for every Judaizing attack on the early Church, in Antioch, Jerusalem, Galatia and Asia; he is stated to have acknowledged only the Gospel of Matthew; and there is a complete fusion between him and the Ebionites. But this is only elaborating what was already the established image of the man and his teaching. And the substantial accuracy of this image is borne out by the thoroughly Jewish millenarian eschatology, held in the crudest materialistic form, which we first find attributed to him by Gaius.[24]

Bardy's conclusion indeed is that 'Cerinthus was a Jewish-Christian and not a Gnostic',[25] or, at any rate, 'a Judaizer much more than a Gnostic'.[26] But this antithesis seems unwarranted, and springs from the deeply rooted assumption that Judaism and Gnosticism belong to different worlds. Thus Law says categorically of Gnosticism that 'while the Church yet sojourned within the pale of Judaism, it enjoyed immunity from this plague'.[27] But one of the things that is becoming ever more clear from recent discoveries is the decisive, though, of course, far from exclusive, part which Judaism played in the origins of Gnosticism.[28] Gnosticism was indeed a movement which left Judaism behind in a conscious striving after a more enlightened, less materialistic, universal religion, and it was to become as much the enemy of Judaism as of Christianity. But an important seed-bed of its early development was undoubtedly the wisdom-mysticism of late Judaism.

In this respect the Qumran literature, and the movement of thought in which the Johannine writings can also be placed, has aptly been styled 'pre-Gnostic'.[29] John saw indeed that the decisive step was taken when the moral dualism of this tradition was transformed into a metaphysical dualism. It was by crossing this line that Cerinthus and his friends became for him the embodiment of antichrist. But this does not in the least mean that

[23]*Haer.* xxxvi.4.
[24]Euseb. *H.E.* iii. 28.1–2.
[25]*Op. cit.,* p. 371.
[26]*Op. cit.,* p. 373.
[27]*Op. cit.,* p. 26.
[28]Cf. e.g. G. Quispel, *The Jung Codex* (ed. F. L. Cross, 1955), pp. 61–78; R. McL. Wilson, *The Gnostic Problem* (1958), esp. ch. vii.
[29]B. Reicke, *NTS* i (1954–5), 141.

they did not regard themselves as Jews, or that in the world of the Johannine Epistles we are not still in a Jewish milieu.

Even if Gnosticism was eventually to lead to 'an acute Hellenizing' of Christianity, we must question the assumption that it was a growth which in New Testament times flourished in Gentile rather than Jewish circles within the Church. All the pointers are in fact the other way. The Colossian heresy was evidently a form of Jewish syncretism, and indeed, in insisting on Sabbath observance and food-laws (Col. 2.16–23), was more Jewish than Paul. Similarly, the gnosticizing opponents attacked in I Timothy who professed 'what is falsely called knowledge' (I Tim. 6.20) are clearly Judaizers, who 'occupy themselves with myths and endless genealogies' and 'desire to be teachers of the law' (I Tim. 1.3–7; cf. 4.1–5). Moreover, they are located precisely in Ephesus (1.3), where tradition places Cerinthus and the Johannine community. In Titus, too, the heretics are said to belong 'especially to the circumcision party' (Tit. 1.10) and to give heed to 'Jewish myths' (1.14), spending their time in 'stupid controversies, genealogies, dissensions, and quarrels over the law' (3.9). The same is true of Jude and II Peter, and of the Letters to the Seven Churches (again in Asia Minor), where an attack is directed against those who 'say that they are Jews but are not' (Rev. 2.9; 3.9).

There is no reason therefore to suppose that the congregations addressed in the Johannine Epistles belong to anything but the Hellenistic Jewish community for which we argued the Gospel was written. This is not, of course, to say that they were exclusively Jewish, or that this kind of Judaism was not wide open to Hellenistic influences. Indeed, any exclusiveness is condemned in the Epistles as expressly as in the Gospel: Jesus is 'the expiation for our sins, and not for ours only, but also for the sins of the whole world' (I John 2.2). But there is no ground for thinking that John was engaged, like Paul, upon a specifically Gentile mission; nor that he was going out of his way to accommodate his teaching to Gentile modes of thought. Indeed, the essence of his contention is that the pass is irretrievably sold once the fundamentally Hebraic categories of his own Gospel are twisted, however subtly, in the interests of a metaphysical dualism. That his particular presentation of Christianity could be seized upon and distorted so easily by the Gnostics (as it was also to be in the second century) makes him the more jealous for its true understanding.

It is not surprising, therefore, that in some respects the Epistles should seem even more Jewish than the Gospel. John is insisting that his Gospel must be Hebraically understood. 'Knowing God', being 'born of God', being 'in the light', and all the other phrases which have been taken up and twisted by the gnosticizers, can be interpreted only in terms of obedience, love, righteousness and doing the truth. Sin can be taken seriously only if it is kept within the intensely personal and moral categories of biblical religion. Real love of God means always, as in the Old Testament, love of one's brother, of the neighbour in need. And there can be no dissipation of the biblical faith in a non-eschatological mysticism that refuses to reckon with the judgment which must accompany the consummation of God's purpose.

All these emphases, so characteristic of the Epistles, can best, I believe, be understood if they are seen as necessary correctives to deductions drawn from the teaching of the fourth Gospel by a gnosticizing movement within Greek-speaking Diaspora Judaism.

X

THE MOST PRIMITIVE CHRISTOLOGY OF ALL?[1]

MR C. F. Evans has recently reopened the question as to how far the speeches in Acts afford ground for reconstructing a primitive apostolic *kerygma*.[2] It is indeed one of those questions that will probably never be closed, and, as Mr Evans himself says, it cannot be decided without taking into account the speeches of Acts as a whole (which he does) and the evidence for a primitive *kerygma* in the Epistles (which he does not). It is not the purpose of this article to discuss the main issue, but to draw attention to a factor which appears to have been under-estimated by those on each side of the debate.

Both those who see in these speeches the marks of an early pattern and those who regard them as evidence for no more than the outlook of Luke have this in common, that they assume them to be fundamentally homogeneous—whether they represent, as Dr C. H. Dodd argues,[3] the preaching of the Church in its formative years or, as M. Dibelius held,[4] a typical sermon of AD 90.

The issue has been debated in terms of whether the theology of the early speeches is the same as that of the author of Acts. On this I would simply say two things. First, it is entirely legitimate and necessary to see these speeches as part of the Lucan design and as subordinate to his theological purpose. And there are points, as I shall be indicating, at which his theology comes out quite specifically in their text. But secondly, there are, as it appears to me, many other points where their theology is demonstrably different from that of the editor of the work as a whole. Moreover if, as I shall be maintaining, these speeches contain at least two *incompatible* Christologies, it is clear that at least one of

---

[1]Reprinted from *JTS*, NS VII (1956), 177–89.
[2]'The Kerygma', *JTS*, NS VII (1956), 25–41.
[3]*The Apostolic Preaching and its Developments* (1936), pp. 17–20.
[4]*Studies in the Acts of the Apostles* (ET, 1956), p. 165.

them must represent material which the author has incorporated. In fact, I believe that neither of them is his own Christology and that both are products of a much more primitive stage in the Church's thinking. In that I agree with Dodd against Dibelius. The latter would reduce the differences simply to variations of *style,* and he confines himself to the statement that 'the use of old-fashioned phrases in the *kerygma* . . . speaks for, rather than against, a dependence upon older texts. But, as far as I can see, the question can only be raised, not answered.'[5] But just to say this is really to trifle with the issue. Mr Evans, in the single paragraph which he devotes to the question, is again content simply to produce later parallels (some of them rather doubtful) for isolated phrases in the speeches. He does not discuss whether their theology as a whole can be regarded as that of Luke, whatever purpose Luke himself may later have made them serve.

But this is not, as I have indicated, the theme of this article, and I must be allowed here to start from the position I have stated and leave the considerations upon which it is based to emerge in the course of the argument. My question is rather whether, within the theology of the early speeches of Acts (which I take to be primitive), there are not divergent strains that require to be more closely analysed.

In Acts 2.36 Peter reaches the climax of his Pentecost sermon with the conclusion: 'So then let the whole house of Israel know for certain that God has made him both *Lord* and *Christ*, this Jesus whom you crucified.' This has been taken with justice to be a fair summary of the Christology of the early preaching; and it was upon this foundation that the Church went on to build, alike in its evangelism and in its theology. In Acts 10.36 the same conclusion stands as the title of the *kerygma* that follows (just as 'The gospel of Jesus Christ the Son of God' prefaces the expansion of that *kerygma* in St Mark's Gospel): 'The word which (God) sent to the sons of Israel when he brought the good news of peace through Jesus *Christ*: he (Jesus) is *Lord* of all.' The original Pauline παράδοσις was in the same terms: 'You received Jesus as *Christ* and *Lord*' (παρελάβετε τὸν χριστὸν 'Ιησοῦν τὸν κύριον, Col. 2.6; cf. II Cor. 4.5). Again, the formula κύριος 'Ιησοῦς χριστός occurs as the climax of the kerygmatic hymn in Phil. 2.6–11, where, as in

[5]*Op. cit.,* pp. 165 f.

Acts 2.32–36, it is made clear that this title is his in virtue of his exaltation. That the raising of Jesus is the moment when he is given his other titles of glory is also brought out in Acts 5.31 (ἀρχηγὸς καὶ σωτήρ), 10.42 (κριτής), 13.33 and Rom. 1.4 (υἱός).[6]

If Acts 2.36 then can stand as a fair summary of the established apostolic preaching, it should be recognized also that in many respects it is not typical. Though the terms 'Lord' and 'Christ' became the settled ones in the Church's preaching and credal formulae, their rarity in the Acts *kerygma* is remarkable.

Except in Acts 2 (and that only in vv. 34 f.), κύριος is not applied in the speeches to Jesus.[7] Its occurrence in the vocative in Stephen's prayer (7.59 f.) cannot be regarded as evidence for its use as a title, any more than the frequent κύριε as a form of address in the Gospels. In this passage the *title* is 'the Son of man'.

In the case of χριστός the situation is more complicated, but not dissimilar. In 10.38 we find the verb ἔχρισεν applied to the baptism of Jesus, but there is no evidence to suggest that the apostolic preaching saw Jesus endowed with the title of χριστός at his baptism, and plenty to indicate the contrary. In 4.27 we do indeed have ἔχρισας (referring to an undefined moment prior to the Passion) used as though in explanation of the phrase τοῦ χριστοῦ αὐτοῦ quoted from Ps. 2.2. But, though this prayer (4.24–30) incorporates primitive phraseology, it bears many marks of being a later, Lucan construction. Like the Nunc Dimittis (Luke 2.29–32), it opens with the rare address δέσποτα, which seems to reflect the Church's liturgical use (cf. Rev. 6.10; *Did.* 10.3; I *Clem.* 59.4). Again, 'thy holy servant Jesus', repeated in vv. 27 and 30, has a liturgical ring, and *in liturgical contexts*—but only in these—παῖς continued to be used long after it may be regarded as a mark of primitive material (cf. *Did.* 9.2 f.; 10.2 f.; 10.7 (Coptic); I *Clem.* 59.2–4; *Mart. Polyc.* 14.1–3; 20.2; Hippolytus, *Ap. Trad.* 4.4 ff.).[8] Peculiarly Lucan features, apart from stylistic traits like μετὰ παρρησίας λαλεῖν τὸν λόγον (v. 29, cf. the Lucan narrative of

---

[6]Acts 9.20 also witnesses to the tradition that the title υἱὸς θεοῦ was peculiarly associated in the apostolic preaching with the person of Paul. It occurs on no one else's lips in Acts. Cf. Gal. 1.16; II Cor. 1.19.

[7]10.36, as we have seen, is a heading to what follows, and represents the considered theology of the Church rather than part of the *kerygma* itself. As in its parallel in Mark 1.1, 'Jesus Christ' occurs as a proper name, a sure sign of a more developed stage.

[8]See. J. Jeremias, *The Servant of God*, pp. 83 f., 96 f.

v. 31), are (*a*) the association of Herod with Pilate in the death of Jesus (found only in Luke 23.6–12) and (*b*) the combination of the people of Israel with the 'peoples' of the Gentiles, forced out of an Old Testament quotation (cf. again Luke 2.31 f.; also Acts 26.17 and 23). In the light of this, it looks as if ἔχρισας is another piece of Luke's theology (cf. Luke 4.18) introduced to explain and justify his quotation. Taken all in all, it would be extremely hazardous to regard this prayer as pre-Lucan[9] or to accept it as evidence for the use of χριστός in the apostolic preaching, especially when it is applied to Jesus prior to the Passion.

In 2.38; 3.6; 4.10; and 10.48 the phrase 'in the name of Jesus Christ' occurs in the narrative *round* the speeches. It is not to be found in the body of the *kerygma* and its use of χριστός as a proper name indicates sufficiently that we have here a developed, if still early, baptismal and healing formula. Similarly, the Lucan summary in 5.42 that 'they did not cease teaching and preaching the good news that Jesus was the Christ' (or 'the Christ was Jesus') faithfully reflects what was undoubtedly the established apostolic case argued in 2.36. But it does not afford further independent evidence for it.

With the exception, then, of a passage about to be discussed, we may say that chapter 2 stands by itself in the kerygmatic summaries of Acts in representing what was to become the accepted thesis of the early Church, that, by virtue of his Resurrection to the right hand of God, Jesus is 'both Lord and Christ'. This conclusion is significant if, as will be claimed, there are also signs of a different Christology within the opening speeches of Acts. The assumption that *within these speeches*, as in the early preaching generally, the theology of Acts 2 is the norm to which other formulations have, consciously or unconsciously, to be assimilated becomes less compelling. The possibility of an alternative Christology must be assessed on its own merits and not simply as an aberration from an otherwise uniform position.

Before arguing this, however, it will be relevant to sketch, in merest outline, the development *from* the position of Acts 2, that it is *by virtue of the Resurrection* that Jesus is Lord and Christ. For the recognition soon followed that at the Resurrection Jesus was

[9]H. F. D. Sparks comes to the same conclusion in his article 'The Semitisms of the Acts' (*JTS*, NS 1 (1950), 24).

merely designated 'with power' what eternally he was (Rom. 1.4); and his pre-existence is explicitly recognized (Phil. 2.6),[10] as the equivalent in Greek terms of his 'foreordination' (Acts 3.20). The next stage is the growing acknowledgement that what he was declared to be at the Resurrection must also have been valid (at least proleptically) even of his humiliation. His designation as Son of God in the voice both at the Baptism and Transfiguration can be shown to belong to early Palestinian tradition;[11] and at least by the time of St Mark's Gospel the whole public ministry is viewed as messianic (though it is still recognized that 'the Christ' is a title Jesus himself preferred to avoid). Finally, in Matthew and Luke, the application of 'Christ' and 'Lord' is pushed back, not merely behind the Resurrection, but behind the Baptism, to the birth of Jesus, so that there is no gap, no moment when χριστὸς κύριος (Luke 2.11) is not the appropriate designation.[12]

There, is, however, evidence that the position even of Acts 2 does not represent the beginning of this process. This brings us to consideration of the speech in Acts 3.12–26, to which insufficient attention seems to have been paid.

This speech is distinctive in a number of ways. In particular, it is the only one to contain a reference to what is normally taken to be the Second Coming.[13] But the further we examine what it says,

[10]Both these passages are widely taken to be pre-Pauline.

[11]Cf. R. H. Fuller, *The Mission and Achievement of Jesus* (SBT 12, 1954), pp. 52–4.

[12]I owe to Professor John Knox (*Christ the Lord* (1945), pp. 89–104) the recognition that this process of 'pushing back' the Church's Christology prior to the Resurrection did not follow a straight line, with pre-existence as the last stage (after the acknowledgement of Jesus as Son of God from birth), as one could conclude from placing the fourth Gospel next in the sequence after Matthew and Luke. Pre-existence, rather, came first (Knox detects it also in Mark); and the gap is then closed during which it was originally thought incredible that Jesus could be acting *as the Messiah*. That '*the Christ* (in contradistinction from "the Son of man") must suffer', that Jesus is distinctively 'the Christ' in his *passion*, is, as we shall see, within the Gospels, late and peculiarly Lucan theology.

[13]Acts 10.42 is often quoted as well. Here, however, the idea is simply read in. The verse does not say that Jesus 'will come to be our judge', but: 'This is he who has been designated (ὡρισμένος) by God judge of living and dead', in exactly the same way as he has been 'designated (ὁρισθέντος) Son of God with power' (Rom. 1.4; cf. Acts 17.31). That he *is* judge is what the apostles are commissioned to 'proclaim and testify'. Clearly his function as judge is not yet exhausted, but there is no suggestion that he will be judge only at some Second Coming.

the less probable it seems that this is in fact the reference. There is no statement that the Christ is to return. Rather, the conception appears to be this: Jesus has been sent by God as Servant and Prophet, in fulfilment of the prediction that God would raise up for his people a prophet like Moses. The purpose of this visitation was to bring the blessing covenanted to Abraham and an opportunity of repentance to Israel. Instead, the Jews have denied and killed God's Servant. But even this has been within his plan: indeed, it has actually fulfilled it. He has not been defeated, but has exalted Jesus to his own splendour in heaven, where he must remain till the day of restoration which the prophets foretold. Meanwhile, because the Jews have acted in ignorance, opportunity for repentance is still open.[14] This they are urged to seize, that the age of renewal may dawn and God may be able to send Jesus, this time as their appointed Messiah.

Jesus is here still only the Christ-elect, the messianic age has yet to be inaugurated. If we put the question 'Art thou "he that should come" or do we look for another?', the answer which this speech seems to be giving is: 'Yes, Jesus *is* the one who shall come. We know who the Messiah will be; there is no need to look for another. To be sure, the Messiah is still to come. But Jesus has already appeared, as the forerunner of the Christ he is to be, in the promised role of Servant and Prophet, with an offer of the covenanted blessing and a final preaching of repentance. Accept that therefore, despite all that you have done, that you may receive him in due time as the bringer of God's new age.'

What are we to make of such a *kerygma* and of such a Christology?

First of all, is it in fact a correct reconstruction of the passage? It has not normally been interpreted in this way.[15] This is partly

[14]This is further evidence of the primitive setting of the speech. Contrast the tone even of I Thess. 2.15 f. It is incredible that this is what was preached in AD 90.

[15]The mass of commentators see no problem here. In his *Jesus the Son of God* (1911), p. 59, B. W. Bacon recognized that the passage means that at the restoration of all things God will send Jesus *as the Christ* (his italics). But he viewed this as the theology of Luke himself, which it clearly is not.

The despair to which criticism can be reduced by the passage is evidenced in *The Beginnings of Christianity* I (1920), 407 f. While in their commentary in vol. IV of the same work Lake and Cadbury apparently detect no difficulties, Foakes-Jackson and Lake are driven to postulate two alternating sources in

because the later Parousia doctrine of the *return* of the Christ has almost inevitably been read into it. But there is also one element in the speech itself which militates against what otherwise appears to be its clear tenor. In v. 18 Peter is made to say: 'But what God announced beforehand through the mouth of all the prophets, that his Christ should suffer, he thus fulfilled.' That Jesus suffered *as the Christ* is clearly incompatible with the idea that he is still, even after the Resurrection, only the Christ-elect.

If we are compelled to accept the words παθεῖν τὸν χριστὸν αὐτοῦ as an integral part of the original speech, then it is difficult on any reconstruction to find in it a consistent theology.[16] But there are strong indications that they are in fact an exegetical

---

vv. 18, 22 f., 26, and in vv. 19–21, 24 f. respectively. In the latter they see an eschatological passage about the sending of the Messiah (they do not appear to be disturbed by the recognition that 'the "sending" of the Messiah Jesus is here clearly regarded as future'). In the former they detect a non-eschatological passage relating to the sending (in the past) of the Servant and Prophet, this being added from a non-Jerusalem source 'affected by Samaritan thought'. Apart from the fact that there is, as they admit, no literary evidence for the presence here of two sources, we may say to this: (a) the supposition that 'the prophet like Moses' was a purely Samaritan expectation is now recognized as groundless; (b) it does not explain the occurrence of the same expectation in Stephen's speech (7.37); and (c) 3.26 is clearly integral to the speech as a whole, taking up the idea of 'blessing' in v. 25 and the title 'servant' in v. 13.

In his commentary on Acts (*Theologischer Handkommentar zum NT* (1939), pp. 66–8) O. Bauernfeind sees the difficulties very forcibly. He cuts the knot by isolating vv. 20 f. as a piece of *Jewish* eschatological expectation referring to the coming of Elijah, and thinks the words τὸν προκεχειρισμένον ὑμῖν χριστὸν 'Ιησοῦν are a Christian substitution for 'Ηλείαν (ἕτοιμον ὄντα ὑμῖν?) introduced when Jesus, at first identified with Elijah, came to be confessed as Messiah. But this is an entirely speculative reconstruction, which raises as many questions as it answers, and the isolation of vv. 20 f. is an arbitrary procedure.

What is certainly true is that the Elijah expectation, as well as that of the Prophet like Moses, does in some way underlie this passage. There is a link between 'the restoration of all things' of v. 21 and the prediction referred to in Mark 9.12: 'Elijah does come first to restore all things.' With this we may compare Ecclus. 48.10 f., which says of Elijah: 'Who art ready for the time, as it is written, to still the heart before the fierce anger of God, to turn the heart of the fathers to the children, and to restore the tribes of Israel' (tr. Box and Oesterley). The function of the forerunner is to restore Israel through a last and great turning of repentance in the spirit and power of Elijah (cf. I Kings 18.37; Mal. 4.5 f.; Luke 1.16 f.). Only when this is completed can the Messiah come (cf. Strack-Billerbeck I, 598). This is precisely what is described in Acts 3.26 and 20, with Jesus acting as forerunner as well as Christ.

[16]Lake and Cadbury (*op. cit.*, IV, 37) regard this verse as evidence that the speech is not authentic.

interpolation by Luke himself. In the first place, the idea of the *suffering* of Jesus plays no part in any other formulation of the primitive *kerygma*.[17] Not only is it not to be found in any of the speeches in Acts (where the betrayal, denial, crucifixion, death, and burial of Jesus are all mentioned), but it is notably absent from I Cor 15.3 f., and from the other Pauline kerygmatic summaries. Secondly, the thesis that *the Christ* should suffer is found on inspection to be a characteristic, and indeed peculiar, feature of Luke's writings. It occurs only in the Lucan summaries of the meaning of the ministry and death of Jesus, placed in the mouth of the risen Lord and of Paul. For him the whole message of the prophets can be summarized in the phrase παθεῖν τὸν χριστόν (Luke 24.26 f., 45 f.; Acts 17.2 f.; 26.22 f.).[18] It would be hardly surprising then should he have introduced the phrase again in Acts 3.18, in parenthetic exegesis of what was foretold by all the prophets concerning the death of Jesus. The supposition that we have here an editorial interpolation is further strengthened by the fact that in Luke 17.25 we find what is generally recognized to be a similar insertion into a block of Q material: 'But first he must suffer many things and be rejected of this generation.'[19]

We may therefore with reasonable confidence detach the phrase about the suffering of the Christ from the main body of the speech in Acts 3. Consciously or unconsciously, Luke is bringing this primitive summary with its heterodox theology into line with his own Christology. In doing so, he is in fact going beyond anything found in the rest of the early preaching, even in Acts 2, which asserts that Jesus is the Christ *by virtue of the Resurrection*.

If what has been set out is therefore a fair statement of the Christology of Acts 3, what, may we suppose, is its relation to Acts 2 and to the rest of the apostolic preaching? I believe it is possible to see in it a first tentative and embryonic Christology of the early Church, as it struggled to give expression to the

[17]Cf. F. L. Cross, *I Peter: A Paschal Liturgy* (1954), p. 14, where he also suggests a special reason for its occurrence in the theology of I Peter.

[18]In each of these instances, as in 3.18, it is made quite clear that ὁ χριστός is a title and not (as in I Peter) a proper name. The Lucan mystery is that it is *as the Messiah* that Jesus should have suffered.

[19]Grounds for regarding this verse as editorial include the fact that here alone in the Gospels is to be found an explicit combination of 'apocalyptic' and 'suffering' sayings about the Son of man.

tumultuous implications of what had happened in Jerusalem in these last days.

From the beginning we may assume that, like John the Baptist, the Church was faced with the question posed above: 'Art thou "he that should come" or do we look for another?' Any confidence the disciples may have acquired in the midst of the ministry and mighty works of Jesus (cf. Matt. 11.2–6 = Luke 7.18–23) must have been shattered by the Crucifixion, and the mood expressed in the words, 'But we had hoped that it was he who should redeem Israel' (Luke 24.21), was no doubt representative. The incredible reversal of the Resurrection reopened the question. But it is facile to assume that it answered it at once.

If the reconstruction of the 'Christology' of Jesus himself argued by Professor R. H. Fuller in chapter 4 of his *The Mission and Achievement of Jesus* is correct (as I believe that substantially it is), then his followers had become accustomed to one who spoke of himself as God's Servant-Son and as the Son of man, whose full and glorious vindication to that heavenly office waited, however, upon the breaking of God's kingdom in power. He had come as the Servant of the Lord and in filial obedience to inaugurate God's mighty act, but always in his teaching the climax lay beyond his present humiliation and death. What the Father was to accomplish through him would indeed be recognized as the messianic act, but the title he declined to anticipate.[20] Those among whom he stood would see the kingdom come with power and the Son of man vindicated in the might and right of God; but to the end of the ministry, even at the Last Supper itself, he was still looking forward and beyond.

We may be sure that the Resurrection restored, and immeasurably deepened, the conviction that Jesus could not have been mistaken. He was, beyond doubt, 'he that should come'. But it is entirely credible that the Resurrection should not at first have appeared so completely to alter the frame of reference that the decisive event was now to be seen no longer in the future, however imminent, but in the past. Jesus *was* indeed 'the Coming

[20]Cf. A. Schweitzer, *The Mystery of the Kingdom of God*, p. 211: 'How is it conceivable that the disciples proclaimed that Jesus had entered upon his messianic existence through the Resurrection, if already upon earth he had spoken of his messiahship as a dignity then actually possessed?'

One', the Christ to be: God had set his seal upon that. But to assert that, by virtue of the Resurrection, he was *already* the Christ, that the messianic act, the eschatological event, *had now taken place*—that was a tremendous leap and required a second major adjustment. Nothing is more natural than that the first Christology should have expressed the Gospel within the same frame of reference in which Jesus himself preached it—namely, that he had come among men as Servant of the Lord and Prophet of the end bringing the good news of God and the final call to repentance, but that all this was but in preparation for the act which would inaugurate the messianic rule of God and vindicate him as the Christ. Indeed, if we had not such a theology as that represented in Acts 3, we should almost be compelled to supply it.

The full Christian gospel of God's act in Jesus waited indeed upon the recognition that the framework within which Jesus himself proclaimed it had itself been shattered by his own action. The Cross-and-Resurrection, incredible as it might seem, *was* the eschatological event of which Jesus had spoken so often to deaf ears. This was the redemptive act, and Jesus was even now the Christ and all else of which prophecy spoke. *From now on* the Messiah reigned at God's right hand and the age of fulfilment had been inaugurated. Such is the proclamation of Acts 2 and the settled gospel of the early Church.

How long it was before this decisive step was taken it is, of course, impossible to say. There is nothing finally to *forbid* its ascription to the day of Pentecost itself, as Acts 2 affirms. It is in any case probable that the two positions, of Acts 3 and Acts 2, represent not chronological stages but conflicting estimates of the Christ-event, one of which was prepared to go further than the other. But, making all allowance for the fact that the epithet 'primitive' may here denote no more than that which failed to develop, there are, I believe, certain features of language which go some way to confirm the priority, in theology if not in time, which we have come to assert of Acts 3 over Acts 2.

On the one hand, as we have seen, of all the kerygmatic summaries in Acts, chapter 2 has a more defined and explicit Christology than any of the others. It alone uses the two terms 'Christ' and 'Lord', which were later to form the heart of the proclamation to Jews and Gentiles respectively. Acts 2 comes to us as the most finished and polished specimen of the apostolic preaching, placed as it were in the shop window of the Jerusalem Church and of Luke's narrative. While there is no longer sound reason for arguing that the term κύριος betrays a Hellenistic origin, yet the carefully compacted argument which by selected *testimonia* leads up to the twin conclusion that Jesus is 'both Lord and Christ' may well represent the fusion of two lines of apologetic current in the early Church. (Indeed, it is possible that the *testimonium* in vv. 34 f. has been appended to the original speech, which elsewhere regularly uses κύριος not of Jesus but of God, and which would reach a very appropriate close at v. 33. In this case v. 36 will have been added to draw together the two lines of argument adduced in vv. 29–31 and 34 f.)

If, on the other hand, we examine Acts 3 in greater detail, we may perhaps detect corresponding signs of its more primitive character.

In the first place, if the prayer of Acts 4.24–30 is discounted as evidence of primitive usage, this is the only speech to use παῖς as a Christological category, a term which finds no place in later formulations. It is retained only in liturgy.

It is interesting, further, to observe that the account in chapter 3 has affinities, not simply with the other Petrine speeches in Acts, but with the sermon of Stephen in chapter 7.

Both of these speeches are more deeply rooted in the theology of the Old Testament than any of the others.[21] Elsewhere[22] the apostolic preaching in Acts limits its appeal to the prophets and the Psalms (using the eponymous figure of David not so much, as in Judaism, as a type of the Messiah but in *contrast* with the Christ (2.25–34; 13.33–37)).[23] Acts 3, like Acts 7, starts from 'the God of Abraham, Isaac and Jacob, the God of our fathers'.[24] And this is no accident. For both speeches are broadly grounded in the

---

[21]The speech of Acts 13.17–41 begins with a broad survey of Old Testament *history*, but theologically it rests on the same foundations as the rest.

[22]Except in the indirect allusion to Deut. 21.22 contained in the word ξύλον in 5.30; 10.39; 13.29.

[23]In this the Church appears to have followed the treatment Jesus himself accorded to the traditional Son of David typology in Mark 12.35–37. Cf. the similar attitude to the Moses typology in Heb. 3.2–5.

[24]Cf. also the explicit quotation of the same passage in 7.32.

pre-prophetic religion of Israel. Both refer to the covenant made with Abraham (3.25 and 7.7) and, in different connexions, to the promise given to his 'seed' (3.25 and 7.5).

But of considerably more significance is their common treatment of Moses. Only in these two passages in the New Testament is there an actual citation of the promise in Deut. 18.15 of 'a prophet like unto Moses' and an application of it to Jesus. There is some evidence that this application was canvassed in Jesus' lifetime (John 6.14; 7.40),[25] and we know that Jesus was prepared to view himself in the role of *a* prophet (Luke 13.33). But it was not retained as a useful Christological category, nor like the prediction of Elijah *redivivus* did it attach itself to John the Baptist (cf. John 1.21). But in Acts 3 and 7 we have the adumbrations of a detailed Moses typology based on the ὡς ἐμέ of Deut. 18.15. Jesus, like the prophet, is 'raised up' (ἀναστήσας in 3.26 is the only application of this word to Jesus *not* with reference to the Resurrection).[26] As Moses was 'denied'[27] by the Israelites and nevertheless 'sent' by God as ἄρχων καὶ λυτρωτής (7.35), so Jesus, 'denied' by the Jews (3.13 f.), is nevertheless raised by God as the ἀρχηγός[28] τῆς ζωῆς (3.15), to be 'sent' as the προκεχειρισμένος χριστός (3.20).[29]

The fact that this embryonic Christology of the Prophet, like that of the Servant,[30] entirely dropped out, in striking contrast

[25]The context makes it clear that 'the prophet' means 'the prophet like unto Moses'. The title is appropriate to Jesus since he appears as the second and greater Moses who (*a*) gives the true manna (6.1–14, 48–51) and (*b*) promises water out of the rock, this time from himself (7.37–40).

[26]Acts 13.33 not excepted.

[27]A. Descamps, *Les justes et la justice* (1950), p. 70, points out that this is not found in the Exodus story and that Moses is here being described retrospectively in terms of Jesus. Thus, though Stephen's speech does not itself draw out the parallel between Moses and Jesus, this reading back of marks of the passion of Jesus into the life of Moses presupposes such a typology. Despite Jeremias (*TWNT* IV, 867 f.), the figure of a suffering and a dying Moses is, I believe, a Christian creation (cf. Rev. 11.1–12).

[28]Descamps (*op. cit.*, p. 71) thinks it probably that ἀρχηγός is simply a variant of ἄρχων (to avoid confusion with the ἄρχοντες of the Jews, e.g., in 3.17) and that this is again intentional typology. But this is highly speculative.

[29]Descamps (*op. cit.*, p. 72) again draws attention to the parallel with the sending of Moses: δέομαι, κύριε, προχείρισαι δυνάμενον ἄλλον ὃν ἀποστελεῖς (Ex. 4.13).

[30]The two are closely associated. Cf. A. Bentzen, *King and Messiah* (ET, 1955), pp. 66–72, who draws attention to 'the influence of the traditional picture of Moses on the Servant Songs' and concludes that it is 'very probable

with the formulations in terms of Lord and Christ, is further evidence that the theology of Acts 3 and 7 represents a form of thinking which failed to establish itself in the Church. Again, the designation of Jesus as a prophet, even as *the* Prophet, heralding the end, is fully in line with what we described as the pre-messianic frame of reference carried over from the ministry of Jesus itself. It comes as no surprise, therefore, that the Stephen tradition, as well as sharing with Acts 3 the only application to Jesus in the early speeches of the primitive title ὁ δίκαιος (3.14 and 7.52),[31] should alone preserve the term which characterizes *par excellence* the outlook of the ministry, namely, 'the Son of man' (7.56). Stephen's sermon is pre-messianic from beginning to end. He does not regard Christology as the central issue dividing the followers of Jesus from other Jews (6.8–14). Christology comes in for him, as it did for Jesus himself, only as the seal and guarantee of his ultimate vindication, and that in terms of seeing the exaltation of the Son of man of which Jesus spoke.

To conclude then. Reasons have been given for thinking that the theology of the apostolic preaching as represented in the early speeches of Acts is not homogeneous. Whether we speak of a stage that was superseded or a line of thinking which was not developed, we may detect in Acts 3, with reflections in Acts 7, an extremely primitive Christology, whose essence may be summed up in the proclamation: 'We know who the Messiah will be.' It has not yet come to recognize the death and exaltation of Jesus as being itself the act of God that inaugurates his kingdom and in virtue of which Jesus is revealed as Messiah. That precisely this *was* the significance of these events to Jesus as he viewed them in advance is, I believe, the conclusion to which Synoptic criticism impels us.[32] The real danger to the message of Jesus was, therefore,

---

that the Ebed Yahweh in the scheme of Deutero-Isaiah played the role of the "new Moses" '.

[31]This also occurs on the lips of Ananias in Acts 22.14, a verse which has other interesting affinities with Acts 3 (ὁ θεὸς τῶν πατέρων ἡμῶν, προεχειρίσατο and ἀκοῦσαι φωνὴν ἐκ τοῦ στόματος αὐτοῦ, which last Descamps takes to contain an allusion to the αὐτοῦ ἀκούσεσθε κατὰ πάντα ὅσα ἂν λαλήσῃ πρὸς ὑμᾶς of Deut. 18.15). In each of its occurrences Descamps sees ὁ δίκαιος as virtually equivalent to ὁ προφήτης and part of the same theology (*op. cit.*, pp. 74–84).

[32]Cf. again Fuller, *op. cit.*, ch. III.

not that the Church would give too exalted a place to his death and his person, but, as Acts 3 illustrates, that it would fail to recognize the former as the eschatological event which it was and would be content to see him merely as the forerunner of himself as the Christ.

Also threatened in this presentation of the gospel was the person and presence of the Spirit. The theology of the speech (though not of the narrative) of Acts 3 is a theology of an absent Christ; that of Acts 2 of a present Christ, active in his Church through the Spirit. For Acts 3 the Christ is inoperative because he has not yet been sent, and there is no mention of the Spirit because its outpouring must wait upon the dawning of the messianic age, the coming of 'the times of refreshment'.

That there could be any doubt that the age of the Spirit had begun, suggests, as we should independently suspect, that the creation of a separate and unmistakable event for the coming of the Spirit (associated with the liturgical feast of Pentecost as the Resurrection was with Passover) is part of Luke's own construction, parallel to his treatment of the Ascension. Neither is so represented elsewhere in the New Testament. Originally, it would appear, the gift of the Spirit, like the exaltation of Christ, was connected with the Resurrection (as indeed Acts 2.33 suggests). And just as it was possible to doubt whether this event was itself the inauguration of the messianic reign, so it could be questioned whether the age of the Spirit yet had dawned; for the baptism of the Spirit was specifically the function of the One who was 'to come' (Mark 1.8 and pars; cf. Acts 19.2).

The purpose of this article has simply been to present the case for recognizing a divergence of theologies within the primitive proclamation. As a doctrine of the person of Christ the theology of chapter 3 lies embedded in the book of Acts like the fossil of a bygone age. Never was the Church to go back on its conviction that Jesus was even now Lord and Christ and that the age of the Spirit had already begun. But it would, I believe, be a mistake to imagine that the kind of thinking it represented was thenceforward extinct. For one thing, the people who were led to formulate it were not extinct. And through these people there may be connexions both forwards and backwards within the New Testament; for they were most probably, I believe, those who entered the Church through the movement of John the Baptist. Again, it has to be asked whether the Church ever resolved the doubt contained in the question, 'Art thou "he that should come"?', with quite the decisiveness that Acts 2 suggests. Yes, he had come —but was he not still to come? I have argued that Acts 3 does not itself contain the idea of a Second Coming. On the other hand, it is, I believe, of crucial importance for the rise of the Parousia doctrine, for the notion, unprecedented in Judaism, that the Christ was to come, not only once, but twice.

But both of these are developments of the theme which belong to a different occasion and require a treatment of their own.[33]

[33]Cf. my book, *Jesus and His Coming,* especially ch. VII.

XI

THE EARLIEST CHRISTIAN LITURGICAL SEQUENCE?[1]

ALL the brethren salute you. Salute one another with a holy kiss. The salutation of me Paul with mine own hand. If any man loveth not the Lord, let him be anathema. Maranatha. The grace of the Lord Jesus Christ be with you. My love be with you all in Christ Jesus. Amen. (I Cor. 16.20–24.)

In this passage v. 22 ('If any man loveth not the Lord, let him be anathema. Maranatha.') appears to be an interruption in an otherwise typically Pauline ending. I suggest that in fact it holds the clue to the understanding and setting of the other phrases, both as they appear here and elsewhere.

It is notable that this short verse (εἴ τις οὐ φιλεῖ τὸν κύριον, ἤτω ἀνάθεμα. μαραναθά) contains three words that do not otherwise occur in Paul.

1. φιλεῖ, a verb which he never uses. In a similar context in Eph. 6.24 he naturally employs ἀγαπᾶν: 'Grace be with all them that love (ἀγαπώντων) our Lord Jesus Christ in uncorruptness.'

2. ἤτω. Paul prefers the form ἔστω. This is particularly significant in the two occurrences of the phrase ἀνάθεμα ἔστω in Gal. 1.8 f. Cf. also II Cor. 12.16.

3. μαραναθά—a ἅπαξ λεγόμενον in the New Testament, though it appears in the *Didache* (10.6) and in translation at Rev. 22.20.

There is general agreement that this last (from its context in the latter two references) is a liturgical phrase surviving in Gentile Christianity from the primitive Aramaic-speaking Church. Now the succession of clauses in the *Didache*, which I set out in what appears to be their dialogue shape, bears a striking resemblance to I Cor. 16.22.

℣ Let grace come and let this world pass away.
℟ Hosanna to the God of David.

[1]Reprinted from *JTS*, NS IV (1953), 38–41.

Deacon(?) If any man is holy, let him come;
   If any be not, let him repent.
℣ Maranatha.
℟ Amen.

This exchange of versicle and response comes at the end of the
prayer 'after you are satisfied'. The probability is that the reference
is to the Agape and that the dialogue forms the introduction to
the Eucharist proper, which presupposes (*Did.* 14.1) prior
confession of sin and mutual reconciliation. *Maranatha* (if, as
seems likely, it is an imperative—'our Lord come!'—rather than a
perfect indicative)[2] is then a prayer to Christ to stand among his
own in his Parousia (anticipated in the real presence of the
Eucharist).

I suggest that in I Cor. 16.22 Paul is quoting a similar liturgical
sequence already current in the Corinthian Church. He is visualiz-
ing the context in which his closing words will reach his listeners.
His letter has been read out in the *ecclesia* (cf. Col. 4.16; I Thess.
5.27), the Christian assembly gathered for worship. As the
synaxis comes to an end, dispositions for the Eucharist begin.
Mutual greetings and the kiss of peace are exchanged[3]—to which
in autograph, Paul adds his own, just as, earlier in the Epistle, he
had vividly portrayed himself in the Corinthian assembly ('For
I verily, being absent in body but present in spirit, have already,
as though I were present, judged him that hath so wrought this
thing, in the name of our Lord Jesus Christ, ye being gathered
together, and my spirit, with the power of our Lord Jesus',
5.3 f.). He then quotes the familiar invitation, with its warning

[2]For the evidence, *vide* K. G. Kuhn in *TWNT* IV, 470 ff. The only plausible
interpretation of the indicative is to take it to mean 'Our Lord is present'
(i.e. in the Eucharist). It then becomes the ground and reinforcement of the
warning. But Rev. 22.20 is against this.
[3]Cf. Justin Martyr, *Apol.* I, 65: 'When we have ceased from prayer, we
salute one another with a kiss. There is then brought to the president bread
and a cup of wine.' Professor E. C. Ratcliff has drawn my attention to the
evidence in Rom. 15.30–3 for the same sequence in the Roman liturgical
gathering a hundred years earlier. Here we have (1) Paul's request for prayer
ἐν ταῖς προσευχαῖς ὑπὲρ ἐμοῦ πρὸς τὸν θεόν, and (2) the kiss formula (cf.
p. 156 n. 5 below) ὁ θεὸς τῆς εἰρήνης μετὰ πάντων ὑμῶν· ἀμήν. He suggests
that the doxology of 16.25–7 (which follows immediately in the Chester
Beatty papyrus) may represent the close of Paul's liturgical sermon (cf. 'my
gospel and the preaching of Jesus Christ') and the γραφαὶ προφητικαί have
reference to the OT lection, still read in Justin's day.

dismissal of all those who 'love not the Lord Jesus'.[4] After this follows the old Aramaic watchword, the prayer by which perhaps from the beginning the note of the Christian Eucharist had been set—*maranatha*! (cf. I Cor. 11.26). And, finally, Paul's closing greeting echoes the words with which the president begins: 'The grace of the Lord Jesus Christ be with you',[5] to which Paul, as it were, once more adds his own response: 'My love be with you all in Christ Jesus. [Amen.]'

If this reconstruction be correct, two conclusions follow:

1. All the phrases of the final greetings take on a new depth and significance. They are the language, not merely of epistolary convention, but of one worshipping community to another, the converse of the saints assembled for Eucharist. The salutations, the kiss, the peace, the grace are all rich with the overtones of worship. The last word of the letter is the first of the liturgy, the one being written to lead into the other. *Omnia exeunt in mysterium.* Of nothing is this more true than of the Apocalypse,[6] whose

[4]The verb φιλεῖν may possibly in this connexion have become the technical one by extension from the φίλημα as the qualification for Communion. Cf. the exchange of greetings in Titus 3.15, 'All them that are with me salute thee. Salute them that love (φιλοῦντας) us in faith', and III John 15, 'the friends (οἱ φίλοι) salute thee. Salute the friends by name.' In Eph. 6.24, 'Grace be with all them that love (ἀγαπώντων) our Lord Jesus Christ', Paul is perhaps alluding to the same qualification, but expressing it in his own words.

[5]The opening salutation of the Eucharist doubtless varied considerably. Later, in the Byzantine rite, we find 'The grace of our Lord Jesus Christ . . .' from II Cor. 13.14, and variations on it in other Syrian liturgies. Most commonly the pre-Nicene rites began either with ℣ The Lord be with you. ℟ And with thy spirit (of which there are traces in II Thess. 3.16; Gal. 6.18; Phil. 4.23; Philemon 25; II Tim. 4.22, and possibly I Cor. 5.4) or with Jesus' own greeting 'Peace be with you'. For the latter cf., in addition to the many closing prayers and exhortations for peace, the sequences in I Peter 5.14, 'Salute one another with a kiss of love. Peace be unto you all that are in Christ,' and in III John 14, 'Peace be unto thee. The friends salute thee. Salute the friends by name.' The frequent occurrence in the final greetings, and nowhere else, of the formula 'the God of peace' (Rom. 15.33; 16.20; II Cor. 13.11; Phil. 4.9; I Thess. 5.23; Heb. 13.20; cf. II Thess. 3.16—'the Lord of peace') suggests that this too may have had a liturgical origin. It looks as if these phrases may originally have formed the words introducing the kiss of peace itself.

[6]It may be said that the Epistles and the Apocalypse represent the contributions of the apostles and prophets respectively to the primitive liturgical gathering. If the NT Epistles are the apostolic liturgical sermons, the Apocalypse may well be a series of prophecies for the Christian assembly on the Lord's day. O. Cullmann (*Early Christian Worship*) has drawn attention to the way in which the book is punctuated by the refrains of the Church's worship.

closing dialogue repeats the familiar pattern, ending with the grace, which from the purely literary point of view here seems strangely out of place:

> And the Spirit and the bride say, Come. And he that heareth, let him say, Come. And he that is athirst, let him come: he that will, let him take of the water of life freely. . . . He which testifieth these things saith, Yea: I come quickly. Amen: come, Lord Jesus. The grace of the Lord Jesus be with the saints. Amen' (Rev. 22.17-21).

2. We have in I Cor. 16.22 (which at all events appears to be pre-Pauline in origin) the remains of the earliest Christian liturgical sequence we possess. The fact that Paul can quote a formula with which he can assume, without explanation, that his audience is familiar, indicates that fixed eucharistic forms were in use at Corinth within twenty-five years of the Resurrection. The fact that that formula includes a word that must have established itself beyond possibility of translation before the rise of Gentile Christianity[7] takes us a great deal farther back still.[8]

---

[7]It is notable that the dialogue of the *Didache* contains no less than three such words: ὡσαννά, μαρανα θά, ἀμήν.

[8]After this note was completed, my attention was drawn to an article by Günther Bornkamm, 'Das Anathema in der urchristlichen Abendsmahls-liturgie', *TLZ* LXXV (1950), 228 f., which anticipates and confirms a number of the points here made and should be consulted for its references to other German discussion of the subject. But cf. more recently C. F. D. Moule, 'A Reconsideration of the Context of *Maranatha*', *NTS* VI (1960), 307-10.

XII

THE ONE BAPTISM[1]

'I ACKNOWLEDGE *one* baptism for the remission of sins.' 'There is one body and one Spirit . . . one Lord, one faith, *one* baptism.' (Eph. 4.4 f.) What precisely is here the significance of the word 'one'? It would clearly be inadequate to see this unity simply as a matter of Church order—though it may yet be more significant than we have allowed that, in spite of everything, divided Christendom still today recognizes a single baptism. We should be nearer the heart of the matter to say that baptism is one because it makes one. Just as it is 'because there is one bread' that 'we, who are many, are one body' (I Cor. 10.17), so it is baptism which in the first place creates this unity: 'In one Spirit were we all baptized into one body, whether Jews or Greeks, whether bond or free' (I Cor. 12.13); 'for as many of you as were baptized into Christ . . . are all one man in Christ Jesus' (Gal. 3.27 f.).

Yet there are other elements in the New Testament doctrine of baptism which suggest that even this does not exhaust the meaning of the phrase. To be baptized 'into Christ' is not merely to find a new and given unity among ourselves. It is to be 'baptized into his death' (Rom. 6.3), to be 'circumcised . . . in the circumcision of Christ' (Col. 2.11). Behind Christian baptism stands the baptism, unique and all-inclusive, undertaken by Jesus himself for the sins of the whole world.[2] Indeed, the fundamental reason why baptism 'makes one' is that it brings men under a baptism 'once made'. The one baptism is that by which the Church is created, before it is that which the Church administers. As Professor Cullmann has put it: 'According to the New Testament, all men have in principle received baptism long ago, namely on Golgotha, at Good Friday and Easter. There the essential act of baptism was carried out, entirely without our co-operation, and even without our faith. There the whole world was baptized on the ground of

[1]Reprinted from *SJT* VI (1953), 257–74.
[2]Cf. W. F. Flemington, *The New Testament Doctrine of Baptism* (1948), p. 72.

the absolutely sovereign act of God, who in Christ "first loved us" (I John 4.19) before we loved him, even before we believed.'[3]

The purpose of this article is to explore the extent to which this conception of the work of Christ as a single, prevenient and all-inclusive baptism is in fact to be found in primitive Christianity. On the face of it, it is not self-evident that *'according to the New Testament*, all men have in principle received baptism long ago'. Has Cullmann's generalization a sound or broad basis? The answer to this question must affect not only his own treatment of the subject but the whole fresh understanding of baptism which is emerging, with such significance for the ecumenical Church, from the revival of biblical theology.

I believe that Cullmann is right. I believe that it can be shown (*a*) that such a conception, though attaching itself pre-eminently and naturally to the death of Christ, is used to interpret his whole work from his baptism in Jordan to the final release of the Spirit at Pentecost; and (*b*) that such an understanding is to be traced in every important literary tradition in the New Testament—in Mark, Q, John, Acts, Paul, the Pastorals, Hebrews, Peter and the Apocalypse. The cumulative evidence suggests that this was one

---

[3]*Baptism in the New Testament,* p. 23. Such a statement, of course, immediately raises many important questions about the relation of this single 'world baptism' to the Church and its sacramental action. It is not the purpose of this article to pursue these. Suffice it to say that the general baptism already undertaken *for* all men has to be made savingly effective, through faith, *in* all men. The instrument through which the work of Christ, already universal in extent, is made universal in obedience is the Church (Eph. 3.10), which is also the pledge and firstfruits of the whole of creation as it will be (James 1.18). The baptism of *all men* in the work of Jesus can therefore be described equally as the baptism of *the Church* (e.g., at Pentecost or in Eph. 5.25–7). By that is not meant that only a section of mankind is after all affected—for the Church is, intentionally and eschatologically, the whole of humanity renewed in Christ. Rather, it is only as mankind becomes the Church, and, this side of the Consummation, only in the Church, that what has been universally achieved is individually effective. A man must therefore be incorporated in the Church if the general baptism is to become savingly his own. Hence the vital place occupied by the sacrament of baptism, as that which, by grafting the individual into the very body of Christ, is for him through faith 'the Christ-event become present'. (O. Cullmann, *Early Christian Worship*, p. 77). It should therefore be clear that emphasis on the general baptism wrought in Christ's completed work is in no way detrimental to a high doctrine of the sacramental action of the Church, but gives to it rather its decisive theological significance.

of the major categories of primitive soteriology and that it had its foundation in the creative interpretation of Jesus himself.

(1) The obvious passage from which to start is Mark 10.38 f., in which Jesus speaks of his own 'baptism'.

Are ye able to drink the cup that I drink? or to be baptized with the baptism that I am baptized with? And they said unto him, We are able. And Jesus said unto them, The cup that I drink ye shall drink; and with the baptism that I am baptized withal shall ye be baptized.

The passage occurs in a context heavily laden with prediction of the Passion. But it would be a mistake to jump too quickly to the conclusion that the baptism of which Jesus speaks is simply his death. In the Matthean parallel the allusion is deliberately so restricted: the reference to baptism is omitted and the cup becomes that which 'I am about to drink' (Matt. 20.22). But in Mark the verbs are in the present—'the baptism that I am being baptized with', 'the cup that I am drinking'. The baptism of Jesus is his whole existence in the form of a servant, all that is included in his being upon earth 'not to be ministered unto but to minister, and to give his life a ransom for many' (Mark 10.45). What lies simply in the future is not the baptism but the apostles' share in that baptism: 'ye shall be baptized'. It is only in the Cross that the baptism becomes inclusive and can therefore be vicarious. In the comment of the fourth Gospel, 'except a grain of wheat fall into the earth and die, it abideth by itself alone; but if it die, it beareth much fruit' (John 12.24).

(2) Along with this must be taken the second passage in which Jesus speaks of the baptism that is laid upon him. Its similarity is particularly striking as it comes from a non-Marcan source.

I came to cast fire upon the earth; and what will I if it is already kindled? But I have a baptism to be baptized with; and how am I straitened till it be accomplished! (Luke 12.49 f.).

In interpreting this passage (which has no parallel in Matthew, though it has a distinctively Q ring),[4] one should probably

[4]Cf. Luke 12.49 πῦρ ἦλθον βαλεῖν ἐπὶ τὴν γῆν with Matt. 10.34 ἦλθον βαλεῖν εἰρήνην ἐπὶ τὴν γῆν. In the latter instance Matthew's version of Q is verbally much closer to Luke 12.49 than is Luke's own εἰρήνην παρεγενόμην δοῦναι ἐν τῇ γῇ in 12.51. It looks as if Luke, having put the two sayings together, has altered (and very much weakened) the second for the sake of stylistic variation.

separate it from the verses immediately following in Luke ('Think ye that I am come to give peace in the earth? I tell you, Nay; but rather division'), which occur at Matt. 10.34 f. in a different context. The verbal association in 'I came . . . I am come' appears to account for the linking of the passages by Luke, for the point of the two sayings—baptism and the division of households—is entirely different. If then they are isolated pericopae, we should clear our minds of the idea that the 'fire' of v. 49 has necessarily the same significance as the 'division' (Matt: 'sword') of v. 51.

I suggest that the words 'I came to cast fire upon the earth' are to be interpreted in the light of Luke 3.16 = Matt. 3.11: 'He shall baptize you in Holy Spirit and fire.' This gives the connexion between the 'fire' of v. 49 and the 'baptism' of v. 50, which is not otherwise apparent. The purpose of Jesus' coming is to loose upon the world the pentecostal fire of the Spirit, which must in the first instance be a fire of judgment. He could wish it were already aflame. '*But* I have a baptism to be baptized with; and how am I straitened till it be accomplished!' The release of the Spirit waits upon the completion of the baptism in Jesus' death. In other words, the teaching is the same as John 7.39: 'The Spirit was not yet given; because Jesus was not yet glorified.' It is also in harmony with our interpretation of Mark 10.38 f. Until the baptism is thoroughly finished (ἕως ὅτου τελεσθῇ: cf. the τετέλεσται of John 19.30), the Son of man is straitened: it is only in the Cross and Resurrection that its confinement to Jesus' person is broken.

These two passages have given us a conception of a baptism undergone by Jesus, which, though it finds its consummation in his death, is not confined to it. Whence did this conception of his ministry derive? We can hardly be wrong in seeking the answer in his own baptism at the hands of John. To this we now turn.

(3) Then cometh Jesus from Galilee to the Jordan unto John, to be baptized of him. But John would have hindered him, saying, I have need to be baptized of thee, and comest thou to me? But Jesus answering said unto him, Suffer it now: for thus it becometh us to fulfil all righteousness. Then he suffereth him. And Jesus, when he was baptized, went up straightway from the water: and lo, the heavens were opened unto him, and he saw the Spirit of God descending as a dove, and

coming upon him; and lo, a voice out of the heavens, saying, This is my beloved Son, in whom I am well pleased (Matt. 3.13-17).

Cullmann has shown[5] the extent to which the baptism of Jesus must be interpreted in the light of the Isaianic Servant Songs. The voice declaring Jesus the beloved or chosen Son of God echoes Isa. 42.1, which continues with a reference to the descent of the Spirit. The essential meaning of Jesus' baptism is precisely that he was 'numbered with the transgressors' and 'bare the sin of many' (Isa. 53.12). He entered upon it 'to fulfil all righteousness' (πληρῶσαι πᾶσαν δικαιοσύνην). That is to say, 'Jesus will effect a general forgiveness' (Cullmann), or, in the words again of Isa. 42.1, 'he will bring forth judgment for the nations'. Cullmann also comments on Luke 3.21 ('Now when *all* the people (ἅπαντα τὸν λαόν) were baptized, Jesus also was baptized'): 'He is distinguished from the mass of other baptized people, who are baptized for their own sins, as the One called to the office of the Servant of God who suffers *for all others.*'

Jesus' acceptance of baptism at the hands of John is therefore the beginning of that baptism of vicarious suffering which could only be completed in the Cross. When Ignatius[6] says of Jesus that he was 'baptized that by his submission (or, by his passion, τῷ πάθει) he might cleanse the water', he rightly divined the connexion between the baptism and death of Christ. The fourth Gospel also sees already in the figure coming to John for baptism 'the Lamb of God, which taketh away the sin of the world' (John 1.29). The baptism is the anticipation of the Cross, in which Jesus in Jordan foresuffered all, and as such it gives to the Cross and all that lies between the two events its own character of a baptism.

But—and this is equally significant for the understanding of Christian baptism as the act in which the Christian not merely dies but also rises with Christ (Rom. 6.4; Col. 2.12)—the baptism of Jesus is likewise the anticipation of his Resurrection and Ascension. As Jesus goes up[7] from the water, God's voice

[5] *Baptism in the New Testament*, pp. 16-19.
[6] *Eph.* 18.2, cited by W. F. Flemington, *op. cit.,* p. 42.
[7] Professor G. W. H. Lampe, in his article '*Baptisma* in the New Testament', *SJT* v (1952), 163-74, draws attention to the significance of this word ἀναβαίνειν in the baptismal narratives (Mark 1.10; Matt. 3.16; cf. Acts 8.39), which occurs seven times in the NT of the Ascension of Christ. At his

declares him his Son in phrases which, as we have seen, designate that Sonship under the form of a servant. But this only prefigures what the primitive preaching was to see fulfilled in the Resurrection, of which it boldly proclaimed, now in the words of the royal psalm, 'Thou art my Son, this day have I begotten thee' (Acts 13.33).[8] This teaching is summarized in the credal formula of Rom. 1.4, which asserts that Christ was 'declared to be Son of

baptism Christ 'goes up', possessed of the promised Spirit which he will pour forth upon the Church after the Ascension (Acts 2.33). In Eph. 4.4–10 there is a similar connexion between the 'one baptism' and the ascended Christ as the giver of the gifts of the Spirit.

This may also underlie the apparently abrupt transition in John 3.9–13 (on which see O. Cullmann, *Early Christian Worship*, p. 77). To Nicodemus' question, 'How can these things be?' (i.e., rebirth through baptism), Jesus replies, 'No man hath ascended into heaven, but he that descended out of heaven, even the Son of man, which is in heaven.' The birth from above (ἄνωθεν) means, looked at the other way round, an ascent into heaven. But that is possible only by union with the crucified Son of man (3.14), who alone can ascend. It is this that baptism affords, namely, participation in the whole descent and ascent of Christ, which was enacted proleptically in the water-baptism of Jesus himself. There is a similar connexion in the ensuing passage (John 3.22–36), where in contrast with John's baptism which is 'of the earth', the Christ (as the true Baptist) comes 'from heaven' bringing the gift of the Spirit which he has received of the Father.

The notion that baptism is the Christian's participation in the descent and ascent of Christ, giving victory over the entire gamut of cosmic forces in heaven and earth and under the earth, is probably the meaning of I Peter 3.18–22 (*vide* E. G. Selwyn, *The First Epistle of St Peter* (1946), *ad loc.*). The little sermon on the meaning of baptism in vv. 20 f. reads like an interpolation into a creed which recites the descent and ascent of Christ shortly to become the candidate's own:

'Christ . . .
Being put to death in the flesh,
But quickened in the spirit,
In the which also he went and made proclamation to the spirits in prison
 [i.e., the angelic forces of darkness];
Who is on the right hand of God,
Having gone into heaven,
Angels and authorities and powers being made subject to him.'
Cf. the closely parallel creed in I Tim. 3.16.

[8]F. J. Leenhardt (*Le baptême chrétien*, 2nd ed., 1947, pp. 27–9) sees this psalm rather than the Servant Songs as decisive for the interpretation also of the Baptism narrative. It is true that it has made its way into the Western text of Luke 3.22 ('Thou art my beloved Son, today have I begotten thee'), but this cannot be accepted as more than an assimilation. Cullmann is surely right in saying that 'Christ at his baptism is not yet proclaimed King but only the Servant of God. His Lordship reappears later, after his Resurrection' (*Baptism in the New Testament*, p. 17).

God with power, according to the Spirit of holiness, by the resurrection of the dead'.

The association at the baptism of Jesus of the gift of the Spirit with the declaration of Sonship is the ground of the connexion between Christian baptism, the Spirit, and our adoption as sons (Gal. 3.26–4.7; cf. Rom. 8.14–16). In Gal. 4.6 the correct translation should in all probability run: 'And to declare that ye are sons of God, God sent forth the Spirit of his Son into our hearts, crying, Abba, Father.' Christian baptism simply reproduces in the life of the Christian the one baptism of Jesus begun in Jordan and completed in the Resurrection. In Eph. 1.5 f. our 'adoption as sons through Jesus Christ' is associated with the grace 'freely bestowed on us *in the Beloved*'. The choice of this title for Christ (found only here in the Pauline writings) may again indicate that the ground of our sonship rests in the baptism of Jesus.

(4) In connexion with the baptism in Jordan, it is natural to consider a catena of Johannine passages which again link this closely with Christ's death, with the giving of the Spirit and with Christian baptism. They are:

This is he that came by water and blood, even Jesus Christ; not with the water only, but with the water and with the blood. And it is the Spirit that beareth witness, because the Spirit is the truth. For there are three who bear witness, the Spirit, and the water, and the blood: and the three agree in one (I John 5.6–8).

If any man thirst, let him come unto me, and drink. He that believeth on me, as the scripture hath said, out of his belly shall flow rivers of living water.[9] But this he spake of the Spirit, which they that believed on him were to receive: for the Spirit was not yet given; because Jesus was not yet glorified (John 7.37–9).

When Jesus therefore had received the vinegar, he said, It is finished: and he bowed his head, and gave up his spirit (or, handed over the Spirit) (John 19.30).

One of the soldiers with a spear pierced his side, and straightway there came out blood and water. And he that hath seen hath borne witness, and his witness is true (John 19.34 f.).

For the purposes of interpretation, the first passage is the decisive one. Its primary purpose is to insist upon the unity of the baptism

[9]So the text of the RV. But the correct punctuation I believe to be that of the RSV margin (and text of the NEB): 'If any one thirst, let him come to me, and let him who believes in me drink.' The reference to '*his* belly' is then to Christ and not to the believer, which accords much better with the Evangelist's subsequent comment and whole theology.

and death of Jesus, against those who held that the divine Christ descended upon the human Jesus at Jordan but left him before his Crucifixion. The water *and* the blood, the baptism and the Cross taken together (conjoined with the witnessing voice of the Spirit) are the testimony that Jesus is the Son of God. Indeed, the baptism of Jesus, as he himself saw, is made complete only in his death. So, in typical Johannine manner, all the symbolism of the baptism is transferred to the Cross itself, where alone it attains its full meaning. It is from the Crucified that the water and the Spirit, as well as the blood, proceed. The Cross is the consummation of the baptism, and consequently, truly considered, it is on the Cross that the world's baptism takes place. Hence the fount and origin of the Church's sacrament is not an isolated word of institution but the body of the Crucified himself.

(5) In the light of this, another Johannine passage becomes significant—the foot-washing of John 13. This incident is linked with great deliberation to the final consummation of Christ's mission in his death and return to the Father (vv. 1–3). Jesus states clearly that its real meaning will become perspicuous only after these events: 'What I do thou knowest not now; but thou shalt understand hereafter' (μετὰ ταῦτα) (v. 7). Then occurs the following dialogue:

> Peter saith unto him, Thou shalt never wash my feet. Jesus answered him, If I wash thee not, thou hast no part with me. Simon Peter saith unto him, Lord, not my feet only, but also my hands and my head. Jesus saith unto him, He that is bathed needeth not save to wash his feet, but is clean every whit (John 13.8–10).

The setting of the incident ('during supper', v. 2); the mysterious reference to the future, the period of the Church; the solemn words, 'If I wash thee not, thou hast no part with me'; and the command to repeat what is described as a ὑπόδειγμα (v. 15); all these strongly suggest that we have here a conscious parallel with the Synoptic account of the institution of the eucharist. The distinction between being 'bathed' (λούεσθαι) and being 'dipped' (νίπτεσθαι) would lead us to suppose that the latter is the symbolic, sacramental act. But if it is the action of 'dipping' (to which too the promise of incorporation is attached) which stands for Christian baptism, what are we to make of ὁ λελουμένος? I suggest that the only intelligible reference for this is to the act of general baptism which Jesus is about to accomplish in his death. It is this 'bathing' which is to be the ground of the Church's sacramental action and which will make it sufficient for salvation. As in the institution of the eucharist, Jesus is here imposing upon his coming death, by an act of prophetic symbolism, its true interpretation and significance. It is to be the great washing which will give the water-baptism of the Church its efficacy, and also its necessity (for without it there will be no incorporation in the person and work of Christ).[10]

Just as the last supper is the fore-ordination of the Christian eucharist, which can be eaten 'new' only in the resurrection order, so the foot-washing is the fore-ordination of baptism, which can become operative only with the giving of the Spirit. In the fourth Gospel this latter event takes place in the Cross and Resurrection (John 7.39; 19.30; 20.22). For the Lucan tradition, however, it is separated temporally, though not theologically, by the space of forty days. Let us then turn to the narrative of Pentecost as recorded in Acts.

(6) The designation of the Whitsun event as a baptism is made explicit from the start.

> He charged them not to depart from Jerusalem, but to wait for the promise of the Father, which, said he, ye heard from me: for John indeed baptized with water; but ye shall be baptized with the Holy Ghost not many days hence (Acts 1.4 f.).

The promise that Jesus would baptize his people in Holy Spirit (and fire) stood in the Synoptic tradition from the beginning (Mark 1.8; Matt. 3.11; Luke 3.16). Neither there, nor when it is quoted in Acts (1.5; 11.16), is there any suggestion that, whereas John baptized with water, *Christians* would not. In fact on each occasion when this prophecy is regarded as fulfilled, the Church at once proceeds to water-baptism (Acts 2.38; 10.47 f.). It is difficult to see why this saying should have been regarded as confusing the

[10]The significance of this passage is lost when it is the act of 'bathing' rather than 'dipping' which is taken to correspond to Christian baptism. Thus Cullmann (*Early Christian Worship*, pp. 105–11; cf. A. J. B. Higgins in *The Lord's Supper in the New Testament*, SBT 6, 1952, pp. 84 f.) interprets the passage as meaning that he who has once been baptized (ὁ λελουμένος) requires only the eucharist for post-baptismal sin. I fail to see how the expression 'needeth only to wash his feet' can naturally describe the eucharist. Cf. my article 'The Significance of the Foot-washing' in the forthcoming Cullmann *Festschrift*, *Neotestamentica et Patristica*, ed. B. Reicke and W. C. van Unnik (1962).

evidence for primitive Christian initiation. For its reference is not to Church baptism at all, but to *Christ's* once and for all baptism of the Church, from which sacramental water-baptism followed without dispute.

In the light of events this activity of Christ in baptizing in Holy Spirit is seen as commencing at his own baptism by John. The fourth Gospel changes the Synoptists' 'he shall baptize' to a present ('he who baptizeth') and makes the point that the Spirit not merely descended upon Jesus but 'abode' on him (John 1.33). From Jordan onwards the great baptism of the Spirit began, even though it was confined till the Cross and Resurrection to the representative figure of Jesus himself. Pentecost represents its final outpouring upon all flesh (Acts 2.17, 33), every nation and tongue being represented *in nuce* in the fellowship of the Church (Acts 2.6–11). It is the last act of the great drama of salvation wrought in Christ. The first act of the new era of the Church follows immediately and necessarily from it, when what has been given is transmitted by water in the name of Jesus (Acts 2.38). The reason why the Apostles and others of the original hundred and twenty did not themselves receive water-baptism is not, as has been suggested, that they had already been so baptized by John (a fact unproven and anyhow irrelevant to the need for Christian baptism; cf. Acts 19.1–6). It is rather that at Pentecost they partook of the *Heilsgeschichte* itself. They had a direct share in the One Baptism, of which the sacrament was to be the effective re-presentation for every *succeeding* person and generation (Acts 2.39).

The incident of Cornelius and his friends in Acts 10 and 11 reopens for the Church the relation between the *Heilsgeschichte* and baptism which seemed thus to be closed.

And as I began to speak, the Holy Ghost fell on them, even as on us at the beginning. And I remembered the word of the Lord, how that he said, John indeed baptized with water; but ye shall be baptized with the Holy Ghost. If then God gave unto them the like gift as he did also unto us, when we believed on the Lord Jesus Christ, who was I, that I could withstand God? (Acts 11.15–17).

This incident is theologically parallel to the share accorded to St Paul in the actual sequence of salvation events, albeit 'to one born out of due time' (I Cor. 15.8). Each case marked a decisive stage in the extension of the Israel of God to include the Gentiles

(Acts 9.15; 10.45). Where the Church would not itself have acted, God declares he is not bound by his sacraments by continuing into the time of the Church the once and for all events of the Resurrection and Pentecost. But the Church must acknowledge and assimilate what God has initiated. The ἔκτρωμα must be incorporated, through the regular instrument of Christian initiation, into the age of the Church into which he has been born. So both Paul and Cornelius, despite the fact that they have been partakers of the decisive saving events, receive water-baptism at the hands of the Church (Acts 9.18; 10.47 f.).[11]

We turn now to the Pauline epistles.

(7) In Col. 2.11–15 Paul writes to his friends that in Christ

> Ye were . . . circumcised with a circumcision not made with hands in the putting off of the body of the flesh, in the circumcision of Christ; having been buried with him in baptism, wherein ye were also raised with him through faith in the working of God, who raised him from the dead. And you, being dead through your trespasses and the un-circumcision of your flesh, you, I say, did he quicken together with him, having forgiven us all our trespasses; having blotted out the bond written in ordinances that was against us, which was contrary to us: and he hath taken it out of the way, nailing it to the cross; having put off from himself his body, he made a show of the principalities and the powers openly, triumphing over them in it.

Here the suffering of Christ is described as his circumcision. In dying, he put right off (ἀπεκδυσάμενος) the body of his flesh,[12] of which action circumcision was the partial, sacramental symbol. It is *in* this general circumcision once undertaken that Christians are circumcised. They thus win, in the complete stripping off of the flesh wrought in the death of Christ, release from sin, the law and powers of evil, whose purchase over man is through the flesh. Baptism, as the Christian circumcision, is the instrument

[11]The grounds for doubting that Cornelius and his friends were in fact baptized with water are valid only if the saying which substitutes Spirit- for water-baptism is understood to refer to the sacramental action of the Church. As we have seen, there is no basis for this. It is true that Cornelius' baptism is not recorded explicitly in the second account; but Peter's words in 11.17, 'who was I that I could withstand God?', surely imply the consequent action taken in 10.47 f.

[12]Following the translation of the RV margin, which I believe to be the interpretation of the words required to make sense of the description of the Cross as a *circumcision*. I have argued the point in detail in my book, *The Body* (SBT 5, 1952), pp. 41 f.

through which the one circumcision or baptism of the Cross is made operative in the believer; for by it he is incorporated into the very body to which all this has happened (Rom. 6.3 f.). The action of the Church in baptism simply releases the action of the One Baptism. In consequence, it is impossible throughout this passage to distinguish what has been done for us by the Cross and Resurrection and what by baptism. This, as we shall see, represents a typical and recurring ambiguity.[13] It is inescapable precisely because Christian baptism is none other than the great baptism of Christ now made individually effective.

(8) The most explicit Pauline description of the death of Christ in terms of a corporate baptism occurs in Eph. 5.25–7.

> Husbands, love your wives, even as Christ also loved the Church and gave himself up for it; that he might sanctify it, having cleansed it by the washing of water with the word, that he might present the church to himself a glorious church, not having spot or wrinkle or any such thing; but that it should be holy and without blemish.

Here the clearly baptismal language of the laver and credal formula is used to describe what has been done to the Church once in the single and sufficient oblation of Christ. The sacramental act only sets forth and sets forward what the Cross as the One Baptism has in principle already perfected.

(9) Closely linked with this passage is the language of I Cor. 6.11:

> And such were some of you: but ye were washed, but ye were sanctified, but ye were justified in the name of the Lord Jesus Christ, and in the Spirit of our God.

Again it is impossible to determine whether this refers to the moment of baptism or to the event in which baptism is grounded. The language of the washing, the mention of the name and of the Spirit all suggest the act of Christian initiation. Yet equally certainly for Paul it is the death and resurrection of Christ itself in which we are sanctified, justified and, as we have just seen, washed. In the parallel words of I Cor. 1.30 ('But of him are ye in Christ Jesus, who was made unto us wisdom from God, and righteousness, and sanctification, and redemption') the reference, as the context of the chapter demands, is clearly to the Cross.

[13]Who can say, for instance, whether in Eph. 2.1–10 the Apostle is referring to the once and for all action in Christ or to the moment of Christian initiation?

There is no contradiction: for the Cross, as in John, *is* the place of the Washing.

Two further Pauline passages deserve attention.

(10) Is Christ divided? Was Paul crucified for you? or were ye baptized into the name of Paul? (I Cor. 1.13).

'Here', as Cullmann comments,[14] 'the two expressions "you were baptized" and "another was crucified for you" are treated as synonymous.' Paul's argument is to stress the impossibility of Christian disunity: 'There is one baptism', he is saying, 'namely, Christ's death, in which you have all been baptized.'

(11) I would not, brethren, have you ignorant, how that our fathers were all under the cloud, and all passed through the sea; and were all baptized into Moses in the cloud and in the sea (I Cor. 10.1 f.).

The point here is that the Israelites, simply by their participation in the saving events of the Exodus, were all automatically 'baptized', even though most subsequently fell away. So, the implication runs, the whole people of God has now been baptized in the new *Heilsgeschichte*, the death and resurrection of Christ, of which the Exodus was the type. There is a *fait accompli*, which has included every one of us, a general baptism, whose very objectivity makes apostasy so serious. Paul bases his warning, not, as we might, on the vows taken at Christian initiation, but on the One Baptism of Christ in which *all* have been involved, whether they have received Church baptism or not.

(12) Moving on to the Pastorals, we find in Titus 3.4–7 the same merging of the action of baptism in that of the saving events that we noted above.

But when the kindness of God our Saviour, and his love toward man, appeared, not by works done in righteousness, which we did ourselves, but according to his mercy he saved us, through the washing of regeneration and renewing of the Holy Ghost, which he poured out upon us richly, through Jesus Christ our Saviour; that, being justified by his grace, we might be made heirs according to the hope of eternal life.

The passage opens with a clear statement of the once and for all action of God 'appearing' and redeeming history in Christ. But before long the language seems to have equally explicit allusion

[14]*Baptism in the New Testament*, p. 15.

to Christian initiation; while, finally, the doctrine of justification by grace (picking up the previous rejection of 'works done in righteousness') appears to relate once again to the single saving act. But in truth there is no such division. I am inclined to think that there is no direct reference to the sacrament as such. 'The washing of regeneration and renewing of the Holy Ghost, which he poured out upon us richly through Jesus Christ our Saviour' I take to be the whole ministry of Jesus from Jordan to Pentecost, conceived as the great Baptism whereby 'he saved us'. Clearly, this is described in the language of Christian initiation, through which alone Christians know this act as saving. But behind the sacrament stands the historical act, the Baptism which is prior to all baptisms and which gives them their efficacy.

(13) The witness of the Epistle to the Hebrews is the same.

Having therefore, brethren, boldness to enter into the holy place by the blood of Jesus, by the way which he dedicated for us, a new and living way, through the veil, that is to say, his flesh; and having a great priest over the house of God; let us draw near with a true heart in fulness of faith, having our hearts sprinkled from an evil conscience, and our body washed with pure water: let us hold fast the confession of our hope that it waver not; for he is faithful that promised (Heb. 10.19–23).

The effect of the Crucifixion is here expressed in phrases which, derived originally from Jewish purificatory rites, carry in Christian parlance obvious baptismal associations—the washing with water, the confession of faith, the cleansing of a bad conscience (cf. I Peter 3.21). The passage, which must be read in conjunction with 9.11–22 and 12.24, appears to be a deliberate combination of Ex. 24.8 ('And Moses took the blood, and sprinkled it on the people, and said, Behold the blood of the covenant, which the Lord hath made with you') and Ezek. 36.25–7 ('I will sprinkle clean water upon you, and ye shall be clean. . . . A new heart also will I give you. . . . And I will put my spirit within you'). That is to say, the author is seeing the blood-shedding of Jesus as itself the new baptism of God's people, in which the Spirit and remission of sins is given (cf. 9.14). The unanimity, particularly with the fourth Gospel, is remarkable.

This interpretation is strengthened by the connexion between baptism and the Crucifixion which comes to light by comparing the opening of this passage with another earlier in the Epistle. In 10.19 the death of Christ is seen as the new Encaenia or Dedication (ἐνεκαίνισεν).[15] In 6.4–6 it is said of those who have once received baptism that 'it is impossible to renew them again (πάλιν ἀνακαινίζειν) unto repentance, seeing they crucify to themselves the Son of God afresh, and put him to an open shame'. The precise connexion is not easy to define, but the underlying thought seems to be of baptism as that whereby the great act of Inauguration or Renewal, achieved once in the Cross of Christ, is made operative in the believer. Its repetition is inconceivable for two reasons. (*a*) Baptism is the communication to the individual of the great ἐφ᾽ ἄπαξ of God's work in Christ: the One Baptism which has finally altered the world-situation (so that beyond it nothing more is either necessary or possible: 9.26; 10.18) has affected in the same manner the status of the person who has accepted it (6.4; 10.26). (*b*) Baptism means being put on the Cross once with Christ: it is absurd to think of renewing it for those who for their own ends are actually crucifying the Son of God again (cf. 10.29). In both arguments the presupposition is that Christian initiation derives its character and meaning from what has been done once and for all in the baptism of Christ's death.

(14) The rudiments of a theology similar to that of Hebrews are perhaps to be found in I Peter 1.2, where 'the sprinkling of the blood of Jesus' occurs in what is agreed to be a heavily baptismal context. What we have learnt to recognize as the typical blurring of baptismal language with that about the saving acts themselves occurs also in this Epistle. In 1.3 the effect of the Resurrection is described in the baptismal term of rebirth; conversely, in 3.21 it is baptism itself which 'saves' 'through the resurrection'—the words δι᾽ ἀναστάσεως here standing parallel to δι᾽ ὕδατος in v. 20.

Finally, there are three passages from the Apocalypse, the first two of which require to be taken together.

[15]The author seems to be conflating the two ideas that the Cross is the dedication (*a*) of the new covenant (cf. 9.18: 'Even the first covenant hath not been dedicated (ἐνκεκαίνισται) without blood') and (*b*) of the new temple (the Encaenia as a technical term (cf. John 10.22) goes back to the rededication of the Temple in I Macc. 4.54–9, and the whole argument of chapters 9 and 10 leads to the climax that Jesus has now 'opened' the new sanctuary in the temple of his body).

(15) And the angel[16] cast his sickle into the earth, and gathered the vintage of the earth, and cast it into the winepress, the great winepress, of the wrath of God. And the winepress was trodden without the city, and there came out blood from the winepress, even unto the bridles of the horses, as far as a thousand and six hundred furlongs (Rev. 14.19 f.).

And I saw the heaven opened; and behold, a white horse, and he that sat thereon, called Faithful and True. . . . And he is arrayed in a garment dipped in blood: and his name is called the Word of God. And the armies which are in heaven followed him upon white horses, clothed in fine linen, white and pure. . . . And he treadeth the winepress of the fierceness of the wrath of Almighty God. And he hath on his garment and on his thigh a name written, KING OF KINGS, AND LORD OF LORDS (Rev. 19.11–16).

It is obvious that behind these passages stands Isa. 63.1–6. But as so often with this writer, the changes he makes in his Old Testament allusions are as significant as the allusion itself. In Isa. 63 it is with the blood of his enemies that the Saviour's garments are sprinkled and it is their life-blood which is poured out on the earth. In Revelation the scene is still one of wrath. But 'John is giving us just a glimpse of the amazing claim of Christianity that the way God judges his enemies is not by killing them but by suffering at their hands.'[17] The winepress, for him the great winepress, is now the Cross, set up 'without the city'(cf. Heb. 13.12), and the blood which flows from it the Saviour's own, sufficient to immerse the whole world.[18] The knights who pass through it emerge, like the baptismal *candidati,* clothed in fine linen, pure and white. 'These', as the author elsewhere tells us, 'are they which come out of the great tribulation, and they washed their robes, and made them white in the blood of the Lamb' (7.14). That is possible only because the Word of God has first

---

[16]If R. H. Charles (ICC, *ad loc.*) is right, the previous verses, 15–18, are an interpolation and ὁ ἄγγελος here is inserted by the same hand. V. 19 would then follow very naturally on v. 14 and the Son of man himself be the one who gathers the vintage of the earth into (his own) winepress. This would add force to the interpretation given below.

[17]R. H. Preston and A. T. Hanson, *The Revelation* (Torch Bible Commentaries, 1949), p. 105.

[18]The significance of the figure of 1600 furlongs is probably that of utter universality. 'Four is the complete number of extent, covering the four points of the compass (as seven is the complete number of quality); the square of four indicates entire completeness. It is multiplied by a hundred as a sign of greatness' (Preston and Hanson, *op. cit.,* p. 105).

arrayed himself in a garment dipped[19] in blood. The verb is βάπτειν, and the blood his own. Here again is the great universal Baptism in which in Christ the whole world has been plunged— a baptism of blood, in fire of judgment, yet a baptism nevertheless from which the nations may finally find healing, through the 'river of water of life, bright as crystal, proceeding out of the throne of God and of the Lamb' (22.1 f.). Once more we seem to be in the presence of a Johannine theology, which sees the 'rivers of living water' flowing from the side of the Crucified on his throne of glory. The water of baptism mingles with the blood— for the Spirit and the water and the blood indeed agree in one, in the One great Baptism in which the world has died and been renewed.

(16) The last passage to be considered is Rev. 16—the pouring out of the seven vials of the wrath of God upon the earth. That this chapter may have baptismal significance[20] is suggested by the recurrence in it of the idea of outpouring. It is noticeable that wherever else the verbs ἐκχέειν and ἐκχύνειν are used in the New Testament with God or Christ as their subject it is in connexion with what we have found designated as a baptism. In Mark 14.24 (and pars) the reference is to the blood of Christ poured out in death; in Acts 2.33 and 10.45 and Titus 3.6 it is quite explicitly to the One Baptism of the Spirit; while in Rom. 5.5 it is probably to this as it has been appropriated in individual baptism.

If we are right in seeing a similar reference here, then we have portrayed once more, this time in a series of stages, a baptism of wrath which engulfs the whole cosmos. On the face of it the scene is again simply one of judgment. Yet the climax, the τετέλεσται, of this baptism reads extraordinarily like a grim parody of the Crucifixion.

And the seventh poured out of his bowl upon the air; and there came forth a great voice out of the temple, from the throne, saying, It is done: and there were lightnings, and voices, and thunders; and there was a great earthquake, such as was not since there were men upon the

[19]The reading βεβαμμένον is certainly to be preferred to ῥεραντισμένον. There is every reason why the new word which the author deliberately introduces should be assimilated to the Isaianic 'sprinkled' but none for the opposite change.
[20]An idea I owe to Professor T. F. Torrance, who is not, however, responsible for the interpretation I have given to it.

earth, so great an earthquake, so mighty. And the great city was divided into three parts, and the cities of the nations fell: and Babylon the great was remembered in the sight of God, to give unto her the cup of the wine of the fierceness of his wrath (16.17-19).

May it be that in the very execution of the wrath the author intends us to see completed that One Baptism of blood in which the world is not only judged but saved? Is this the astonishing Divine righteousness—and not merely the surface vindication, which at its own level is also true—that provokes the wonder of vv. 5–7?

> And I heard the angel of the waters saying, Righteous art thou, which art and which wast, thou Holy One, because thou didst thus judge: for they poured out the blood of saints and prophets, and blood hast thou given them to drink: they are worthy. And I heard the altar saying, Yea, O Lord God, the Almighty, true and righteous are thy judgments.

The enemies of God have poured out the blood of the saints 'like water round about Jerusalem', says the Psalmist whom he quotes (79.2 f.). So blood they must drink. The allusion is to Isa. 49.26: 'I will feed them that oppress thee with their own flesh; and they shall be drunken with their own blood, as with sweet wine: and all flesh shall know that I the Lord am thy saviour, and thy redeemer, the Mighty One of Jacob.' But once again how subtle and how total is the change! The blood is still the blood of wrath, just as the Crucifixion is seen by Jesus as recapitulating in judgment all the righteous blood shed from the foundation of the world (Luke 11.50 f.; Matt. 23.35 f.). But it is no longer merely their own blood. It is given them by God— poured out in the Cross like water round about Jerusalem. So this is the amazing requital of which God has deemed men worthy! Once more the bath of blood and the bath of baptism are one; and in the work of redemption so understood we have a category of interpretation among the most profound and universal in the New Testament.

INDEX

Abraham, 46, 51, 110 f., 113, 115 f., 144, 149 f.
Agape, 155
Allbright, W. F., 26, 64 f., 101
Allegro, J. M., 11
Allen, W. C., 84
Angels, 78–81, 87 f., 90 f., 173
    fallen, 85 f., 163
Antichrist, 45, 131–3, 136
Antinomians, 131
Apocalypse, The, 25, 137, 156 f., 172–5
Apocalyptic, 76, 103 f., 132, 172–5
Apollos, 48–50
Aramaic, Aramaisms, 90, 98, 112, 114, 123, 154–7
Audet, J.-P., 23
Ascension, 162 f.

Bacon, B. W., 65, 144
Baldensperger, W., 49
Baptism, Christian, 16–18, 41, 48, 158 f., 161–75
    of Jesus in Jordan, 20, 39, 60, 143, 159, 161–4, 167
    of the Passion, 21 f., 44 f., 158–63
    of John the Baptist, 12–27, 64
    Proselyte, 16, 19
    at Qumran, 16, 18–20
Baptist sects, 18 f., 49 f., 52, 64, 101, 108, 153
Bardy, G., 135 f.
Barrett, C. K., 25, 94, 96, 104, 107 f., 118, 120
Bauernfeind, O., 145
Benedictus, The, 48 f., 51 f.
Benoit, P., 49, 51
Bentzen, A., 150
Bevin, E., 104

Bornhäuser, K., 118
Bornkamm, G., 157
Bousset, W., 45
Bowen, C. R., 52
Braun, F. M., 26, 99
Brooke, A. E., 134
Brown, R. E., 26, 30, 99
Brownlee, W. H., 11, 14, 23, 26, 101
Bultmann, R., 65, 67 f., 97, 105, 133
Burrows, M., 24, 26

Cadbury, H. J., 112, 144 f.
Caiaphas, 120
Cain, 130 f.
Cerfaux, L., 67
Cerinthus, 134–7
Charles, R. H., 24, 173
Christology, Primitive, 46 f., 49–52, 139–53
Church, The, 46, 129, 146–9, 151–3, 158 f., 163, 165–70
    as shaper of tradition, 61 f., 75, 120
    as the true Israel, 58–60, 69, 115, 121 f., 130, 167
Clement, First Epistle of, 141
Clementines, 50, 65
Colwell, E. C., 124
Cornelius, 167 f.
Cross, F. L., 146
Crucifixion, see Passion
Cullmann, O., 22, 26, 33, 37, 48, 50 f., 61–63, 156, 158 f., 163, 166

Dahl, N. A., 16
David, House of, 52
    Son of, 37, 149

Descamps, A., 150 f.
Devil, The, 54–58, 85 f., 115, 128
Diaspora, 116–21, 125 f., 138
Dibelius, M., 35, 139 f.
Didache, 20, 141, 154 f., 157
Dionysius bar Salibi, 135
Docetism, 134 f.
Dodd, C. H., 25, 30, 51, 74, 77, 89, 96, 98, 100, 103, 115, 118, 132 f., 139 f.
Drag-net, Parable of the, 76, 83–85, 91
Duncan, G. S., 31

Ecclesiasticus, Book of, 36, 39, 44, 47
Edwards, H. E., 41, 104, 122
Edwards, R. A., 104
Elijah, 28–52, 145, 150
Enoch, Apocalypse of, 25, 36, 44, 76, 81, 85
Epiphanius, 135
Ephrem Syrus, 50
Eschatology, 14, 18–21, 37 f., 71–74, 76–93, 103 f., 132, 136
Eucharist, 155–7, 165 f.
Eusebius, 65, 135 f.
Evans, C. F., 139 f.

Father, God as, 82 f., 86, 131
Fison, J. E., 103
Flemington, W. F., 158, 162
Foakes-Jackson, F. J., 144 f.
Foot-washing, 92, 165 f.
Forerunner, 29, 31, 34–37, 46 f., 145
Fuller, R. H., 143, 147, 151

Galilee, 38 f., 41–43, 64, 118, 123
Gardner-Smith, P., 96
Gentiles, 108–21, 131 f.
Geyser, A. S., 11
Gnosticism, 26, 98 f., 108, 124, 133–8
Goguel, M., 11, 40, 50
Goodenough, E. R., 102

Green-Armytage, A. H. N., 104
Groussow, W., 26, 99
Gyllenberg, R., 26, 105

Hanson, A. T., 173
Harnack, A. von, 133
Hawkins, J. C., 77, 83 f.
Headlam, A. C., 104
Hebrews, Epistle to the, 17, 59, 130 f., 156, 159, 171–3
Heilsgeschichte, 59 f., 167, 170
'Hellenists', 62, 116 f.; see also Judaism, Hellenistic
'Hellenized' Christianity, 133, 137, 149
Herod Antipas, 33, 142
Higgins, A. J. B., 94, 166
Hippolytus, 18, 135, 141
Hoskyns, E., and Davey, F. N., 67, 72
Howard, W. F., 94, 96
Hunt, B. P. W. S., 119
Hunter, A. M., 94

Ignatius, 162
Incarnation, The, 134
Irenaeus, 104, 134 f.
Isaiah, First, 38, 113
    Second, 34, 38, 43, 46, 151, 162
Israel, 14, 18 f., 21–23, 47, 54–60, 69 f., 71 f., 74, 110 f., 113, 119, 121, 140, 144
    Christ as the true, 19, 60, 113 f.; see also Church

Jacob, 110, 149
James, 46, 119 f.
    Epistle of, 131
Jeremias, J., 22, 35, 37, 41, 43, 45, 67–69, 72, 74–76, 79, 83–86, 97, 100, 102, 120, 141, 150
Jews, Judaism, 16, 58, 64, 107–25, 126–33, 135–38
John the Apostle, 46, 95, 104–6, 119
John the Baptist, 11–27, 28–52,